ENGLISH COUNTRY HOUSES

BAROQUE

1685–1715

Burghley House, Northamptonshire. The Heaven Room, by Antonio Verrio, c. 1696, looking east.

ENGLISH COUNTRY HOUSES

BAROQUE

1685 – 1715

JAMES LEES-MILNE

COUNTRY LIFE

Published for Country Life Books by
The Hamlyn Publishing Group Limited
London · New York · Sydney · Toronto
Hamlyn House · The Centre · Feltham · Middlesex

© *Copyright The Hamlyn Publishing Group Limited 1970*

ISBN 0 600 43123 1

Printed offset litho in Great Britain
by Jarrold and Sons Limited, Norwich

PREFACE

'And should I be so mad to go about
To give account of ev'ry thing throughout,
The Rooms of State, Stair-cases, Galleries,
Lodgings, Apartments, Closets, Offices;
Or to describe the splendors undertake,
Which ev'ry glorious Room a Heaven make,
The Picture, Sculpture, Carving, Graving, Guilding,
T'would be as long in Writing as in Building.'

Charles Cotton, 'The Wonders of the Peake', 1681.

A word of explanation is needed about the composition of this book. It is primarily concerned with the chief country houses built between 1685 and 1715, i.e. that interval between the Caroline and Early Georgian periods, already dealt with in the *English Country Houses* series by Oliver Hill and John Cornforth, and Christopher Hussey respectively. Only secondarily is it concerned with country houses that can be termed wholly Baroque. The title, in a sense misleading, has been chosen for convenience. Its connotation should perhaps be understood chronologically rather than stylistically. Whereas I have seldom been tempted to include houses built before 1685, I must confess to having often left out with much reluctance houses built after 1715. So many of George I's and even George II's reign are in fact just as Baroque as, even at times more Baroque than those which belong to Queen Anne's reign. My rule, therefore, has been not to include any Baroque houses described in Mr Hussey's *Early Georgian*, and only to include those belonging to the reigns of the first two Georges if the architects of them had previously been building in Queen Anne's reign. For instance, it would clearly have been a mistake to omit Seaton Delaval and Grimsthorpe from a volume so largely concerned with Vanbrugh. On the other hand I have not included any houses by Gibbs (undoubtedly a Baroque architect) because he built none before 1715.

Again, in order to be consistent, I have not included any houses, no matter how important in themselves, in the Palladian style even when built by architects who in Queen Anne's reign were actively working in the Baroque idiom. Wricklemarsh by John James of Greenwich and Linley Hall by Henry Joynes belong to this category, and therefore find no place here.

The claim of a country house to a full section has largely depended upon its present-day condition. It seemed to me purposeless to describe at length those which have been demolished or are so greatly spoilt that they cannot be illustrated. It is true that not all those I have selected remain family homes, but they are all preserved. Most indeed contain the furnishings and works of art for which they have long been renowned.

In addition to innumerable *Country Life* articles the following books of reference have proved absolutely indispensable: H. Avray Tipping's *English Homes*, Period IV, vol. I, *Late Stuart*, 1929, and (with Christopher Hussey) vol. II, *Vanbrugh and His School*, 1928; H. M. Colvin's *Biographical Dictionary of English Architects*, 1954; Kerry Downes's *English Baroque Architecture*, 1966; Edward Croft-Murray's *Decorative Painting in England*, vol. I, 1962; Laurence Whistler's *Sir John Vanbrugh*, 1938 and *The Imagination of Vanbrugh*, 1954; Marcus Whiffen's *Thomas Archer*, 1950; Kerry Downes's *Hawksmoor*, 1959; David Green's *Blenheim Palace*, 1951; and Francis Thompson's *A History of Chatsworth*, 1949.

Finally, I am indebted to more people than I can possibly acknowledge for help and kindnesses of one kind and another, including many owners, tenants and custodians of 'Baroque' houses. To Mr Christopher Hussey, the pioneer editor of the series it would be impertinent to offer praise. I gratefully offer him thanks for much help and encouragement. To Mr Geoffrey Beard, Mr John Cornforth and Mr John Harris my gratitude for unstinted generosity in material vouchsafed and valuable time spared towards furthering my efforts cannot adequately be expressed. Mr Giles Clotworthy's part in the production of the book has gone far beyond the usual courtesies of a publisher towards an author. I am deeply grateful for his advice and co-operation.

J. L-M., Alderley Grange, Wotton-under-Edge, 1968

CONTENTS

NOTES ON THE PRINCIPAL BAROQUE HOUSES

HOUSES ILLUSTRATED

ACKNOWLEDGEMENTS

The publishers are indebted to the following owners of paintings, drawings, engravings and works of art for permission to reproduce them. This list does not include pictures, drawings or objects at the principal houses illustrated in the book.

Reproduced by Gracious Permission of Her Majesty the Queen 32, 33, 393; Warden and Fellows of All Souls College, Oxford 12; Cooper-Hewitt Museum of Design, Smithsonian Institution, Washington D.C. 204; County Record Office, Huntingdon 169; Mr A. Galliers-Pratt 24; Mr George Howard 253, 254; the Marquis of Exeter 99, 107, 108, 109; National Portrait Gallery 14; Petworth Collection, 69, 71, 77; Mr J. C. F. Prideaux-Brune 448; R.I.B.A. Drawings Collection 50, 95, 178, 330, 417, 444, 448; Sabin Galleries Ltd 428; William Salt Library, Stafford 13; Lord Sandys 111; Trustees of the British Museum 5, 9, 429, 451; Trustees of the Devonshire Collection 113, 120, 122.

Most of the photographs in the book are the copyright of *Country Life* but the publishers would like to acknowledge the following for additional photographs: Aerofilms 67, 161, 181, 260; Alinari, Florence 26; Architectural Press 377; Clive Barda 461; Courtauld Institute of Art 3, 225; Christopher Dalton 302, 304, 307, 308, 309, 310, 311, 312, 313, 314, 316, 443, 459, 466; Dr Kerry Downes 18, 19, 22, 447; English Life Publications, Derby 422; John R. Freeman 40; Hamlyn Group Photo Library 6, 7, 11, 13, 15, 21, 30, 39, 430, 455; Hawkley Studio Associates 82, 83, 88, 89; Cyril Howe Studios, Bath 149; A. F. Kersting 70, 74, 78, 79, 88, 219, 220, 226, 228, 231, 233, 234, 263, 265, 266, 271, 275, 276, 281, 282, 283, 284, 285, 287, 296, 360, 418; King's Lynn Camera Centre 28; James Lees-Milne 437, 456; Millar and Harris 41; Ministry of Public Building and Works (Crown Copyright) 8, 20, 38; National Monuments Record 194, 207, 209, 230, 289, 290, 292, 294, 298, 380, 381, 388, 392, 393, 396, 445, 450, 465; R.A. Postcards Ltd 278; A. de Rahm, Transglobe Ltd 274; A. J. Roberts, Barnsley 376, 378; Edwin Smith 1, 269, 286; Thomas-Photos, Oxford 12, 413; Victoria and Albert Museum 377; C. V. Wardell 346.

INTRODUCTION

I. THE POLITICAL BACKGROUND

It is a mistake to assume that with the Restoration of the Merry Monarch in 1660 the constitutional changes that had taken place during the dismal years of the Protectorate were now completely shelved and forgotten, and that England blithely accepted again the divine right of kings and government by autocracy. Charles II may well have hoped that this would be the case. On the contrary the outward calm of his reign was often menaced by grave political rumblings. Ever since the Restoration the nobility of England had been developing in stature and territorial ownership. They began by swallowing up the estates of the small landowners who, farming their few acres and enjoying no rents, were finding difficulty in raising capital for the agricultural improvements then needed. Those little men, nearly all of whom had been Cavaliers and were now Tories, were in a sad plight. Economically everything was going against them: the enclosure system, the inequitable game laws, and later in the century the high land taxes imposed in order to pay for William III's wars which they resented in consequence. At the expense of the Tory squires the great landowners—on whose budget the taxes incidentally made no appreciable inroads—were flourishing. A result of their increasing prosperity was a lust for power and rule and an ambition to limit the authority of the Crown. An open conflict was only avoided before 1685 by the astuteness of Charles II; with the accession of his foolish and reactionary brother James II, it fairly broke loose.

Between 1685 and 1688 the country was in a very unsettled state. One pointer to political uncertainty and doubt was the pause in country-house building. Almost the only large house being built during James II's reign was Boughton, if we except Chatsworth whose owner waited until he foresaw as a certainty William of Orange's successful invasion of England. Even Boughton, supposedly begun before Charles II's death, was not fully under way until the early 1690s. Indeed the Glorious Revolution of 1688 established the power of the territorial nobility in Britain and marked the passing of authority from an absolute monarchy to a Whig oligarchy. A very significant sequel was the immediate spate of country houses on a monumental scale.

In spite of having wrested the Crown's authority into their own hands the Whig nobility nevertheless accepted the monarchy as the pivot of the new constitution and the fount of their recently augmented honours. Between 1688 and 1714 the peerage was strengthened by the creation of a number of dukedoms, among them Brandon, Bolton, Buckingham, Montagu, Manchester, Devonshire, Leeds, Shrewsbury, Kent and Marlborough—as many indeed as existed, including the royal bastards, at Charles II's death.[1] William III was recognized by the nobility to be more than

[1] At least two more, Kingston and Ancaster, were created in 1715.

1 *Statue of Queen Anne by J. M. Rysbrack, c. 1736, in the Gallery at Blenheim Palace.*

a figurehead: he was a great military hero, the saviour of their country from Stuart tyranny and papistry, the bulwark against the depredator of Europe, Louis XIV, and the instrument, willing or unwilling, of their greatness. It was in their interests and in their justification to install the reconstituted monarchy in settings worthy of its changed role. So they encouraged the King, who did not happen to be particularly interested in architecture and the arts, to house himself appropriately. But he had no English palace worthy of the name, apart from Windsor Castle which was too far from London, in which to live most of the year. The old palaces of St James and Whitehall were in disrepair and hopelessly out of date; besides, their closeness to the river affected the King's asthma. Something had to be done. As luck would have it the Surveyor-General of the King's Works was, in spite of his Tory connections still the highly respected Sir Christopher Wren. And Queen Mary II unlike her husband had considerable knowledge of architecture and love of the arts. The Wren family records, *Parentalia*, bear testimony that 'there were few arts, or sciences, in which Her Majesty had not only an elegant taste but a knowledge much superior to any of her sex, in that, or (it may be) any former age. This is not said as a panegyrick, but a plain and well-known truth, which the Surveyor had frequent experience of. . . .' Hampton Court and Kensington House—the last bought by William from Lord Nottingham—were transformed by Wren into fitting classical residences for the sovereigns. On Mary's premature death in 1694 William, for love of her, continued the operations at both palaces. Furthermore, in the good Queen's memory he launched her long-cherished scheme, which was the creation under Wren of the Royal Hospital for Seamen at Greenwich (Fig. 2). As a public building of monumental character the Hospital was to become England's most integrated Baroque achievement, in spite of falling short of Wren's original plan. This was to have been a recession of two open courts into quadrant colonnades joined to a portico before a central dome. The spirited exercise was based on an amalgam of ideas culled from the Collège des Quatre Nations in Paris, and above all the Château of Versailles. Although not carried out it undoubtedly influenced Vanbrugh's first great country-house projects.[1]

In fact the palaces of the royal hero who eventually brought the redoubtable Louis XIV to heel with a series of resounding victories, were largely—if not recognizably —inspired by that of England's arch-enemy himself. The compulsive motive, chauvinism, was certainly the same. And we can to some extent discount Matthew Prior's boast on being conducted round Versailles, where on every side Louis was depicted in marble, plaster and fresco as Apollo the Sun King, that 'the memorials of my master's actions are to be found everywhere but in his own houses.' For to be truthful, William III's glorification is to be met with on

[1] Sir John Summerson—*Architecture in Britain, 1530–1830*, 1963.

2 *The Royal Hospital, Greenwich, from the Thames.*

the pediment of the east front of Hampton Court, in the role of Hercules casting out envy, hatred and malice. The hero King, who was not remarkable for his muscular physique or beauty, is also represented on several painted ceilings in the houses of his flattering subjects as triumphant Caesar and, even more surprisingly, as Mars sleeping naked in the lap of Venus. It is one of history's established ironies that nations are inclined to adopt the manners—and often the principles—of those they have defeated in battle.

Where the King, prompted by the Queen, gave a lead, the great Whig lords were quick to follow suit. The Peace of Ryswick in 1697 opened the way to a revived interest in French culture. A limited amount of travel once more across the Channel was highly welcomed, for the nobleman's hobby in this reign had turned from science to art. It is astonishing what vast sums were shortly to be spent by the English on decorating and furnishing country houses; Lord Nottingham, having purchased the Burley-on-the-Hill estate for £50,000, lavished no less than another £30,000 on a new house in spite of the original estimate having been half that amount. Bubb Doddington spent as much as £140,000 on embellishing Eastbury Park.

II. THE BAROQUE ACHIEVEMENT

The period in England with which we deal has been termed the *Baroque*, a word of which its contemporaries were of course totally ignorant. On the other hand they were extremely conscious of a change in architectural style from the homely to the stately, a change which they deliberately sought to bring about. Yet how different in meaning is the Baroque of England from that of France and above all, Italy, the land of its origin! There the Baroque, first manifest in the early seventeenth century, was a joyous exclamation of the Catholic Church's renewed spiritual authority, its recovery from the disruption caused by the Reformation and the scarcely less deadening decrees of the Council of Trent. In France and northern Europe the Baroque architectural style had no sacred significance. It was rather an expression of monarchical absolutism. Charles II would dearly have liked to echo the sentiment in England, but lack of funds and a watchful,

jealous Parliament prevented him. The building of the abortive Winchester Palace (Fig. 3) and the decoration of the state rooms at Windsor Castle constituted his sole attempt. It was a half-hearted one. When the English Baroque was eventually to flower in William III's reign it was motivated by still different ideals. Professor Geoffrey Webb has pointed them out in his penetrating study, *Baroque Art.*[1] 'To the mind of Vanbrugh', he writes, 'Greenwich Hospital was the rival of the Invalides in splendour, but built by freemen, and all the resources of baroque eloquence were only fitting to celebrate at Blenheim the victory of their faith that freedom is as consistent with an effective state as any absolutism, however imposing.' Nevertheless the age of democracy was still far distant. And however much the unrepresented common man felt convinced that Britons even then were

[1] *Proc. Brit. Acad.,* XXXIII, 1947.

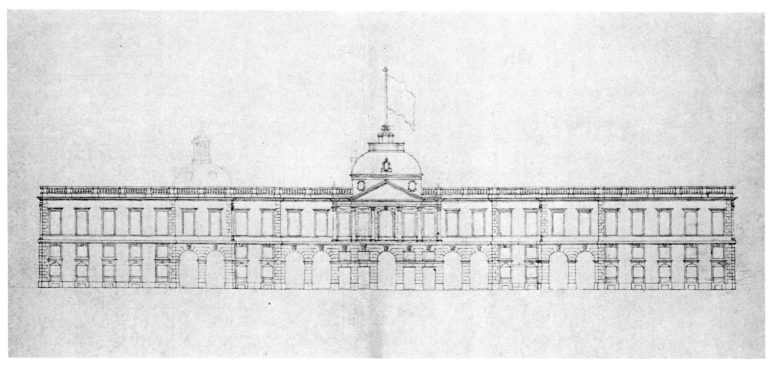

3 *Wren's preliminary design for Winchester Palace, 1682–3.*

never slaves, they were in fact merely living under a different form of absolutism—one transferred from the monarch to a handful of Whig noblemen.

Many of the great landowners and their architects looked for inspiration to Paris and Versailles. Scarcely any at this time went to Italy direct. The Duke of Shrewsbury, it is true, visited Rome where Paolo Falconieri gave him in 1704 a plan for a royal palace, which may have influenced the elevations of Heythrop House. And the Duke of Manchester was in 1707–8 Ambassador to Venice whence he brought back Pellegrini and Marco Ricci to decorate Kimbolton Castle. More significant is the fact that only one important architect of the period, Thomas Archer, actually got to Rome. As a consequence his architecture alone echoes the language of Bernini and Borromini of a previous generation.

Lively and inventive though it be the English Baroque style is not generally distinctive. It is variable and may be said to lack order. Hence very probably its originality, for the visitor never knows what next to expect from William III and Queen Anne buildings as he moves from one county to another. There was in England no co-ordinating authority corresponding to Colbert's French Academy of Architecture, founded in 1671 to elaborate doctrine and control stylistic movement. There was at home no philosopher-exponent of its meaning, like the 3rd Earl of Shaftesbury who acted in that capacity for the ensuing Palladian movement. There was no Addison, no Pope to contribute essays to *Tatler* and *Spectator*, or to correspond with noble owners about its classical derivations. There was not even any propaganda treatise, like Campbell's *Vitruvius Britannicus* or Leoni's *Palladio*, which so loudly trumpeted and clearly enunciated the refinements of the coming culture. The first volume of Kip and Knyff's

Britannia Illustrata which appeared in 1707 made no special pleading whatsoever, and was merely intended to be a useful catalogue of country houses of all styles and dates. The only influential organization—if such a term may be applied to so loose an assembly—was the Kit Cat Club, whose heyday coincided with the reign of Anne. This was a convivial circle of Whigs, mostly noble patrons, with a sprinkling of men of letters, like Congreve and Steele, and of artists like Kneller and Vanbrugh. The common political interest of the members inevitably dictated a certain common attitude to art and architecture. But the attitude was never clearly defined. The Club nevertheless helped Vanbrugh to numerous commissions, and his buildings are in effect the movement's most eloquent expression.

Another factor which forms a thread linking country house to country house and at times a clue as to authorship when otherwise unspecified, is the close family relationship of the Whig owners. For instance, the 1st Duke of Devonshire (Chatsworth) was a kinsman of the Earls of Kingston (Thoresby) and brother-in-law of Lord Exeter (Burghley). Lord Nottingham (Burley-on-the-Hill) was uncle of Lord Bingley's wife (Bramham), and Sir John Langham (Cottesbrooke) first cousin of the Duke of Chandos's first wife (Cannons). The Duke of Montagu (Boughton) was first cousin of Lord Exeter, and his first wife was the mother of the Duchess of Somerset (Petworth). Lord Lempster (Easton Neston) married a daughter of the 1st Duke of Leeds (Kiveton). The ramifications of upper-class society in a small and under-populated country like England at the turn of the eighteenth century were almost infinite. There is every evidence, too, that during a time of strong political feeling family ties between great houses were drawn exceedingly close.

III. THE ARCHITECTS' STATUS

If political circumstances allied to vast increases of territorial wealth favoured the new outcrop of country houses, the perfection of craftsmanship now attained in England was a wonderful stimulus to the new style. We owe this happy outcome to Wren who over the years had trained at the Board of Works an army of skilled artificers for the royal palaces, the City churches and St Paul's. He had been quick to realize that what these men needed was education in drawing and design, and, with his close associate Robert Hooke, an inveterate collector of French engravings, he supplied it. The bias of their education was overwhelmingly French. 'It is not to be considered', Wren wrote in 1692 in his rather casual style, 'that the country men are not altogether so handy in plain worke & in good worke scarce to be trusted till they are well practised.' The town men were, he conceded, in 'good worke' unsurpassed. Never before or since had this country produced individuals of the calibre of Pierce, Gibbons and Goudge and the many other excellent craftsmen whose names will crop up in these pages. It is significant that with the dominance of the Burlingtonians and the imposition of standard Vitruvian patterns after 1715 such individuals tended to disappear.

When our period opened in 1685 Wren was already fifty-three years old. His authority as Surveyor-General of the King's Works and his prestige were as yet unassailed; his position was unique and his influence as great as his achievements. Gentleman, amateur, scientist, artist, genius, he was beyond compare. What then, if we leave him aside for a moment, was the status of most architects in 1685? Pretty well the same as in the sixteenth century—and by 1715 it had barely changed. Until about the middle of the eighteenth century the majority of practitioners had received no training at all. What is more few described themselves as 'architects'. Talman, for example, in a petition of 1708 to the 2nd Duke of Devonshire claimed that 'for near Tenn years' he had acted as 'chief overseer and surveyor' to his Grace's father. Throughout our period architects can be put very roughly into three categories—craftsmen-architects, gentlemen-architects and Board of Works architects.

The craftsmen-architects were, in the words of Frank Jenkins, 'men who had served an apprenticeship in one of the building trades, generally bricklaying or carpentry, had graduated as master craftsmen, and who undertook the designing of buildings, as well as contributing directly to their erection in their own particular trade.'[1] John Prince who drew an accurate upright of Cound Hall was a bricklayer. William Coleman who worked at Kimbolton Castle and William Etty at Newby Park were joiners by profession. James Withenbury (if it was he who built Hanbury Hall), and John Hunt who worked at Hinwick Hall, were both sculptors of repute in Worcester and Northampton. These master-craftsmen would lift designs from well-thumbed copybooks, or deliberately imitate some house in the neighbourhood particularly admired by the client. The prototype might be a modest residence like Bourne Park (Fig. 4), or a seat of national repute like Thoresby Hall, Castle Howard or Buckingham House.

The gentleman-architect is not quite so easily defined. He sometimes originated from the first category, like the Warwickshire Smiths, the Dorset Bastards, and the Oxfordshire Townesends and Strongs, who, becoming extremely successful, bettered themselves socially. Sometimes he had a foot in the third category, being attached in a minor or semi-professional capacity to the Crown, like Archer, who came of landed stock and being well off undertook private commissions only when it suited him. The best of the gentlemen-architects were well-educated men. They were either artists or intellectuals who regarded the orders not as decorative appendages but as structural fundamentals providing a modular basis for an architectural composition. Dr George Clarke, Fellow of All Souls, was in all senses one of these eclectic amateurs and, from what we know of him, William Wakefield was another.

Lastly the Board of Works architects formed the most professional category. They had the best pretensions to architectural training; in fact the Board of Works was the only institution to provide anything of the sort. Moreover all its officers who designed country houses within our period—namely Talman, Hawksmoor, Vanbrugh and James—had enjoyed the inexpressible benefit of training under Sir Christopher. The superiority of these men can be measured by the incompetence of the dilettante William Benson who, without previous training or experience, managed through shameless political jobbery to oust Wren from the surveyorship in 1718. Within twelve months he was obliged to resign for making a 'false and groundless' report that the House of Lords was falling down, having as Hawksmoor put it, 'got more in one year (for confusing the King's Works) than Sir Chris Wren did in 40 years for his honest endeavours'. His successor Sir Thomas Hewett, again an untrained nonentity, is only known to have built a stable block at Thoresby, described also by Hawksmoor as 'the most infamous that ever was made'.

4 *Bourne Park, Kent, built in 1701. The doorway has been altered.*

---

[1] *Architect and Patron*, 1961.

IV. NATIONAL ARCHITECTS

In spite of the estate agent's persistent reference to the 'Wren-style' country house, no such type ever really existed. What is generally implied by this vague description is an astylar, two-storey house with broad eaves, hipped roof, dormer windows and sometimes a cupola. This homely, infinitely endearing pattern originated in Pratt's Clarendon House, Piccadilly (1664–7) (Fig. 5). It was repeated at Belton House (1684–8), Stanford Hall (1697) and, with modifications, even at Hanbury Hall after the turn of the century. Its deserved popularity made it a type of long-enduring tradition. Wren, however, had no hand in its formation.

Apart from Tring Manor (now altered out of all recognition) which was built to his design in 1669–71, only Winslow Hall can unquestionably be attributed to Wren's personal supervision. And its block-like design with a slight central salient under a pediment and high pitched roof is (apart from the grouping of the chimneys) noticeably old-fashioned for 1702. But in this year Wren was seventy-two years old. It is because he was by now old-fashioned that the Duchess of Marlborough with her contempt for new-fangled nonsense, as well as her desire to snub Vanbrugh, commissioned Wren to design a house overlooking St James's Park in 1709 (Fig. 6). So long as Wren held office his quiet influence, whether out of date or not, always made itself felt; the Surveyor-General's advice and approval were still the ultimate standard and seal of excellence. In 1696 ugly disputes between the Duke of Devonshire and Talman at Chatsworth were submitted to Wren for his intervention. About the same time the Surveyor-General sent by letter advice to Sir William Fermor on the building of Easton Neston, and he evidently discussed points of detail with Lord Nottingham over Burley-on-the-Hill.

Easy-going, generous and great, the Surveyor-General readily recommended and delegated his subordinates to design and build houses for prominent landowners, irrespective of their political party. Thus architects from the Board of Works were freer to take up unofficial commissions than at any previous time. Their names and those of the Board's craftsmen are frequently associated with the greatest houses of this period. Of the country-house architects the oldest and about the most prolific was William Talman.

This very important architect still remains, after much recent research by scholars, an enigma. We now know a good deal about his difficult nature, but nothing to explain why his style was so very variable. There can be little doubt that the unfortunate rows with his patrons and colleagues ruined his chances of developing his art to its fullest expression. For he quarrelled with, amongst others, the Dukes of Devonshire, Buckingham, Newcastle and Chandos, and the Earl of Carlisle, and against Devonshire's son and Carlisle he brought lawsuits, both of which he lost. Differences over money seem to have been the burning causes of dispute. A letter from Chandos to Talman of December 1714 at least makes it clear what the owner of Cannons was complaining about. 'I desir'd Mr Zollicoffe [Chandos's secretary] to wait on you for the ballance of the £1500, advanct you for the works at Cannons, of which you had given me an account of the expenditure of £1400. He tells me you hope I will allow you the remaining £100 as a reward for your pains. As I cannot believe anyone who has the character of a gentleman can make so ridiculous and extravagant a demand, I must believe Mr. Zollicoffe must have mistaken your answer. . . .' The character of a gentleman was the very thing Talman, with his preposterous self-importance, was constantly and tactlessly endeavouring to impress upon his patrons. It was remarkably absent in his disloyal efforts, made in the very year of his appointment as Comptroller of the Works, to discredit his superior the Surveyor-General himself.

Talman, who was not travelled, was none the less responsive to numerous architectural influences, both vernacular and foreign. Chief of these were the country houses of his immediate predecessors, and Dutch and French engravings; they are apparent throughout his working life

5 *Clarendon House, Piccadilly, London. Designed by Roger Pratt, 1664–7. (Demolished.)*

6 *Marlborough House, St James's, London, as designed by Sir Christopher Wren, 1709.*

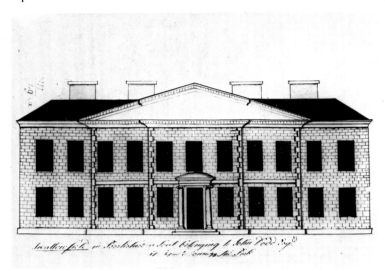

7 (left) A survey drawing of Swallowfield Park, Berkshire. Designed by William Talman, 1689–91. (Remodelled.)

8 (below) A painting of Thoresby Hall, Nottinghamshire, attributed to Pieter Tillemans. Designed by William Talman, 1689–91. (Rebuilt.)

9 (bottom) Buckingham House, London. Possibly by William Winde, 1703–5. (Rebuilt.)

10 (opposite top) Wotton House, Buckinghamshire; the west front. Designed by John Keene or James Thornhill (?), 1704–14. The attic storey and first-floor windows were altered by Soane after a fire.

11 (opposite centre) William Talman's project for a Petit Trianon at Hampton Court, c. 1699.

irrespective of dates. That is to say Talman built in the Caroline, Dutch-Palladian or French style, using or ignoring the orders as and when he felt inclined. Swallowfield Park (1689–91) (Fig. 7), Stansted Park and Uppark are conventionally vernacular, pertaining to the old Clarendon House formula of projecting wings, pedimented centre, hipped roofs and dormers. Kiveton (1694–1704) with its temple-like centrepiece follows in the wake of May's Berkeley House, Piccadilly and Eltham Lodge. With Thoresby Hall, begun in 1683 and damaged by fire shortly afterwards, Talman moved to a different formula in providing a continuous attic storey with flat, balustraded roof line (Fig. 8). The tall rectangular front so contrived marked a new departure in English domestic architecture. The derivation was probably Dutch, taken from Vingboon's *Gronden en Afbeeldsels*, etc. (published in 1665), or from Ruben's *Palazzi di Genova* (1622). The theme was repeated by Talman at Dyrham in 1700 with a difference. Whereas the Thoresby elevation had a three-bay centrepiece, the east front of Dyrham was given three-bay wings. Furthermore it is astylar.

It is not improbable that Talman gave Winde the idea of his famous Buckingham House front (Fig. 9), since the owner's name was included by Vanbrugh in the list of patrons who had fallen foul of him, and the elevation is unlike any other design by Winde. Again at Buckingham House, like Thoresby, we find an attic storey above the cornice and under a balustraded parapet. But here the giant order is used throughout. The Buckingham House formula was at once copied in different parts of the country. It appeared at Waldershare Park, Kent in 1702–10, at Cottesbrooke Hall, Northamptonshire and Wotton House, Aylesbury (Fig. 10). In the last two even the quadrant colonnades linked to pavilions are included. Hinwick House and Cound Hall are likewise imitations but without pavilions.

To illustrate the further diversity of Talman's erudition and talent we need merely consider his south front of Chatsworth, a revolutionary design based on Bernini's proposed Louvre river front, and possibly suggested by Wren; his little Trianon project for William III at Hampton Court (Fig. 11), inspired by designs given to Lord Portland by J. H. Mansart; and the extraordinary Italian Mannerist, rather than Baroque, courtyard elevation at Drayton. Talman was unquestionably a man of original and inventive mind who, without going abroad, looked overseas for new ideas. Some of these were in his later life supplied by his son John, a traveller and avid collector of continental drawings of architecture and the antiquities generally.

When, however, we speak of the English Baroque we are thinking particularly of Hawksmoor, Vanbrugh and Archer. The last has little association with the first two, who in most people's minds are inseparably connected. The plodding, practical, scholarly Hawksmoor (Fig. 12) is held to be subordinate in creative power to the flamboyant, empirical, imaginative Vanbrugh. Hawksmoor's identity only asserts itself before the other's astonishing burst upon the country-house scene and after his death—

12 *Bust of Nicholas Hawksmoor by Sir Henry Cheere, c. 1730, at All Souls College, Oxford.*

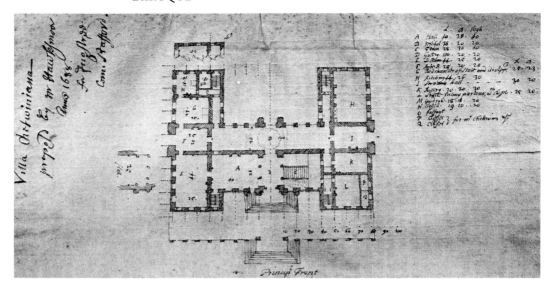

13 (above) A plan for a projected remodelling of Ingestre Hall, Staffordshire, by Hawksmoor, 1688.

14 (right) Sir John Vanbrugh by Sir Godfrey Kneller. The Kit Cat Club portrait of 1704–10 in the National Portrait Gallery, London.

15 (opposite) The château of Vaux-le-Vicomte, designed by Louis Le Vau, 1657–61. A contemporary engraving by Perelle.

in other words, in those buildings which are solely and indubitably his, namely Easton Neston and the great Mausoleum at Castle Howard. Vanbrugh's brilliance has in truth most unfairly eclipsed Hawksmoor's less effulgent but equally potent star.

At the age of eighteen Hawksmoor, a Nottinghamshire farmer's son, was in Wren's service and at twenty-one his assistant at Chelsea Hospital. From early youth then he received the best architectural training available. In 1688 when he was twenty-seven Hawksmoor was already engaged in country-house practice according to a plan (Fig. 13) in Robert Plot's grangerized copy of his *Natural History of Staffordshire* for a projected recast of Mr Walter Chetwynd's Jacobean Ingestre Hall.[1]

Hawksmoor was no more travelled than Talman: he never crossed the Channel. Like the other he greatly relied upon published prints and engravings, of ancient and modern Italian buildings, the works of Jean Marot, and upon books of voyages. Above all archaeology was his passion and he was obsessed by the monumentality of the buildings of classical Rome, largely gleaned from Perrault's *Vitruvius* (published in 1684), a copy of which he owned. Nowhere is this influence more pronounced than in the Castle Howard Mausoleum. Hawksmoor worked out his peculiar handling of masses which he inculcated on Vanbrugh, but precisely how their architecture was interrelated remains a mystery. Their joint achievements are the result of one of the most fruitful partnerships in architectural history, a partnership not without its element of personal tragedy. For Hawksmoor was the victim of class distinction: he was not a gentleman born. He enjoyed none of Vanbrugh's aristocratic connections, nor was he blessed with social graces and convivial manners. As a matter of course he accepted the humbler role in the duality, not without occasional grumbles to which his chronic gout contributed. In the Board of Works he never rose higher than the secretaryship which he then only filled during the years 1715–18.

Yet Hawksmoor was always amenable. He listened with attention and deference to the views and complaints of clients. Vanbrugh while genuinely valuing his partner's sterling qualities ('What wou'd Monsr: Colbert in France

[1] In the William Salt Library, Stafford. Did the young Hawksmoor have a hand in the design of St Mary's church, Ingestre, built for Chetwynd in 1676?

have given for such a man?') nevertheless referred to him as a subordinate. 'As for the ornaments on the top,' he wrote to Lord Carlisle regarding the centre block of Castle Howard, 'I'll get Mr Hawksmoor to add them there.' With the same sweeping indifference to the module as to the detail of architecture he wrote on another occasion, concerning his patron's desire to enlarge the scale of the Belvedere in the park, 'If you Ldp has a mind to extend the area from a cube of 20 ft to one of 22, it needs have no regards to the columns, or the other parts of the architecture, which will do as they stand at present.' This casual attitude must have deeply shocked Hawksmoor, if he heard of it. But then Vanbrugh knew that his scrupulous partner would put such tiresome matters to rights, just as he relied upon him to turn his hasty, brilliant sketches into competent working drawings. In truth Vanbrugh could not manage without Hawksmoor, whereas Hawksmoor could do perfectly well without Vanbrugh. Does not this affirmation strengthen Sir John Summerson's view that the leader of the partnership was really Hawksmoor?

With Vanbrugh (Fig. 14)—and here the credit is his rather than Hawksmoor's—a novel development of the Baroque country house appears in the plan. He evolved, on an enormous scale and to an integrated design, the spread palace. The first exemplar is Castle Howard; the next and more perfect is Blenheim. Seaton Delaval, Grimsthorpe and Eastbury follow suit. Hitherto the great country house had been block-like, having a rectangular façade, without basement, sitting firmly on the ground and articulated by a giant order embracing two storeys. It probably derived from Webb's Charles II block at Greenwich. Kiveton and even Easton Neston were of this sort, although the last was distinguished by those advancing and receding planes which are Hawksmoor's rhythmic contribution to the Baroque façade. The Castle Howard plan was certainly not inspired by Italy where Vanbrugh never went and, apparently, never wanted to go. On the contrary it came directly from Wren's Winchester Palace, begun in 1683 for Charles II, and indirectly from Le Vau's Vaux-le-Vicomte (1657), the château in the Ile-de-France which both Wren and Vanbrugh had doubtless seen, and Talman probably knew from French engravings (Fig. 15). For the latter had prior to Vanbrugh, prepared plans for Castle Howard which incorporated

16 *The chimney-stacks of Kings Weston, Gloucestershire.*

17 *Vanbrugh Castle at Greenwich. Designed for his own use, 1717.*

an oval saloon on the garden front like that at Vaux-le-Vicomte. Vanbrugh abandoned the saloon but adopted on the entrance front the Vaux-le-Vicomte hall with dual flanking staircases. He also kept on the entrance front the quadrant corridors of the French château linking centre blocks to wings, and of course greatly projected the end wings so as to form an ample forecourt. If these motifs were Vanbrugh's, as seems likely, the masterly handling of the façade masses was probably Hawksmoor's.

Several other French influences are detectable in Vanbrugh's houses, such as Antoine Le Pautre's grouping of units and rustication, Le Muet's ringed Doric columns, and Bruant's Invalides arcades. But if in his early practice Vanbrugh eschewed Italian and cultivated French influences, he infused his buildings with a monumental quality unmistakably his own. For he alone of English architects of our period, if we except the ageing Wren, was possessed of genius. Robert Adam, Reynolds and Soane were aware of it, however much they deplored his lack of refinement and taste. Adam called his buildings 'rough jewels of inestimable value'; Reynolds praised his versatility and imagination as the attributes of a poet, and Soane referred to him as 'the Shakespeare of architects', and rightly so for his buildings are brimful of poetry. What could be more inspired than the rhythm of those twenty arched chimney-stacks (Fig. 16) on the skyline of Kings Weston? Or more dramatic than the through-views to the stairs from the hall at Grimsthorpe? Not for nothing had he been a playwright and promoter of opera. Professor Webb was the first scholar to touch upon the connection between his country houses and his Haymarket opera-house, where he took immense pains over the scenery, poring over the

English edition of Pozzo's *Perspective*, and even engaging theatre designers, as well as singers, from Italy.

Poetic and dramatic Vanbrugh's buildings undoubtedly are; they are also imbued with history and romance. He was fascinated by associations with the distant past. His 'Reasons Offer'd for Preserving some Part of the Old Manor' of Woodstock in the park at Blenheim reveal it. 'There is perhaps no one thing,' he opens his treatise, 'which the most polite part of mankind have more universally agreed in; than the value they have ever set upon the remains of distant times nor amongst the severall kinds of those antiquitys, are there any so much regarded, as those of buildings; some for their magnificence, or curious workmanship; and others; as they move more lively and pleasing reflections . . . on the persons who have inhabited them; on the remarkable things which have been transacted in them. . . .' He was strongly drawn to the mediaeval. His preposterous appointment as Clarenceux King of Arms filled him with delightful, romantic notions. Certainly in Queen Anne's reign the old aristocracy were developing a retrospective interest in their ancestors, and the new families were busily acquiring them. Vanbrugh fostered this spirit in a practical sense, often by preserving whenever he could the Gothic core of the houses he was called upon to rebuild, as at Lumley Castle, or by simulating the mediaeval, at Vanbrugh Castle (Fig. 17), and the Tudor, in the corner towers of Seaton Delaval.

Beyond a sentimental attachment to Woodstock Manor, which had been 'rais'd by one of the bravest and most war-like of the English Kings [Henry II]' and 'tenderly regarded as the scene of his affections [Fair Rosamund's Bower]', Vanbrugh had respect for its signal landscape value. With

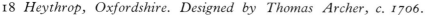

18 *Heythrop, Oxfordshire. Designed by Thomas Archer, c. 1706.*

19 *Heythrop. Borrominesque detail on the south-west front.*

the help of judiciously disposed plantations he saw it could supply 'all the wants of nature in that place'. This first of the romantics was also the first to relate a great country house to its natural setting in terms of landscape painting. Nowhere was he more successful in the attempt than at Blenheim. Reynolds again was quick to appreciate Vanbrugh's special skill in painterly composition of house and park, so as to make the latter form the scenic background to the former; and he also praised his understanding of light and shade. 'No architect took greater care than he that [his buildings] did not abruptly start out of the ground without expectation or preparation.'

Only in Vanbrugh's later houses is an Italian influence perceptible. Even then it is second-hand, being a concession, seemingly reluctant, to the prevailing Palladianism of Lord Burlington and his followers. The portico of the south front of Seaton Delaval, the projected garden front and the executed Venetian windows of the entrance front at Grimsthorpe are feminine incursions upon the sturdy independence of his designs. Vanbrugh was always keenly alive to the ephemeral requirements of high society, and towards the end of his life he allowed fashion to intrude upon his style, somewhat to its detriment.

As has already been pointed out the only important English Baroque architect to have studied in Italy was Thomas Archer. He signed his name in the visitors' book at Padua University on 13 December 1691. That he stayed also in Rome we hardly need documentary proof. Archer's interest in Roman seventeenth-century Baroque architecture is distinctly registered in his own buildings, but

unfortunately there are too few of Archer's surviving country houses from which to trace the development of his style. On the other hand his churches afford an extraordinary variety of plans and structural detail.

Archer was an isolated figure who belonged to no vernacular school. He was not a professional, although appointed in 1711 one of the commissioners to administer the Act for building Fifty Churches in London and the suburbs. Towards this number he contributed St John's Smith Square, and St Paul's Deptford. He was essentially a gentleman-architect, being the younger son of a Warwickshire county family. He was a man of means derived chiefly from sinecures; and in 1705 he was given the nicely lucrative and unexacting post of Groom Porter to Queen Anne. Although he lived until 1743 he may not actually have built anything after 1715.

In 1706 Archer began Heythrop House for his friend and fellow Romanophil, the Duke of Shrewsbury. To this great house (Fig. 18) the influence of Bernini's Louvre design was basic but much of the detail was lifted from Borromini. It cannot be claimed that Heythrop was entirely successful or that it had lasting influence upon country-house architecture. The grouping of the parts was clumsy and much of the detail too eccentric for English taste. Nevertheless no English architect before or since Archer made such extravagant experiments, and he remains one of our most interesting and enigmatic designers. Gigantic broken pediments, canted doorways, tapered pilasters, bulbous console brackets, lugged window heads and involuted capitals were his stock-in-trade' (Fig. 19). His water pavilion at Wrest Park (Fig. 20) is comparable with Borromini's Sant' Ivo chapel, Rome, being a masterpiece

of geometrical curves and rectangles containing a triangular core. From whatever direction you look at it the little domed building writhes with movement.

By contrast John James, called of Greenwich, and the last of the period's architects of national stature, is staid. He began his career as a carpenter in the office of Matthew Banckes, Master-Carpenter to the Crown and in this capacity he basked in the aura of Wren at Greenwich. He fell more particularly under the influence of Hawksmoor, having worked many years with him at the Royal Seamen's Hospital. In 1711 he joined the Board of Works. Yet he professed to dislike the extravagant style, claiming Inigo Jones as his guide. Notwithstanding this pretension his own buildings are markedly un-Palladian. His finest house, Appuldurcombe (Fig. 21), now a silvery disembodied ghost, looks back to the Webb block at Greenwich Hospital with additional Baroque touches in the niches and the coupled chimneys. The carved stonework throughout is exquisite. His own house, Warbrook, of red brick is strikingly individual. It is a skilful composition of unadorned masses with, again, coupled chimney-stacks prominent in the design.

There are echoes of James's style in his native county of Hampshire, at Hursley Park, Hinton Admiral and even Herriard Park.

20 *(left) The Pavilion at Wrest Park, Bedfordshire. Designed by Thomas Archer, 1711–12.*

21 *(below) Appuldurcombe, Isle of Wight. Probably designed by John James, 1701–10. (Now a ruin.)*

V. PROVINCIAL ARCHITECTS

The provinces evolved their several interpretations of the Baroque. As we should expect, the regional variations in a minor key lasted long after the final notes of the metropolitan theme had died away. Thus the style lingered in remote districts well into the fourth decade of the century when nearly all its great national exponents were dead and Palladianism was firmly rooted in the Home Counties. The provincial men who still built in the old manner could invariably boast some link with the national architects whom we have been considering.

Curiously enough the influence of Archer was widespread, considering how alien, quirky and eccentric he could be. We find the Bastards in Blandford, and Ireson at Ven House and Crowcombe Court in distant Somerset, adopting in the 1730s his weighty window-aprons and Borrominesque capitals (Fig. 22). In Shropshire the almost aggressive tympanum of Hardwick Hall (Fig. 23), and in Buckinghamshire the swept parapet of Chicheley Hall, are undoubted Archerian echoes. There are reasons for attributing both these houses to Francis Smith, an extremely versatile and prolific Midlands architect who worked mostly for the old-fashioned Tory squires. Smith of Warwick, as he was called, would repay closer study than he has yet received. His Stoneleigh Abbey, Sutton Scarsdale and (Fig. 24) Mawley Hall (if indeed this most Baroque of provincial houses is his), all distinguished by supreme craftsmanship, raise Smith among the immortals of English architects. Most of his professional career however falls within the Early Georgian period

22 (left) A capital at Crowcombe Court, Somerset. Begun 1734 by Nathaniel Ireson.

23 (top) The central block of Hardwick Hall, Shropshire, c. 1715. Possibly by Francis Smith.

24 (above) Mawley Hall, Shropshire. Attributed to Francis Smith, c. 1730.

25 *(top) The centrepiece of the main façade of Aldby Park, Yorkshire. Possibly by William Etty of York. The arcaded windows would seem to derive from those on the main front of the Palazzo Barberini in Rome.*

26 *(above) A section of the entrance façade of Bernini's Palazzo Barberini.*

(see Christopher Hussey, *English Country Houses, 1715–1760*).

Archer's social contacts certainly took him to Yorkshire. His friendship with Lord Bingley and the Earl of Strafford led to some fundamental influences at Bramham, Wentworth Castle and even Beningbrough. The owners of these houses were, in contrast with the squires of Ven, Crowcombe, Hardwick and Chicheley, travelled and sophisticated men, with distinct claims to architectural knowledge. Archer and his friends' experiments with Roman *settecento* motifs were at least actuated by sound scholarships, as the sections on some of their houses will show. The central bays of Wentworth Castle and Aldby Park (Fig. 25) have an affinity in their superimposed arcaded windows with the frontispiece of Bernini's Palazzo Barberini (Fig. 26). Both houses are distinguished by the superb carving in which the York masons and joiners excelled. Wentworth was designed by Jean Bodt, a French Protestant refugee who settled in Berlin; Aldby may have been built by William Etty of York, who deputized for Vanbrugh at neighbouring Castle Howard and at Seaton Delaval.

Indeed the Archerian merges with the Vanbrughian influence in Yorkshire. There are unmistakable traces of the last inside Aldby in the monumental hall chimney-piece and the Doric order of the Breakfast Room. Thoroughly Vanbrughian in style is the architecture of William Wakefield, an East Riding squire, who bears out Sir John's remark that, 'There are several gentlemen in this part of the world that are possessed of the spirit of building.' Wakefield's Duncombe Park and Gilling Castle have been much altered, but in the former the stout use of the Doric order and massing of units, and in the latter the treatment of the forecourt wings in canted bays so as to harmonize with the Tudor polygonal towers on the garden side, are clearly inspired by Vanbrugh.

In the early eighteenth century a great house would often breed lesser houses in the vicinity. At Blenheim Palace a vast army of master-masons and master-craftsmen of a superior kind were employed at intervals over a long period. Sir Thomas Wheate, baronet of Glympton four miles away to the north, got one of them—he is unknown—to add a garden front to his modest seat, having tried and failed to engage Vanbrugh himself. The man who acted at Blenheim as 'comptroller and conductor' for over ten years was Henry Joynes. He began work there as a young man of twenty-one and remained deep in the confidence of Hawksmoor, who instilled into him the rudiments of architecture and draughtsmanship. Joynes assisted his master with the Clarendon Building at Oxford and succeeded him as Clerk of the Works at Kensington Palace. Yet Joynes's only surviving country house, Linley Hall in Shropshire, is basically a compact Palladian villa—it was built as late as the 1740s—of which the façade breaks and recessions are the only reminders of the training of his Baroque youth. On the other hand Hawksmoor's protégé, William Townesend, member of a large Oxford family of master-masons, and like Joynes employed for many years at Blenheim, was faithful to the Hawksmoor style whenever he built to his own designs. Had he not been older than Joynes and had he lived later than 1739 he might likewise have departed from it. Townesend was in constant demand by the University. He built to the designs of Hawksmoor at Queen's and All Souls Colleges, as well as at Christ Church (Peckwater Quadrangle) under Dean Aldrich, and Worcester College under Dr George Clarke, but the interiors of hall and chapel at Queen's were to his own draughts. He was a hard-working, hard-headed, unambitious mason-architect who amassed a great deal of money. He seems to have been content to remain fairly anonymous, yet recent researches suggest that he designed and built Shotover Park, Woodperry

27 *The south front of Compton Verney,*
Warwickshire, 1714.

28 *Part of the elevation of the Duke's Head, King's Lynn. Originally Sir*
John Turner's house, it was designed by Henry Bell, 1683.

House, Britwell Court and Haseley Court in Oxfordshire;
he may even have built Compton Verney in Warwickshire (Fig. 27). All these houses have inherited the sound,
common-sensical robustness of Hawksmoor, without his
originality and learning.

All over England the mason-builders were busily engaged in raising houses for the nobility and gentry. Seldom
were they at liberty either to present a draught entirely out
of their own heads or to carry it out unaltered. Nearly all
worked at the dictation and under the guidance of exacting
clients who knew pretty well what they wanted and were
determined to get it, or if they did not know, prevaricated
and repeatedly interfered with the designs submitted. The
wonder is how seldom the architecture went seriously
wrong. The client, while proudly brandishing a letter of

advice from Sir Christopher Wren's office on the seasoning
of floor-boards or the laying of roof-tiles, would perhaps
rough out a scheme which the mason-builder perfected
with the help of Le Petit Marot or Blondel's *Cours*
d'architecture, for until 1728 when Gibbs's *Book of*
Architecture appeared, few up-to-date manuals in English
were available. Lord Nottingham acted like this with his
supervisor, John Lumley, who drew innumerable sketches
of moulds and details. It is unlikely that Lumley was very
creative at Burley or at Ampthill Park to whose owner,
Lord Ashburnham, he was sent on Nottingham's recommendation. Even Counsellor Vernon seems to have tried
out at least three local builders who submitted sketches for
a main front to Hanbury Hall. The sketches all agree as to
the prerequisite size and shape of the house down to the

29 *Trewithen, Cornwall. Begun 1715 and finished by Thomas Edwards in 1738–40.*

30 *Wellesbourne Hall, Warwickshire, c. 1700.*

details of the exact number of floors and windows.

It is astonishing how far the influence of the Board of Works architects penetrated the provinces. Not until we get right away from London and the Home Counties into remote pockets of the country where no great palaces were arising do we come upon a purely vernacular architecture. Even Henry Bell of King's Lynn, possibly the author of the Kimbolton Castle quadrangle, and certainly of the Customs House and other buildings in Lynn, was known to Robert Hooke who referred to him as an 'ingenious architect' and 'a witt'. Bell's architecture, which at first sight looks distinctly provincial, emerges on closer scrutiny as being quite sophisticated. Dutch in flavour, it is characterized by slight salients, garlanded Ionic capitals, broken pediments over doors and curious acanthus crests and grotesque masks over windows (Fig. 28). These are not the quirks of an ignorant mason but motifs culled from wide learning. Thomas Edwards, who built up a flourishing practice in Cornwall, originated from Greenwich and was to some extent under the influence of Gibbs to whose book he was a subscriber. Nevertheless his clean-cut, linear and flat façades, with the minimum of ornament, like granite Trewithen (Fig. 29), reflect the rugged quality of the peninsular duchy. Only the remoter and lesser country houses are free from metropolitan influences. Red-brick Wellesbourne Hall, Warwickshire (Fig. 30), Acton Round Hall, Shropshire and Bourne Park beyond Canterbury, whose designers and builders remain nicely anonymous, can perhaps be described simply as no more and no less than William and Mary or Queen Anne.

VI. ROOMS OF STATE

On the whole the interiors of English Baroque houses are dull compared with the exteriors. The visitor, having been excited by the movement of the courtyard and façade of Blenheim Palace, is, on entering the hall, greeted with stony anti-climax. With Palladian houses the emphasis is in reverse. The grimly ordered front of, say, Holkham, is forgotten once you are within the voluptuous hall with its aisles of pink and green alabaster columns on a deep plinth banded with damson marble and its richly coffered apse. Yet in country houses of our period much attention was paid by owners to the apartments of state. These were intended and usually reserved for display. In his daydreams the great Whig lord looked forward to the occasion when he might receive his sovereign in a fashion that would bring him credit. Or if, like Lord Carlisle, he were already playing a prominent part in affairs of state, he would deem it incumbent upon him to receive his neighbours, tenants and petitioners in a manner suited to his dignity, which was that of a petty prince. Even Mr Secretary Blathwayt, no great aristocrat, must have at Dyrham, a house of medium size, 'not more than six or seven Apartments more for state than use except upon extraordinary occasion', according to a description by his nephew in 1700. Mr Blathwayt's letters make it clear that he always hoped to persuade Queen Anne whenever she took the Bath waters to visit him. Alas, he was not successful! At Petworth no distinc-

tion was made between rooms of state and family living rooms because no doubt the proud Duke of Somerset never lived in any other way but state. All the principal rooms there are on the ground floor. In most large houses the grand suite was kept apart, usually on the first floor as at Boughton, Burghley and Wentworth Castle. At Chatsworth, an Elizabethan house reconstituted, it is on the second floor.

We would expect therefore the staircase leading to the state rooms to be very magnificent. Certainly much thought was given to it, as we learn from the papers at Chatsworth where the approach received the most lavish treatment that the space allowed. Yet English stairs of this period are modest beside French ones. None is grander than those at Petworth and Burley-on-the-Hill, which, oddly enough, led to no important suite of rooms, if we exclude the single upstairs saloon of the latter house. On the staircase and the hall from which it usually sprang the owner concentrated the highest form of art or craftsmanship procurable, sometimes, as at Hanbury, almost to the exclusion of the other apartments. Iron balustrades for stairs were a novelty. Inigo Jones had, it is true, used one of simple tulip pattern in the Queen's House, Greenwich; but they do not appear again until our period. Balustrades by Tijou himself are a rarity; only those of the great staircases at Hampton Court, Kensington Palace (Fig. 31),

Chatsworth and Kiveton were wrought by the master. The west staircase balusters at Chatsworth are the work of his pupil, John Gardom of Derbyshire. The lyre-shaped rails at Cottesbrooke and Easton Neston owe their inspiration to Tijou, as do the balustrades by the little-known Joshua Lord at Burley-on-the-Hill.

This was the age *par excellence* of the decorative painter. It became the fashion to have the stairwell of a great house covered with mythological scenes from the classics, such as Hercules between Vice and Virtue, or Achilles among the daughters of Lycomedes. Only rarely, if the owner were a national hero like the Duke of Marlborough, or a stupendously rich heiress like the Duchess of Somerset, was he or she apotheosized amid clouds or drawn in a triumphal car accompanied by winged *amorini*. It was typical of the English to adopt with fervour a fashion that was already played out on the Continent. It was a pity, too, that with few exceptions the foreign practitioners engaged were second-rate. The exceptions were Jean-Baptiste Monnoyer and Jacques Rousseau, brought from Paris by the Duke of Montagu, and Pellegrini and Marco Ricci from Venice by the Duke of Manchester. Pellegrini's staircase at Kimbolton has a Rococo sparkle and liveliness not found in any other large mural composition, but unfortunately little of the foreigners' work in this country has survived. The majority of owners were not such discriminating virtuosi as these two Dukes and merely regarded large painted surfaces as we would a superior wallpaper. Celia Fiennes never looked closely into decorated ceilings unless it was to cry out in shocked surprise against the nakedness of the limbs displayed. She complained that 'its enough to break one's neck' to make the effort. What had been good enough for King Charles II at Windsor Castle was good enough for most owners of the next generation. So Verrio, whom Montagu likewise first introduced to England, having decorated the Windsor state rooms (Fig. 32) during the seventies and early eighties, was in perpetual country-house demand until his death in 1707. Although his illusionism was often feeble and his figures were stiff—towards the end of his life he had cataracts in both eyes—Verrio was the first painter to bring to this country a watered version of that Italian decoration which he had once helped Le Brun to reproduce at Versailles. His assistant and junior, the Frenchman Laguerre, was almost as popular. He was a no less capable painter, especially when engaged on restricted surfaces like ceiling coves. Chéron and Lanscroon followed in their wake. Curiously enough the native Thornhill was the best artist of the group, although he did little to develop the particular form of scenographic decoration which he inherited from the foreigners. He had a surer understanding of architecture and was a more delicate colourist than his predecessors.

The apartments at Windsor Castle form a landmark in the evolution of English Baroque culture because they were a fusion of the three arts of architecture (under Hugh May), painting (under Verrio) and carving (under Grinling Gibbons). They set an example which for the ensuing thirty years and more was followed by the nobility and gentry with varying degrees of success. In the Royal Chapel at Windsor (Fig. 33) illusionism and naturalism

31 *The King's Grand Staircase at Kensington Palace. Wrought-iron balustrade by Tijou, 1692–3, murals painted by William Kent, 1725–7.*

32 *A detail of the ceiling of the Queen's Audience Chamber, Windsor Castle.* Catherine of Braganza as Britannia in Triumph, *painted by Verrio, c. 1678.*

were so cunningly mingled that the spectator was left wondering whether the apse, the organ pipes, the ceiling and the carved stalls were genuine or feigned. The covering of entire walls and ceilings in *trompe l'œil* of one sort and another was the very essence of Italian Baroque decoration. The confusion engendered in the spectator's mind was its very purpose. Because the Heaven Room at Burghley and the staircase at Reigate Priory (Fig. 34) create an illusion of illimitable space, they come closer to Italian than to French prototypes, where painted scenes are usually confined within an architectural framework of stucco, and so delude nobody.

Typically Baroque was the treatment of woodwork which to be really elegant had to look different from what it really was. Thus Celia Fiennes remarks that at Newby Hall 'the best roome was painted just like marble'. Fir-panelled walls were frequently grained to simulate a superior wood. An agreement of December 1695 between Lord Nottingham and Charles Blunt of Nottingham, painter, stipulated for 'Oak wainscot colour grained & walnutt tree colour grain'd & all other wood-colours grained & laid three times in oyl proper for the said colours for eight pence for every square yard.' A room treated in this manner is the Balcony Room at Dyrham;

another painted to simulate rockwork is at Hill Court, Herefordshire. In great houses panelling was usually of oak, the moulds of door-cases often exquisitely undercut in acanthus foliage (Fig. 35). And of course the crowning achievement was that of Grinling Gibbons and his school of carvers. Their patterns, naturalistic and of extreme delicacy, were applied in pear or limewood to the oak background. The Gibbons practice, unique to England, disappeared with the onset of Palladianism which preferred repetitive patterns like the Vitruvian scroll and the money mould.

Towards the end of the seventeenth century plaster-work falls out of favour. It is true that the Gallery (now Library) ceiling at Chatsworth is composed of stucco compartments by the leading London plasterer, Edward Goudge, framing painted roundels. But it is interesting that in a letter dated 1702 Goudge attributed the decline of stucco decoration as much to the demand for ceiling paintings as to lack of money on account of the wars.

Pictures, apart from ancestral portraits, were few and far between in all but great houses. Tapestries on the other hand were until the turn of the century still a favourite wall covering. The first Dukes of Montagu (he purchased the Mastership of the Wardrobe in 1671 and took over the

33 (above left) The Royal Chapel, Windsor Castle. Designed by Hugh May, 1682–4. (Destroyed.) Watercolour by C. Wild, c. 1818, in the Royal Library, Windsor.

34 (above) The staircase at Reigate Priory, Surrey, decorated by Verrio, c. 1685.

35 (above right) Carved ornament on the moulding of a door-case at Beningbrough Hall, Yorkshire.

36 (below) The silver chandelier, 1694, in the State Dressing Room at Chatsworth.

Soho works) and Devonshire hung the state rooms of Boughton and Chatsworth with Mortlake panels. But in 1710 a traveller noted that 'now in England tapestry is no longer in fashion, [and] all is painted at great cost'.

Lack of variety is a criticism that may reasonably be levelled at English state rooms of the period. It is true that they usually lead one into another through doorways set exactly opposite each other so as to present an enfilade of brown monotony. Yet we should remember that against the grained fir panelling and the 'drab' painted backgrounds there was originally much fresh and vivid colouring. The ceilings were rich with painted figures and gold highlights; the tapestries were alive with gold and silver thread; silver chandeliers (Fig. 36) hung from ceilings and coroneted sconces twinkled on the walls. The candlelight from both was reflected in Venetian mirrors with frames of *verre églomisé* in red and green. Chairs were upholstered

in needlework *point de Hongrie*, or turkey work of bright floral patterns, and in Genoese cut velvet of crimson and saffron (Fig. 37).

Although Daniel Marot's name never appears in English account books his influence here was considerable long before the engravings of his works were published in 1712. This young French Huguenot who entered the service of William of Orange in 1685 was brimful with decorative schemes derived from Jean Berain and Jean Le Pautre, 'dessinateurs et ornemanistes du roi Louis'. By 1692 he had gained control of the decoration of Het Loo Palace in Gelderland and the layout of its gardens. In 1694–6 he was in England where he may have designed the sumptuous delftware vases now in the Queen's Gallery at Hampton Court (Fig. 38). Lesser blue and white delftware was supplied to Chatsworth and Dyrham, at both of which houses, as well as at Hampton Court, Talman was engaged. The corner chimney-pieces at Hampton Court (copied at Beningbrough, Hanbury and elsewhere) with tiers of shelves for pottery and porcelain were taken from Marot's designs (Fig. 39). So too were the great plumed beds (Fig. 40) with their convoluted testers, embroidered head-pieces and heavy hangings. Tables and upholstered chairs and gilt-framed mirrors assumed a new refinement after the accession of William III. We ought not to assign credit for these things exclusively to Marot, for after the

37 (above left) Three chairs of c. 1690, with loose covers of Italian velvet, formerly at Kimbolton Castle.

38 (left) Two delftware bulb holders in the Queen's Gallery, Hampton Court. Probably executed after designs by Daniel Marot by Adriaenus Kocks, 1687–1701.

39 (above) Engraved design for a wall and fireplace to display porcelain, by Daniel Marot, c. 1690.

40 (above right) The Melville Bed in the Victoria and Albert Museum, 1692–1707. The State Bed, made for the 1st Earl of Melville, is hung with white silk damask and red silk velvet, both trimmed in crimson.

Revocation of the Edict of Nantes numbers of Huguenot craftsmen—among them the cabinet-makers Gerreit Jensen and Jean Pelletier—fled to London direct from France. Furthermore rich noblemen brought back from Paris furniture they had ordered to be made for them there. The Duke of Manchester sent from Venice walnut and parcel gilt chairs, the arms, legs and stretchers of which were carved with wildly extravagant foliage, and several looking, or 'seeing' glasses, as they were called, elaborately coloured, painted, etched and moulded.

With more luxurious furnishings to look after owners developed a greater house pride than in Caroline days. The 2nd Earl of Nottingham's *Orders for ye Groom of ye Chambers* throw some light on a nobleman's concern for his possessions. There is only space here for quotation of the first two orders:

1. You must be careful of the furniture, brushing and cleaning every morning that which is in constant use, and the rest also once or twice in the week or oftener if need be.
2. You must make fires in the hall, parlour, etc. where required, keeping clean the hearths and often coming in to repair them and at night to snuff ye candles. [And for prayers] lay the cushens and take them away when done, and keep them and all the furniture of the chappell clean.

VII. THE DECLINE OF THE BAROQUE

That the English Baroque survived in official circles after 1714 was due to Vanbrugh's status as Comptroller of the Works until his death, and as Surveyor to Greenwich Hospital in succession to Wren early in George I's reign. But as I have already intimated, even Vanbrugh's once uncompromising architecture was affected towards the end of his life by the new Palladianism. In domestic building the Baroque was still accepted for another generation by the Tory squires in silent, unconscious protest against the hated Whig magnates who in their eyes represented Dissent, trade, war and the excess profits thereby accruing. What on the other hand the English Baroque meant to the Whigs, when its course was almost run, is best summarized by its critics.

The famous letter from the 3rd Earl of Shaftesbury to Lord Somers of 1712 was written when the Whigs were temporarily in opposition. It does not of course contain the word 'Baroque', which was then totally unknown, but in identifying art with politics Lord Shaftesbury laments that with the Revolution of 1688—'when the spirit of the nation was grown more free'—the bad old style, which came to the fore with Charles II's autocracy, had not then been rejected out of hand. A new 'correct' architecture to coincide with a reformed standard of popular conduct was long overdue. Without mentioning the Tory Wren by name the Earl inveighs against the taste of 'one single court architect' being imposed upon the nation. The public, he says, is becoming indignant 'at the hearing of a new palace spoilt [Hampton Court?] or a new design committed to some rash or impotent pretender [Vanbrugh at Greenwich?]'. He expresses the fear that in consequence of the Act of 1711 more church spires will arise in the City, 'retaining much of what artists call the Gothick kind of relish', by which he means that debased taste to be associated with the dark, tyrannical past.

Then he touches upon an interesting new development in an enlightened public voice. When a great man builds for himself a country house he need expect little quarter from the masses if the style does not meet with their approval. In other words the Earl, in bracketing the Baroque style with the vested interests of an exclusively landed class represented by the Jacobite and High Church statesmen, Harley and St John, is hinting at an urban democracy based on manufacture and material progress.

Colen Campbell is equally censorious, and since his first volume of *Vitruvius Britannicus* was published in 1715 just after the Hanoverian succession he assumes a new patriotic tone. For his famous condemnation of 'capricious orna-ments, which must at last end in the Gothick', and of the 'shockingly licentious' designs of Borromini, 'who has endeavoured to debauch mankind with his odd and chimaerical beauties', is as much a parting shot at the High Church Tories and Catholic Stuarts who patronized this style of architecture as at the architecture itself. Of Baroque buildings he has this to say: 'the parts are without proportion, solids without their true bearing, heaps of materials without strength, excessive ornaments without grace, and the whole without symmetry. And', he concludes with a deep sigh over the state of contemporary architecture abroad, 'what can be a stronger argument that this excellent art is near lost in that country [Italy], where such absurdities meet with applause?'

Finally, we have the wretched experience of the Italian Alessandro Galilei who, at the invitation of his patron the Irishman John Molesworth, reached England just after Queen Anne's death and the reinstatement of the Whigs. In spite of recommendations to various noblemen and the Court, the designs of this Baroque Papist architect for country houses, a royal palace and even seven City churches (some rivalling Guarini's in their play and counter-play with segments and ellipses) met with a frigid reception. In disgust Galilei wrote home that the English were 'grandissimi asini', and England 'non è paese dove la virtù sia apprezzata'. Unappreciated himself he returned to Italy where he immediately received important commissions and added the great façade to the Lateran church in Rome. A letter which his friend Molesworth wrote to him in 1726 sums up the change that had finally taken place in England. 'For here the reigning taste is Palladio's style of building and a man is a heretick that should talk of Michel Angelo or any other modern architect. You must diligently copy all the noted fabricks of Palladio for those very drafts would introduce you here, and without them you may despair of success.' Doubtless by now, having put behind him his shabby treatment in England and being hailed as a star in his own country, Galilei could not care less.

Shaftesbury and Campbell may or may not have been right in seeing the source of the English Baroque style in Stuart autocracy. They certainly overlooked the fact that its most mature expression coincided with the reign of their hero King William III, and the triumph of those Whig liberties they so loudly proclaimed. It is always tempting, but rash, to identify artistic styles with political creeds. The two seldom run parallel for long. And we are invariably left as we began our diagnosis with many anomalies unresolved.

41 *The entrance front from the south.*

WINSLOW HALL, BUCKINGHAMSHIRE

Begun for Secretary William Lowndes in 1699 and finished in 1702. This red-brick house was almost certainly designed by Sir Christopher Wren. 'Accompts of the Charge of Building, etc.' give full details of expenses and the names of the craftsmen employed. (The home of Mr and Mrs Edward Tomkins.)

The claim of Winslow Hall to be the first country house described in this series rests upon its undoubted association with Sir Christopher Wren. His proven domestic work is extremely scanty. Fawley Court, also in Buckinghamshire, is a very dubious claimant. Tring Manor, Hertfordshire, was long ago altered out of all recognition. Both these houses belong chronologically to the Caroline period and, stylistically, were typical of it. Winslow Hall, although dating well within the Baroque period, is nevertheless untypical, apart from one distinctive feature which will at once be evident when we come to look at the exterior.

The house is for its date singularly old-fashioned. When

it was begun Sir Christopher was rising seventy years of age, its owner rising fifty. William Lowndes was born in 1652 and had for sixteen years been employed in the Treasury before he became Secretary in 1695. This put him in close touch with the Surveyor-General, who had in fact designed Tring Manor for Lowndes's predecessor in office, Secretary Henry Guy, as long ago as 1669.

William Lowndes was a native of Winslow where his family had lived in modest circumstances since the early sixteenth century. His financial adroitness brought him a tidy fortune. He originated the funding system and coined the phrase 'Ways and Means', which he adopted as the family motto. In 1697 he bought the manor of Winslow, but he must already have leased the land because two years previously he began laying out the garden of his new house on the extreme eastern edge of the town. Building, however, did not start until 1699.

Winslow Hall is well documented. William Lowndes's building and garden accounts, discovered before the last war, have been published by the Wren Society (vol. XVII,

42 (above) The garden front.

43 (left) Detail of the south doorway, inscribed 'William Lowndes A.D. MDCC'.

44 (below) Plan of the ground floor.

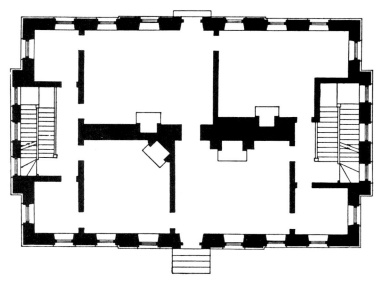

45 *Decoration in the style of Daniel Marot, in the Painted Room on the first floor.*

1940). From them we learn the whole cost of the operation —it amounted to £6,585. 10s. 2¼d. in all—from 1699 to 1702. Not only are bills included but also the names of the craftsmen employed, Richard Mapletoft, London mason and John Yemans, bricklayer from Hampton, Middlesex. The first worked the quoins and door-cases in stone brought from Cosgrave in Northamptonshire and provided most of the chimney-pieces; the second laid over a million ordinary bricks and nearly a thousand rubbed bricks round windows and doors. These men were directly responsible to Lowndes. Moreover, three other craftsmen employed were Board of Works men who had toiled under Wren at St Paul's and elsewhere—namely Matthew Banckes, King's Master-Carpenter, Charles Hopson, King's Joiner, and Joseph Roberts, King's Serjeant-Plumber. Again, John Churchill, whose job was equivalent to that of a quantity surveyor, was a carpenter employed on the royal palaces and, oddly enough, on Marlborough House for his namesake the 1st Duke of that title.

While, however, no payments for designs are noted in the accounts, and no payments to Wren himself, yet several of the bills, particularly Hopson's, were 'abated by Sir Chr Wren's Judgmt', which certainly implies that he closely scrutinized what was going on. If Wren had provided draughts and plats these may well have been paid for before Lowndes's account book opens. And there is evidence in the design of Winslow as well as the quality of the workmanship to suggest that he did provide them.

The house is sited so close to the Aylesbury road that a proper view of the entrance front (Fig. 41) can only be obtained by walking into the field opposite. From there the pronounced verticality of the building is more fully apparent than in the garden front (Fig. 42), which is an exact duplicate, apart from not being raised on a terrace owing to the higher ground level. Seemingly unsophisticated these two fronts are most expertly handled. The three central bays under an acutely pointed pediment are just perceptibly broken forward. The undressed windows and the door-case (that on the entrance front has 'William Lowndes A.D. MDCC' carved under the elliptical hood, for the cutting of which mason Mapletoft charged 5s.) are framed within bands of rubbed orange brick against deep plum walls. In fact the elevations are nearly identical with the front of the house which Wren built for the Master of the Temple, London, more than thirty years previously. But there is one additional feature at Winslow which lends this house a Baroque distinction lacking in the earlier. It is the four enormous panelled chimney-stacks riding upon the steep-pitched roof. In all other respects the 'design of Winslow is truly old-fashioned.

For two hundred years the flanking pavilions for kitchen, brewhouse and laundry, and for stables, coach-house and 'milkhouse' remained detached from the centre block. A single tall chimney-stack dominated each. In 1901 the pavilions were linked by clumsy abutments, the removal of which would restore a proper balance to the original composition.

The plan of the house is rectangular, with forward breaks of a foot or two on the side elevations. These accommodate two staircases of modest dog-leg plan and surprisingly slender balusters (Fig. 47). The reception rooms, although generously proportioned, lack spectacular decoration. Most of the rooms are wainscoted in oak fielded panels common in this period, and doubtless the work of joiner Hopson and carpenter Banckes (Fig. 46). The most

46 (below left) Oak panelling in the dining room (as in 1951).

47 (below right) One of the two staircases.

remarkable apartment is the large Painted Room (Fig. 45) on the first floor facing north. Four wide spaces over the dado are filled with canvases (c. 1700) by an unknown artist inspired, according to Mr E. Croft-Murray, by the famous series of tapestries of the 'Château du Roi' by Le Brun. They have been cut and were evidently not painted for this room. The central landscapes are overwhelmed by the heavy grotesque frames of scrolls, cartouches, masks, herms and draperies.

Nothing now remains of the garden layout by the well-known firm of London and Wise. From 1695 to 1701 they sent William Lowndes fruit trees and plants, and in 1702 charged him £20. 7s. 10d. for stocking 'the largest garden, ye Kitchen garden and the Platts before ye house'.

William Lowndes's great-grandson, another William, on succeeding to the Whaddon estates in 1813, added the prefix of Selby to his patronymic. After that date Winslow became a secondary home of the Selby-Lowndes family. In 1898 it was sold to Mr N. D. McCorquodale. In 1948 it was virtually saved from demolition by Mr G. Houghton Brown who acquired it in the nick of time. He sold it in 1959 to Mr Edward Tomkins, the present owner.

48 *The house and stables from the north.*

BOUGHTON HOUSE, NORTHAMPTONSHIRE

After 1528 a successful lawyer, Sir Edward Montagu, began the huge house. Ralph, 1st Duke of Montagu, transformed Boughton between 1683 and 1709 in the French taste. The architect of this remarkably unaltered house is unknown. (A seat of the Duke of Buccleuch and Queensberry.)

Of Boughton's remarkable qualities the most apparent are, I think, these. Firstly, its Frenchness. Secondly, in spite of immense size and occasional grandeur, its contrasting homeliness, both in situation and architecture. Thirdly, its timeless, arrested beauty which gives it, of all our great Baroque houses, a peculiar magic. The Frenchness of course was deliberate owing to Ralph, Duke of Montagu's close ties with and love of France. The homeliness may

partly be due to the fact that this palace was never finished, and the magic to its having been neglected and left undisturbed practically for two hundred years.

The lay manor of Boughton was in 1528 conveyed to a successful lawyer, Sir Edward Montagu, who in 1539 became Chief Justice of the King's Bench, and subsequently of the Common Pleas. He accumulated large estates in Northamptonshire and died in 1557. He built round a number of courtyards the large, straggling house which serves as the core of the Boughton of today. Parts of the mid sixteenth-century building are visible in the enclosed Fish Court to the south of the great hall, the Bell Court, the south front, and of course in several rooms untouched by later owners. Sir Edward's eldest grandson and namesake became 1st Lord Montagu of Boughton; his fourth

49 *The entrance façade.*

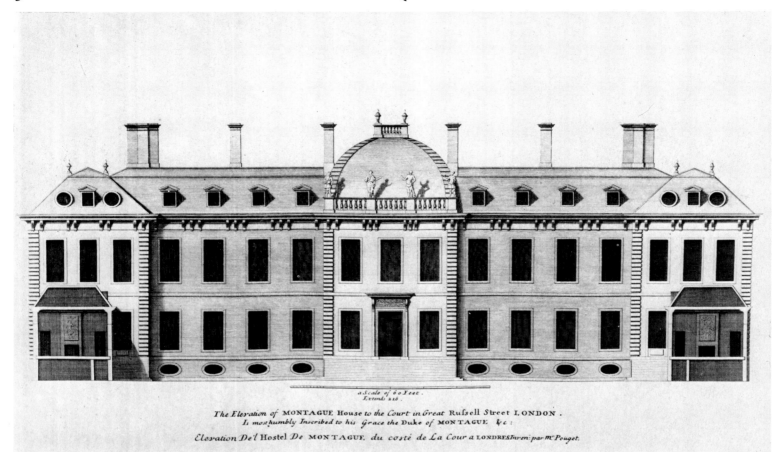

50 *(above) The elevation of Montagu House (from Vitruvius Britannicus).*

51 *The stable block lying to the east of the house.*

52 (top) The pediment over the stable arch.

53 (centre) The west front.

54 (left) The north-west pavilion.

55 *Inside the entrance arcade.*

56 *(opposite) The Great Hall.*

grandson was an ancestor of the Dukes of Manchester, and his seventh an ancestor of the Earls of Sandwich.

It was the 3rd Lord Montagu (Fig. 58) who transformed Boughton after his succession in 1683. Ralph Montagu was according to Bishop Burnet 'a man of pleasure'. He may have been 'coarse, sallow, fattish', but he was also 'gifted with charm' and had an undoubted love and understanding of the arts. On equivocal terms with his Stuart sovereigns Charles II and James II he was sent abroad whenever opportunity offered, and in 1669 was made Plenipotentiary Extraordinary to France. His entry into Paris was accompanied by seventy-four pages, twelve lead horses, coaches and chariots 'as costly as art and workmanship could

contrive'. In 1677 he was back there as Ambassador. After the Rye House Plot in 1683 he again went to France in exile. On the accession of William and Mary he was rewarded with a viscountcy and earldom for his services in the Glorious Revolution. In 1705 he was created Duke of Montagu by Queen Anne.

Ralph Montagu's contemporaries and posterity have all agreed that he assiduously cultivated French tastes which he endeavoured to introduce to his own country. It was he who brought Verrio from Paris to England in 1672. His Bloomsbury town house, which was first built in 1674–9 by Robert Hooke in what Evelyn described as 'the French pavilion way', was burnt down and rebuilt in

57 *The ceiling of the Great Hall;* The Marriage of Hercules and Hebe *by Louis Chéron.*

58 *Portrait of Ralph, 1st Duke of Montagu.*

1686–8 with mansard roofs and a *cour d'honneur* in a style even more French than before. According to Colen Campbell and Vertue[1] a mysterious personage named Monsieur Pouget was the architect, but probably it was again Hooke,[2] whose tastes in architecture were notably Gallic. Montagu House was decorated by a team of Frenchmen under Charles de la Fosse, Jacques Rousseau the landscape painter, Jean-Baptiste Monnoyer the flower painter, and Jacques Parmentier.

Precisely in which year after his succession Ralph Montagu began operations at Boughton is not known, nor was the name of his architect recorded by him. But the strong probability is that whoever redesigned Montagu House, whether Pouget or Robert Hooke, extended and improved Boughton soon afterwards.[3] This would be in the early 1690s. The resemblance of the north front (Fig. 49) to the façade of Montagu House (Fig. 50) is more than superficial. We have the same long two-storey block, shallow basement and mansard attic floor with pedimented dormers. At Boughton, it is true, the pavilions project by four bays as though to initiate the *cour d'honneur* so conspicuous at Montagu House. And it seems that the curiously unpompous arch entrance which we drive through was originally sited to face the entrance door of the north front, and was shifted to its present off-centre position by the 2nd Duke. The ground floor of the Front is an open loggia. The horizontal rustication and the Doric pilasters—with entablatures broken forward and grouped at the corners—are peculiarly French.

The stable block (Fig. 51) away to the left is attached to the house by a long wing (by contrast modest and traditionally English) running from behind the north-east pavilion of the entrance front. The stable block, which faces west, has two storeys and slightly projecting wings. The angles are horizontally channelled like those of Montagu House. Similarly channelled is the monumental opening with the ducal arms (carved by Gideon du Chesne after 1704 for £15) in the pediment (Fig. 52). Above it the distinctive, four-sided dome is a flattened version of the one at Montagu House, which Hooke in his turn may have taken from a design by Wren for Winchester Palace.

Presumably the 1st Duke intended to finish off the west front (Fig. 53) of the house in the same symmetrical style as the north front. As it was, he got as far as three bays beyond the north-west pavilion (Fig. 54), and abruptly halted. We should perhaps be grateful that he spared the low, old range on account of the charming earlier rooms and chimney-pieces which it contains.

The gentle undulations of the surrounding parkland lent themselves to ambitious garden projects and Duke Ralph seized with both hands the opportunities nature offered him. As early as 1684 he had begun a layout in a westerly

59 *The Stone Staircase Hall decorated by Chéron; it leads to the state apartments.*

and south-westerly direction on such a gigantic scale that comparison with Versailles was inevitable. John, 2nd Duke of Montagu, was a no less enthusiastic gardener than his magnificent father. Indeed, he was known as 'The Planter', and during the forty years of his reign extended the avenues for miles into the country. He was according to his mother-in-law Sarah, Duchess of Marlborough, a simple individual given to childlike pranks. 'To get people into his gardens and wet them with squirts, to invite people to his country house and put things in their beds to make them itch', never failed to arouse in him infinite merriment. On the other hand, the well-known antiquary William Stukeley considered him an extremely cultivated and civilized being.

Duke Ralph may have been inspired by Versailles in transforming the exterior of his ancestral home, but what he did inside only faintly recalls the splendour of the Sun King's apartments. His rooms are not so much French as English, being really unambitious versions of the state apartments at Hampton Court and Kensington Palace.

A large, central, winged door in the north loggia leads through a passage to the north-east end of the Great Hall (Fig. 56). Here Duke Ralph hid the sixteenth-century roof with a vaulted ceiling, which after 1695 he engaged Louis Chéron, a young Protestant who had left France because

[1] Who writes, 'the Architecture conducted by Monr. Pouget 1678'. Vertue certainly got the date wrong. Mr John Harris tentatively suggests that Pouget was a misreading of Boujet, a late seventeenth-century designer whose few drawings are among the Smithson collection in the R.I.B.A.

[2] Hooke's master-joiner at Ragley, by name Roger Davies, did extensive work at Boughton between 1687 and 1692, and at Montagu House.

[3] Sir Anthony Blunt sees the source of the Boughton north front in plate 83 of Jean Marot's *Recueil des Plans, Profils, etc.* (1660–70). Hooke would undoubtedly have known this book.

60 (above) The High Pavilion Ante-Room.

61 (right) The State Bedroom in the High Pavilion.

62 (opposite) The First State Room or Great Chamber.

of the religious persecutions, to decorate with *The Marriage of Hercules and Hebe* (Fig. 57). Effectively the bright dawn is made to sweep her way across the great purple mantle of the night. For once Chéron was influenced by his compatriot Charles Le Brun instead of Raphael and the Roman antique. The panelling is twentieth century. Over the marble fireplace, also modern, the dashing equestrian portrait of the Duke of Monmouth is attributed to Wissing. The ceiling of the Egyptian Hall to the east—*The Triumph of Bacchus*—is also Chéron's work; so is that of the Little Hall to the west. The ground floor on the garden front of the old west wing contains drawing rooms, whereas upstairs are the library and bedrooms. These are the present family's living rooms.

The ceremonial approach to the state rooms, however, was by way of the Great Hall, the Little Hall to the west of it, and the Stone Staircase. The Stone Staircase Hall (Fig. 59), within the recessed three bays of Duke Ralph's unfinished west wing, is entirely decorated by Chéron. The ceiling is his best. Discord throws the apple among the gods, whose robes of yellow and mauve have an almost Poussin-like clarity. The walls are decorated with two

feigned reliefs of barbarians captured by Roman soldiers, as well as with statues and busts in niches.

The balustrade of the Stone Staircase is formed of a wrought-iron handrail, rods with scrolling extremities, and curious thin, twisted newels. The stairs lead to the first-floor suite of state rooms on the north front. The north-west and north-east pavilions (the latter (Fig. 65) was never finished and remains open to the roof) were intended not for state, but family use. In these apartments is found much of Duke Ralph's original furniture and hangings. In the High Pavilion Ante-Room (Fig. 60), panelled from floor to ceiling in oak, are the blue Boulle cabinet, given to the Ambassador by Louis XIV; silver-gilt Charles II firedogs and a dressing-table service; and a magnificent pair of mirrors with scrolled cresting, bordered with gilt-bronze acanthus and carrying a female mask, in the style of Marot. In the adjoining bedroom (Fig. 61) hang panels of tapestry of the Four Elements bearing Montagu's cipher and earl's coronet. These were woven in Soho especially for him between 1689 and 1704 and are simplified versions of Le Brun's cartoons made for the Gobelins factory.

63 *(opposite page) The Second State Room or Drawing Room.*

64 *(left) The Fourth State Room.*

65 *(above) Part of the unfinished north-east pavilion.*

The five state rooms of the north front are seen in enfilade (Fig. 63). In a house the size of Boughton they can only have been used, as they still are today, for occasional entertainment and the display of works of art. Ostensibly they led through ante-rooms and a guard room to a state bedroom in which to accommodate the sovereign or a particularly important guest. The actual state bed is now in the Victoria and Albert Museum. The state rooms are remarkably unchanged since Chéron painted the ceilings—not perhaps among his most inspired work—and, we may suppose, the cornices in a brown mud colour, described in late Stuart times as 'drab'. The marble fireplaces have bolection moulded surrounds; the walls are panelled in oak, but not carved as at Chatsworth and Burghley. Indeed the state rooms show evidence of hasty preparation for a visit from William III. Against a sombre background the sumptuous contents stand forth in a glow of pristine gold and colour. The needlework table covers, Isfahan carpets and *point de Hongrie* upholstery of the late Stuart chairs are hardly less abundant and rare than the wall tapestries here and elsewhere in the house. Their number is explained by Montagu having bought the management of the Mortlake factory in 1674. His director was Francis Poyntz. There are in the west wing two sets of the 'Playing Boy' series, and in the state rooms panels of the famous 'Acts of the Apostles' series. These have side borders of terminal figures and top borders of fruit and foliage carrying the arms of the 6th Earl of Pembroke.

The 2nd Duke's chief contribution to the house was to load overmantels (Fig. 67) and staircases with armorial bearings, a practice which on overmantels at least he inherited from his Tudor predecessors. The effect, as upon the library chimney-piece, was often exceedingly pretty. The heraldry he imposed upon the 'Chinese' staircase occasioned Horace Walpole's quip about 'the descent of the Montagus'. Alas, Duke John's three sons all died in childhood, and the dukedom expired with him. His daughter Mary was married to George Brudenell, 4th Earl of Cardigan, who in 1766 was made Duke of Montagu of the second creation. Brudenell's only son predeceasing him, the dukedom again died out in 1790. His daughter Elizabeth having married the 3rd Duke of Buccleuch brought Boughton into that family.

66 The 'Chinese' staircase, c. 1740.

67 (right) The Library overmantel; it traces the descent of the Montagus from Edward I.

68 Aerial view from the south showing that Boughton is still basically a Tudor manor house.

PETWORTH HOUSE, SUSSEX

A Percy stronghold since the twelfth century, Petworth was largely rebuilt and decorated by Charles Seymour, 6th Duke of Somerset, husband of Elizabeth Percy, from 1688 until George I's reign. (A property of the National Trust and the home of Lord and Lady Egremont.)

The anomaly of having to guess who was the architect of a great house where building accounts may abound in the names of craftsmen employed is often brought about by a simple factor. Artisans, even master-craftsmen, were usually paid through the client's clerk of works, whose job it was to keep scrupulous record lest his master might at a moment's notice query a particular item. The architect and superior artists, on the other hand, were usually engaged and so paid direct by the client, who more often than not did not bother to keep accounts at all. A distinguished architect in late Stuart times might well provide an overall scheme from London, and after paying one visit to the site leave the execution to others and never even see the work in operation, or completion. These reasons will explain why up to date the name of Petworth's architect has not been disclosed, and how that of England's most famous carver is only twice mentioned, as it were by chance, in the 6th Duke of Somerset's private account book under the year 1692.

The authorship of Petworth has, like that of Boughton, long been a mystery, the solution of which may one day be arrived at through the relationship between the owners of the two houses. The style of Petworth like that of Boughton has a distinct French flavour.

In the previous section Ralph, Duke of Montagu's close ties with France and patronage of French artists were discussed. This Duke's first wife was Elizabeth, widow of Joceline Percy, 11th and last Earl of Northumberland, to whose family Petworth had belonged since the twelfth

69 *Turner's vision of Petworth, 1810.*

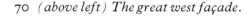

70 (above left) The great west façade.

71 (below left) A painting in the house thought to represent the west front before the fire of 1714.

72 (above) The centre of the west front and plan; a detail of Laguerre's decoration on the Grand Staircase.

73 (above right) The centre of the west front today.

century. The heiress to the immense Northumberland possessions was the Duchess of Montagu's only surviving Percy child, Elizabeth. After two outrageously dynastic marriages little Lady Elizabeth, aged fifteen and twice widowed, was wedded in 1682 to Charles Seymour, 6th Duke of Somerset. The ceremony took place in her step-father's home, Montagu House, Bloomsbury. Somerset, known as the Proud Duke, a preposterously snobbish fellow—he never addressed servants directly and was served on bended knee—and his infant bride went to live at Petworth, a late thirteenth-century house altered in Jacobean times by the 9th Earl of Northumberland (known as the Wizard Earl on account of his alchemical researches).

As soon as the Duchess of Somerset came of age in 1688 she and her husband set about improving Petworth. However limited their original intentions, these developed as the years went by into drastic full-scale reconstruction. All that is left of the mediaeval house, apart from several walls, the undercroft of the fourteenth-century hall, and a

long barrel-vaulted corridor under the great west front, is the chapel built after 1293. Even so the chapel was to receive embellishments of the most Baroque sort to be seen in any English country house.

Everything about Petworth speaks of patrician pride and disdain for the common herd. The manner in which the house presents its rather unseemly back towards the town cowering as it were close at heel, and the imperious, not to say impervious look of the entrance gates are calculated to make the visiting stranger quail in the legs. On either side of the high, solid gates a pair of magnificent trophies[1] of outsize cuirasses and plumed helms confront him. They are the first intimation of Petworth's French bias, and were undoubtedly carved for the Duke of Somerset. They were brought to their present position about 1870, but are shown in an early eighteenth-century oil painting (Fig. 71) to be standing at the entrance of the west fore-court.

The estate accounts[2] relate that Mr Fulkes, or Flukes, was resident supervisor of works from 1688 to 1696, and that in the year 1690 payment was made to 'Mr Scarbrow a surveyor for 8 days measuring . . . £10. 15. 0', which was quite a tidy sum of money. These names are significant. Samuel Fulkes, or Foulk, was one of Wren's master-masons under contract at Winchester Palace in 1683 and at work

[1] Pevsner and Nairn attribute them to V. Prost of Dijon (1842–1912). He designed for the 2nd Lord Leconfield similar trophies, which were never made.

[2] G. H. Kenyon—'Petworth, Town and Trades', Sussex Arch. Colls., vols. 96 and 99.

74 *The north end of the west front.*

75 *(opposite) The Grand Staircase decorated by Laguerre.*

on St Paul's between 1688 and 1695: he may, or may not, be the the same man as Mr Fulkes, the Petworth supervisor. But 'Mr Scarbrow' is almost certainly John Scarbrough, measuring surveyor on Wren's staff at divers City churches, and Winchester and Hampton Court Palaces.

In the summer of 1688 John Selden, a local carver, was already shaping stone for the 'frontishpeice', which he fixed the following year. In March 1689 Edward Dee was paid for pulling down parts of the old house. Work began at the north end and proceeded southwards. By 1691 the roof of the new west front (Fig. 70) was on, and finishing touches were being put by Selden to the great centrepiece. By July 1694 the 'new south front'—to be rebuilt by Salvin in 1869–72—was nearing completion. In June 1695 coping and cornice were being added and John Pike was cutting 'the plinths that the potts [since removed] stand on'. The stone used for the walls was a local greensand; for all dressings and the west centrepiece, with its horizontal rustication and groups of channelled brackets in the cornice, the familiar silver Portland. The deliberate chromatic contrast between the stones and the outstanding quality of the carving give the west front a distinction of which the undue length cannot deprive it. The twenty-one bays of only two storeys and an attic do not seem unduly horizontal. The slightly projecting end wings (Fig. 74) and Selden's centrepiece (Fig. 73), only broken forward by a matter of inches, provide a vertical emphasis which is astonishing,[1] although it is true that the verticality has been accentuated by a later prolongation of the lower

[1] They repeat the theme of the south front of Hampton Court.

windows practically to ground level. The masterly handling of the deep cavetto reveals, and the extension in the wings of the panels between the windows are further contributory factors. The panels hold busts and the Seymour phoenix. Over each first floor is a superbly carved basket of fruits.

In spite of its extraordinary merits the tremendous length of the Petworth front cries out for some dominating feature to crown it, and this is what it once had. In the New Year of 1714 a fire gutted the whole south part of the house, including a dome above the centrepiece. In the early eighteenth-century painting of Petworth, as well as in one of Laguerre's panels of the staircase hall (Fig. 72), this dome is shown—a four-sided affair with balustraded crest and sculpture at its base, closely resembling the very dome at Montagu House. It is a great pity that this crowning feature was not replaced.

Mr John Harris has pointed out that an elevation drawing (from the Bute Sale of 1951) of Wren's Winchester Palace, 1683–5 (Fig. 3), shows just such a four-sided dome. Moreover, the drawing has other affinities with the Petworth front in the continuous skyline balustrade and the vertical linking of windows by panels. Incidentally the only comparable treatment of such carved panels is to be found on Talman's courtyard front at Drayton. Now master-free-mason Fulkes and surveyor Scarbrough were working at Winchester Palace only a year or two before Petworth was begun. Mr Harris's inference is that the Petworth front was designed by a Board of Works man, whether Hooke, Wren or Talman has still to be established. As Mr G. H. Kenyon has suggested, Fulkes and Scarbrough carried

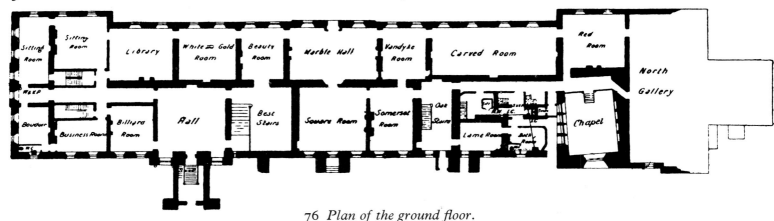

76 *Plan of the ground floor.*

out the design of their superior, whoever he was, on the spot under the vigilant eye of Stiles acting on the Duke's behalf. Its French flavour, like that of Montagu House, is readily explained by the notable influence upon the Wren school of the Sun King's Versailles.

The fire must have consumed the Grand Staircase which, the detailed accounts tell us, was originally constructed in 1692–3, and the Beauty Room (so called after the portraits of the ladies of Queen Anne's court) to the south of it. The redecoration of both suggests the early years of George I's reign. The whole stairwell was painted by Louis Laguerre in the full English Baroque manner; the concept is extremely grand and the quality of the painting uniformly high (Fig. 75). The feigned architecture is predominantly buff with gold highlights. The ceiling subject is the story of Prometheus, possibly in reference to the recent disaster, and a main wall is devoted to the apotheosis of the Duchess of Somerset whose children attend the triumphal car in which she is drawn by a white charger. The stair balustrade is not contemporary, and is presumably to Salvin's design.

To the north of the Beauty Room and behind the centrepiece of the west front is the Marble Hall (Figs. 78 and 79), originally styled the Hall of State. This splendid apartment and those to the north of it escaped the fire. In fact Vertue tells us that Selden lost his life in saving the carvings to which he had so signally contributed in this part of the house.

By the end of 1691 the Hall of State was ready for the decorators. In the following spring the floor was paved in white and black marble, and '2 dove-coloured' fireplaces were set in place and polished by one Bullock. Thomas Larkin was paid for executing and fixing the wainscot (it rests upon skirting of Purbeck marble) and John Selden, who turned his hand from stone to wood with equal dexterity, received £50 'for carving work in the Hall of State'. By midsummer 'Mr Tourner' was painting the walls. The combined result is glacial perfection; Selden's carving (with or without the help of Larkin) is without flaw. The question arises whether it was he who designed the rather top-heavy, reredos-like overmantels with the ducal bull and unicorn reclining uneasily upon the curved pediments, the deep acanthus brackets of the frieze, the Brobdingnagian egg and tongue moulding and the over-doors and door-cases, which running together induce that vertical effect we noticed on the wings of the facade. Or

were these features dictated by some architect overseer imbued with Gallic tastes?

The next room we come to, moving north, is the Little Dining Room, formerly the Vandyke Room, with richly foliated cornice and frieze carved by Selden. Here the brass door-locks (Figs. 80 and 81), like others about the house which are chased and incised with the Somerset cipher, coronet or phoenix crest, are doubtless the work of John Draper, a smith paid in 1690 for locks and hinges.

Horace Walpole considered the Carved Room (Fig. 82), which occupies four bays of the long west front before the north wing is reached, 'the most superb monument of [Grinling Gibbons's] skill'. Few will disagree with him.

77 *The 6th Duke of Somerset, by Riley and Closterman.*

78 *(right) The north end of the Marble Hall.*

79 *(opposite above) The Marble Hall in the centre of the west front.*

80 & 81 *(opposite below) Two brass door-locks by John Draper.*

82 *(above) The Carved Room.*

It was originally the eating room, and its decoration, begun in 1689, was finished by 1692. During these years Grinling Gibbons was working on the Library of Trinity College, Cambridge, for Somerset in his capacity as Chancellor of the University. His bills for the Petworth carving were paid out of the Duke's personal account, which explains why there is no mention of the great craftsman's name in the building accounts.

The scheme adopted in this great apartment, 60 feet long by 24 feet wide, was to adorn three groups of full-length portraits on the east wall, a pair of overdoor portraits and one full-length portrait on each end wall; also the surrounds of the four windows. The three portraits which are in conspicuous central settings are of Henry VIII on the east wall, and Charles I and Henrietta Maria on the

end walls. Members of the family, including the Duke and Duchess of Somerset, take hardly less honoured positions. The Kit-Cat-size portraits by Reynolds and others are later additions.

The paired portraits of the Duke and Duchess of Somerset and of the 1st Lord and Lady Seymour of Trowbridge, the Duke's grandparents, on the east wall are adorned with crests, swags and trophies of a beauty of design and skill of craftsmanship unsurpassed by Gibbons anywhere else in England. Putti heads and baskets of flowers, ciphers, coronets, the Duke's 'George', birds and foliage are, after nearly three centuries, as crisp and naturalistic as when first applied. The composition reminds Mr David Green[1] of 'a Mozart symphony, gay and triumphant'. Not only in the grouped detail does he find the carver's handling superb, but also in the spacing, 'for Gibbons' pauses and intervals are as deliberate and as telling as are rests in music'. Indeed, between the Seymour portraits the carver has included a lute, flute, violin, horns and a music score among a medley of beads, a quiver of arrows, oak leaves, medallions and his favourite lace cravat (Fig. 85).

[1] *Grinling Gibbons, His Work as Carver and Statuary*, 1964.

83 (opposite) The centre of the east wall of the Carved Room.

84 (above) Grinling Gibbons's cypher (?) in the Carved Room.

85 & 86 (left) Two details from the Carved Room.

Not all the carving here is Gibbons's work. The slightly less skilled hand of John Selden may be detected in the surround of King Henry's portrait; whereas the scrolls in the ceiling cove and a good deal of infilling were added by Jonathan Ritson who worked at Petworth between 1815 and 1847. Ritson, like Selden, and Watson at Chatsworth, was no metropolitan, but a provincial and belated follower in the Gibbons tradition. Eccentric and bibulous but undoubtedly talented, Ritson, who came originally from Whitehaven, was engaged to restore and remained to confuse the Petworth carving. Often his work can only be isolated by the trained eye quick enough to detect a quality only a little coarser than Selden's, and distinctly less refined than Gibbons's.

The chapel (Fig. 88) of the late thirteenth-century Percy house was given immensely thick walls in order to align it with the new Petworth. It occupies the east portion of the north wing. The early pointed windows survive, those on the north wall being blocked and painted, probably by 'Mr Tourner' with feigned casements and armorial glass.

87 (opposite above) The Somerset pew at the west end of the Chapel.

88 (opposite below) The north wall with painted decoration and woodwork of 1690–2.

89 (below) Detail of the reredos and altar rail.

90 (below right) The east end of the mediaeval chapel, as refitted by the 'Proud' Duke, showing the barrel vault divided into stucco panels.

Much was done to introduce the style of William and Mary's reign. The ceiling was given a barrel vault and divided into stucco panels, probably by Edward Goudge and his master-plasterer, Daniel Lance, both of whom were working here in 1691–2. Panelling, pews and reredos were made by Larkin in 1690 and carved by Selden; the wainscot is deal grained to resemble walnut. The altar rail (Fig. 89) with imitation fringes is more imaginative than the reredos drops embracing the elements of the Eucharist. Selden, too, must have been responsible for the ducal escutcheon upheld by angels and the folded curtains over the Somerset pew, the whole of which is carved out of solid wood, coloured crimson and gold. It is one of the most operatic compositions to be found in this country and its realism is comparable with those marble hangings on the pulpit of the Gesuiti church in Venice.

The Proud Duke survived his wife by many years and lived till 1748. His son, the 7th Duke, reigned for only two years, whereupon his subsidiary title of Earl of Egremont and the Petworth estate devolved upon his sister's son, Charles Wyndham. The 3rd Earl of Egremont ruled at Petworth for sixty-five years, dying in 1837. He patronized artists and men of letters and he entertained Turner who painted many of his most important pictures here.

He also built the North Gallery which he filled with pictures and sculpture, and 'landscaped' the exceptionally beautiful park. His illegitimate son was created Lord Leconfield in 1859 and it was the 3rd Lord Leconfield who gave Petworth to the National Trust in 1947. His nephew, Mr John Wyndham, created Lord Egremont in 1963 and who succeeded as the 6th Lord Leconfield in 1967, now lives in part of the house.

BURGHLEY HOUSE, NORTHAMPTONSHIRE

Built between 1553 and 1587 by William Cecil, Lord Burghley. John Cecil, 5th Earl of Exeter, refashioned the interior between 1681 and 1700. The state rooms decorated by Verrio are the finest Baroque suite in England. (Seat of the 6th Marquess of Exeter.)

In 1697 Celia Fiennes visited 'my Lord of Exeters Burly House eminent for its Curiosity'. After describing the formal gardens, 'you go thence', she says breathlessly, 'into parlours dineing roomes drawing roomes and bed-chambers, one leading out of another at least 20 that were very large and lofty and most delicately painted on the top, each roome differing, very fine Carving in the mantlepieces and very fine paint in pictures but they were all with Garments or very little. . . .' Her rather garbled description is exactly the unrehearsed sort one would probably give today, if asked unawares by a television reporter at the front door what impression the inside of Burghley had made. One is in fact dazed by the quantity of the rooms decorated by that Lord Exeter who was still alive when Celia paid her visit.

John, 5th Earl of Exeter, was forty-nine years old in 1697, and he lived another three, to die suddenly in Paris after a surfeit of fruit. In 1678 he had inherited the enormous Elizabethan palace built between 1553 and 1587 by his famous ancestor and Queen Elizabeth's chief minister, William Cecil, Lord Burghley. It cannot have been a style of building much to his liking, for John Cecil had a great passion for the painting and architecture of his own day. He travelled three times to Italy where he struck up an intimate friendship, based on a mutual love of art, with the reigning Grand Duke of Tuscany. He was, through his Countess, a brother-in-law of the 1st Duke of Devonshire and a first cousin of Ralph, Duke of Montagu, both of whom were altering Chatsworth and Boughton in the contemporary manner. Unlike these Dukes with their ancestral homes Lord Exeter had the good sense to make the minimum alterations to the exterior of Burghley. It remains with its towers, octagonal turrets, ogival cupolas, columned chimney-stacks, spikes and spire a reminder of what Nonesuch and old Sheen Palace must have looked like in their heyday—namely a Mannerist fantasy. Within this setting Lord Exeter contrived the finest Baroque suite of apartments after those at Windsor Castle begun for Charles II in the 1670s.

The south front (Fig. 94), far from being rebuilt by Lord Exeter, remains substantially as it was left by Lord Burghley at the end of the 1580s, although the 5th Earl probably repaired it. He certainly imposed the rather clumsy pedimented door (Fig. 92)—it bears his shield

91 *The south and west fronts seen across Capability Brown's lake.*   94 *(opposite below) The south front.*

92 *(above) The pedimented doorway added to the south front by the 5th Earl.*

93 *(above) The Golden Gates by Tijou in the west gate-tower.*

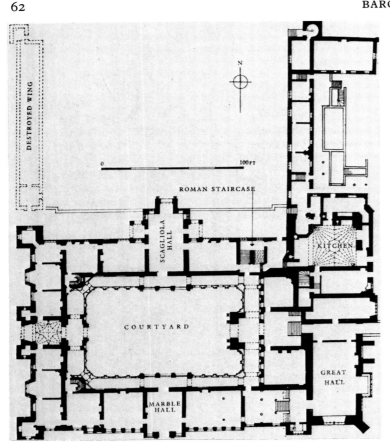

95 *Plan of the ground floor. The state rooms occupy the first floor of the south range.*

96 *Portrait of John, 5th Earl of Exeter.*

of arms impaling Cavendish—upon the centre of a loggia which he enclosed in order to accommodate three ground-floor rooms behind. For two reasons Mr Hussey[1] believes that the architect of these alterations may have been William Talman. In 1688 Talman is stated in the Fitz-william Papers to have been sent from Burghley to Milton, near Peterborough; at this date he was also rebuilding Chatsworth for the 5th Earl's brother-in-law, the Duke of Devonshire.

The 5th Earl was not responsible for the curious fact that the top-floor windows of the Burghley south front are dummies, the roof lying far below the balustraded parapet. Behind the first-floor windows are those state apartments called the 'George' Rooms, over the ceilings of which the dates 1681 and 1684 were recently found inscribed. Above them traces of a late Elizabethan ceiling suggest that the roof level has not been altered since Lord Burghley's time.

The 5th Earl's only other exterior contribution to Burghley was the magnificent pair of ironwork gates (Fig. 93) by Tijou in the west gate-tower. When Celia Fiennes went to Burghley they were the main entrance to the house (now the entrance is from the north forecourt) and were duly noted by her. 'The door you enter', she observed, 'is of iron carv'd the finest I ever saw, all sorts of leaves flowers figures birds beast wheate in the Carving.' The rampart lions supporting a garb in the overthrow, all now painted in gold leaf, stand forth proudly against a surround of sombre Barnack stone.

If the ceilings of the state or 'George' Rooms on the first floor of the south front were constructed by 1681, which was soon after the Earl's succession, decoration of the rooms by Verrio was certainly incomplete at the time of his death. Before Exeter embarked upon their very ambitious treatment, which we shall deal with shortly, he formed on the ground floor with easy access to the gardens, apartments for family use and adjoining bedrooms on the west front. The family apartments are lower, and therefore easier to keep warm, than those of the floor above and although not painted in the grand manner, are scarcely less splendidly decorated. The Earl and Talman, if he was the architect, relied for their enrichment upon carved wainscoting, plasterwork and tapestries, all of a very high order indeed.

How much of the carving was worked by Grinling Gibbons we have no means of telling. Mr David Green[2] estimates that the overmantel in the Marble Hall (Fig. 98), entered from both garden and inner court, is his. Composed of game birds, flowers, shells and fruit it is a tumble of rich luxuriance which frames a portrait by Wissing of the 6th Earl as a boy holding a long-barrelled gun. Lord Exeter paid Gibbons £50 in 1683 for unspecified work, and two years later the same sum again, the total being, Mr Green points out, little more than a quarter of what he also paid to Jonathan Maine and Thomas Young between 1682 and 1687. Both these craftsmen worked for Talman at Kiveton and Chatsworth. The bolection-moulded panelling and the cornice of this room, as of others through-out the house reach an excellence typical of work known

[1] *Country Life,* 17 Dec. 1953.   [2] *Grinling Gibbons,* 1964.

97 *Part of the ceiling of the Marble Hall, 1682–3.*

98 *The overmantel, attributed to Grinling Gibbons, in the Marble Hall.*

to be by these master-carvers elsewhere.

The ceilings of the Marble Hall, and of the Red Drawing Room and Dining Room on either side are of heavily ornamented stucco in what Walpole termed 'the good loose taste of Charles II'. Those of the two first rooms have deeply recessed compartments hung with festoons (Fig. 97). Mr Geoffrey Beard[1] attributes them to Edward Martin, master-plasterer, whose bills were paid in 1682–3 and who had worked on the chapel at Arbury Hall in 1678.

The 5th Earl was a leading patron of English tapestry weaving under John Vanderbank who in 1689 took over management of the Great Wardrobe Looms in Soho. He commissioned at least four sets of Soho panels, of which one panel of *Venus and Pallas* and another of a formal garden were observed by Celia Fiennes in the Blue and Silver Bedroom of the west front. The tapestry, which 'was all blew Silke and Rich Gold Thread, so that the gold appeared for ye Light part of all the worke', remains in the bedroom to this day, even if the gold has tarnished after nearly three centuries. Other superb pieces are the large panel in the Dining Room of *Venus's Armoury* in the French Gobelins style, and the very early Soho arabesque panels in the Black and Yellow Room on the north front (Fig. 103). In this room the Charles II bed is hung with black satin—now faded to brown and purple— sewn with silk and wool sprays of butterflies and urns of flowers. The lining is of yellow silk. These hangings were worked by Lord Exeter's mother-in-law, Lady Devonshire around 1670.

Mention of the north front is a timely reminder that the state rooms at Burghley occupy the first floor of three sides

[1] *Georgian Craftsmen*, 1966.

of the great inner courtyard. They are approached by
Lord Burghley's Roman staircase in the north-east angle,
and lead from one to another as far as the Grand Staircase
in the south-east corner. The north rooms were probably
decorated simultaneously with the rest, except for the Ball
Room, now called the Second Billiard Room. It is approached from the First Billiard Room, of which the
carved panelling is of the same high quality as that of the
Marble Hall. The panels contain portraits of the family
and members of the Honourable Order of Little Bedlam,
a convivial club founded by the 5th Earl in 1684 and which
included amongst its members relations and the painters
Kneller, Wissing and Verrio. Each was referred to by the
name of an animal, which appears prominently in his
portrait.

The Second Billiard Room (Fig. 99) lies at right angles
to the front, for it extends over the north porch. It was
entirely decorated by Laguerre who was to succeed Verrio

99 The Meeting of Antony and Cleopatra; *part of
Laguerre's decoration in the Ballroom, or Second Billiard
Room.*

100 *(opposite) The State Bedroom; the Vanderbank
tapestry depicts* The Element of Air, *the bed was prepared
for Queen Victoria's visit in 1844.*

at Burghley in 1698. Walls and ceiling relate to events in
the story of Antony and Cleopatra. After Verrio's breezy
compositions these are strictly academic, and architectural:
colonnades enclose each scene; captive figures support the
large frame above the fireplace and a curtain hangs de-
murely over one cornice. There are busts and urns on
brackets under the coffering of a semi-dome within the
window niche. Two sons of the 5th Earl are introduced
before a globe.

When built by Lord Burghley the long west front

101 (above) Detail of the tapestry in Fig. 100, showing a view of Burghley in the border.

102 (above right) The State Bed in Queen Elizabeth's Room.

103 (right) The Black and Yellow Room.

Opposite Page

104 (above) The ceiling of the State Dining Room (the Fourth George Room); The Feast of the Gods *by Verrio.*

105 (below left) The State Dining Room.

106 (below right) The Third George Room.

107 *Verrio's self-portrait in* The Cyclops' Forge; *detail of Fig. 108.*

108 *The Heaven Room, looking east.*

contained an unbroken gallery. The 5th Earl divided it into a suite of bedrooms. The Green Damask Room has a corner fireplace garnished with blue and white china in the fashion introduced by Queen Mary at Hampton Court. The most notable bedroom is called after Queen Elizabeth (Fig. 102), who, of course, never saw it. The green and gold bed with broken tester cornice, quilted soffit and gold cherubs at the angles, is one of a number of superb beds at Burghley. Chairs and stools are *en suite* and the Soho tapestries are referred to in the inventory of 1688.

Mr Hussey has surmised that the famous 'George' Rooms on the south front were so named on the occasion of the 1st Earl of Exeter receiving the Order of the Garter in 1601. In any event they were entirely redecorated by the 5th Earl after completion of the family apartments on the floor below. For the purpose he engaged Antonio Verrio, whose services with the Crown had been abruptly terminated with the abdication of James II. As a Papist Verrio loathed the Prince of Orange and gladly accepted protection from Lord Exeter who, although a supporter of the Glorious Revolution, refused to take the oath to William and Mary. For ten years, from 1688 to 1698, Verrio carried out his largest single task since decorating the Windsor Castle state rooms for Charles II. By now he was thoroughly spoilt. He demanded and received extraordinary attentions. He settled in at Burghley with his two sons and five assistants. He demanded a coach, horses, expensive furniture, choice wines and brandy. Delicacies like Parmesan cheese, Bologna sausages, olives and caviar were specially imported for him. Although his insolence provoked Lord Exeter to call him an 'impudent dogg', his great reputation induced the Earl to put up with his behaviour until it could be borne no longer.

Evidently Verrio had visited Burghley before the Revolution when he actually began work upon the First George Room, or Dressing Room, with communicating Jewel Closet at the west end of the south front. These are the only rooms of the suite in which the painter shared the decoration with those carvers who had been busy on the ground floor in the early 1680s. The carved overdoors comprising trophies of musical instruments and scores, doves, a quill, watch and chain, have their counterparts at Chatsworth; they may be by Young who worked at both houses. The rich acanthus cornice is of natural oak gilded. The walls of the State Bedroom (Fig. 100) are hung with Vanderbank tapestries of *The Elements*, specially woven for them, upon the borders of which views of Burghley and Wothorpe Manor (Fig. 101) on the property have been inserted. The ceiling depicts *Romulus Received on Olympus* and the coves, probably by Réné Cousin, display gilt cupids and bronze Michelangelesque ephebes leaning against medallions of *grisaille*. The architectural treatment of curved pediments in the middle of each wall, and broken pediments at the corners is the most advanced form of the Baroque of all Verrio's ceilings. The Dining Room ceiling—*The Feast of the Gods*—is supported by a feigned balustrade against which gold plate is piled on purple cloth. In the corner fish, fruit, flowers and game are thrown in heaps (Fig. 104). The State Dining Room leads to the Saloon, or Heaven Room (Figs. 108 and 109).

109 *The north wall of the Heaven Room;* Neptune and His Court.

This is by far the most ambitious of all Verrio's apartments, including those at Windsor which were destroyed by Wyatville, and the most sensational to survive in England. Verrio, compared with Cortona and the Roman *seicento* school, was pretentious and second-rate. Here the actual execution of his painting leaves much to be desired. But the composition is spirited and grand. It covers the entire room, there being no division between walls and ceiling. Illusionism has completely conquered space and dimension. From the sky the assembled gods look down upon a colonnaded enclosure, before and behind which are enacted the capture of Mars and Venus in Vulcan's net, the delivery of Mars by Mercury, and the forging by the Cyclops of Achilles' armour. In a corner of the last scene Verrio sits, naked to the waist without his wig, sketching (Fig. 107). In the east corner a shaft of light descends upon two polished shields hanging beside the forge. All around figures are depicted flying and striding into the room in Baroque defiance of reality. The Heaven Room was completed in 1695–6.

Verrio began to paint the adjoining room but did not get beyond the ceiling. In contrast with his previous subject the artist here conceived a classical hell wherein the deities pile up before, and are spewed out of, a ghastly fiery mouth. Assistants painted the feigned cornice and possibly the supporting columns. Then Verrio and his gang were dismissed. Soon afterwards Lord Exeter died, and for over fifty years the 'George' Rooms remained in a sad state of neglect, the floors not even fully laid. In the 1750s his great-grandson the 9th Earl came to the rescue, relaid the floors and provided fireplaces where these were wanting. It was he who got Capability Brown to landscape the park.

In 1800 Henry, 10th Earl (husband of the Cottage Countess) who became 1st Marquess of Exeter, commissioned Thomas Stothard to decorate the walls of the Hell Room, which had subsequently been turned into a staircase. Stothard's subject was *The Horrors of War*. Thus the Baroque scheme of the 5th Earl was completed a hundred years later by his great-great-grandson.

CHATSWORTH, DERBYSHIRE

The Elizabethan house of Bess of Hardwick, wife of Sir William Cavendish, was entirely rebuilt by their descendant William, 1st Duke of Devonshire, between 1685 and 1707. Talman and Archer were the architects, employed with many other artists and craftsmen. (A seat of the Duke of Devonshire.)

Few English country houses so dominate their surroundings as Chatsworth. The vast palace is set at the eastern foot of a great basin of hills on the left bank of the river Derwent (Fig. 110). It commands wide views over a vast park, beyond which the savage moorlands roll away in all directions. Everything about it is ample and generous. It looks, and virtually is, the capital of a principality.

The present Chatsworth owes its form and character chiefly to three members of the Cavendish family, Bess of Hardwick, the 1st Duke and the 6th Duke of Devonshire. The 6th Duke's extensive additions to the north of the house and alterations of the main block at the hands of Wyatville and rearrangement of the gardens, with Paxton's help, are not our concern. As for Bess of Hardwick little

of her building is visible (her prominent hunting stand on the brow of the east hill is, however, still intact).

Elizabeth Barley of Hardwick Hall, which she brought to the Devonshires through her father, John Hardwick, was the third wife of Sir William Cavendish, a successful agent of Henry VIII in the appropriation of monastic lands. Sir William had bought Chatsworth from the Leche family in 1549 for a trifling £600. At the time of his death in 1557 his new house at Chatsworth was only just begun. His widow lived another fifty years to complete it. Their second son, William Cavendish, who was created Earl of Devonshire by James I, bought the estate from his elder brother Henry soon after their mother's death in 1607.

The 3rd Earl of Devonshire, a staunch supporter of Charles I, suffered the confiscation of his properties during the Commonwealth. On his reinstatement at Chatsworth after the Restoration he modernized the rooms and substituted sashes for the old casement windows. It was his son William, the 4th Earl, who between 1685 and his death in 1707 demolished the house of his ancestors and built the present Baroque palace on the old foundations. The 4th

110 *The house, set in the valley of the Derwent, from the south-west.*

Earl, who was created Duke of Devonshire in 1694, was no chip off the old block. He was an advanced Whig and avowed enemy of autocratic monarchy and Romanism. He opposed James II as Duke of York and flouted his authority as King. Enforced retirement to Derbyshire throughout James's short reign enabled him to intrigue for William of Orange's usurpation and occasioned the rebuilding of Chatsworth.

The 1st Duke was handsome, gifted and contrary. A hater of tyranny he himself behaved like an autocrat to his subordinates. He was violent and quarrelsome, given to brawls and duels, yet extremely musical and artistic. He was an infallible chooser of talent, and patronized numerous young artists and craftsmen who later became famous.

Like its re-creator Chatsworth is full of contradictions. It has come to epitomize the English Baroque in domestic architecture, decoration and furniture. In Sir John Summerson's words, 'It inaugurates an artistic revolution which is the counterpart of the political revolution in which the Earl was so prominent a leader.' Yet this great symbol of a new autochthonous style deriving from territorial Whig-

111 *Chatsworth in 1707. Siberechts' painting shows the south and east fronts and the gardens laid out by the 1st Duke.*

112 *Talman's south front : the steps were built by Wyatville.*

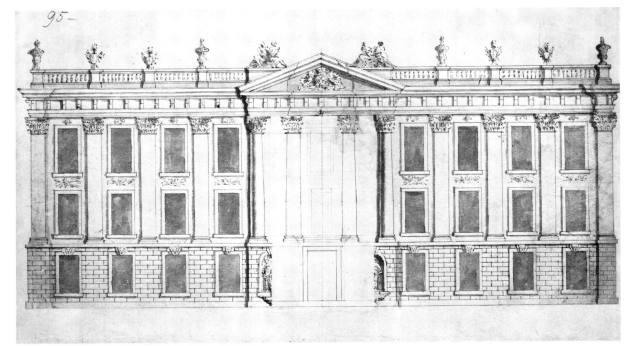

113 *A design for the west front.*

114 *(below) The west front.*

115 & 116 *(left) Two details of the centrepiece of the west façade; carving by Nadauld and Watson.*

117 *(below) The frost-work 'Grotto' and west terrace steps.*

gery arose, as it were, by accident. It started because its owner had nothing better to do. The house's plan of four fronts round a courtyard was absolutely determined by its Elizabethan predecessor, for at first the Duke never meant to go beyond rebuilding the south wing. Gradually however he pulled down and rebuilt the remaining three wings, protesting as he proceeded that each was the last to be altered. In consequence all the outside walls and those of the inner court follow the Elizabethan contour, if they do not incorporate the old material. Perhaps after all English Baroque is not so remote in spirit from English Mannerism, from which it is separated by the short-lived Classicism of Inigo Jones and its subsequent misinterpretation by Caroline artisan builders.

A further contradiction in this seemingly so English house is its French, or at least Continental, emphasis. For the south front (Fig. 112) derives from Jean Marot's engraving of Bernini's unexecuted project (1665) for the Louvre river wing. The Earl himself had been in Paris in 1669—he was involved in a skirmish in the Opera House that year—when he may well have studied it. The architect whom he engaged in 1685 was William Talman, who came from finishing Thoresby Hall in Nottinghamshire, bringing with him his master-mason Benjamin Jackson. Talman had also been working at Burghley for Devonshire's brother-in-law, Lord Exeter. The south front is without question a revolutionary design for an English country house. Gone are attics and all vestiges of hipped roofs and instead a rusticated basement carries a two-storey block. The slightly advanced wings are articulated by Ionic pilasters. The even number of the central bays, the greater height of the upper over the lower-floor windows and the very ponderous entablature and balustrade are disturbing elements. Unfortunately the angular stone stairs are Wyatville's substitute for a horseshoe perron,

of which the iron balustrade was wrought by Tijou.

Talman stayed long enough to begin the east front in 1694 (it was rebuilt by Wyatville in 1823) and the west terrace with its monumental stairs in 1696. In this year the Duke finally broke off relations with his architect. The reasons were twofold—Talman's undoubted intransigence and his alleged extravagance. Until his dismissal all work at Chatsworth was under contract, a system which the Duke, who was accustomed to giving orders direct, found insupportable. For a time Jackson continued with the terrace until he, too, with nearly all the London craftsmen, was dismissed in 1699. The boldly conspicuous frostwork of the terrace (Fig. 117) was finished by the carver Taylor in this year.

For the west front (Fig. 114) the Duke in 1700 fetched from Kiveton in the West Riding a master-mason named John Fitch. He undertook 'to doe and pforme all the worke contained in the Estimate according to a ground plan and upright prepared to set forth the fforme thereof'. It is most unlikely that Fitch was responsible for the design (Fig. 113) which the Duke chose out of three uprights submitted. The façade was clearly inspired by Louis XIV's pavilion at Marly built by J. H. Mansart in 1680. It consists of nine bays in three units over a rusticated basement; the two storeys are embraced by a giant Ionic order of pilasters and columns in the centrepiece. The rich carving of the keystones, central window-surrounds and pediment is by Nadauld (who was to work at Castle Howard) and Samuel Watson, a Derbyshire craftsman who spent a lifetime at Chatsworth working in stone, marble and wood.

It is just possible that Thomas Archer was the author of the west front. One of the rejected uprights displays cornice brackets and window-heads characteristic of his later architecture. He almost certainly built the Cascade

118 (above left) The east side of the courtyard.

119 (above right) Detail of one of Watson's carved trophies on the east wall.

120 (left) A drawing of the north front by Wyatville; it shows Archer's original treatment of the fenestration.

121 (right) Plan of the second floor.

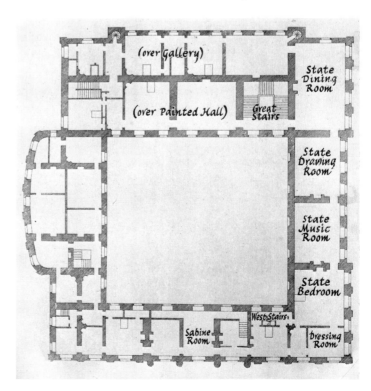

House (Fig. 135) in the east garden, and in 1705 definitely built the north front (Fig. 120)—it was much altered by Wyatville in 1821—with its great elliptical bow cleverly linking the two end surfaces of different alignments. The Duke's relations with Archer remained cordial to the end and he left him £200 by will.

Each one of the four fronts was built by the Duke on a sudden impulse. It is amazing, if we take into account the frequent changes of architects and workmen, not to mention the changes of design, how the great block maintains a degree of consistency. The rebuilding of the courtyard elevations was equally piecemeal. First, a one-storey, closed gallery was built on the south side in 1691. It lasted twelve years. It was replaced by a two-storey gallery, open below, closed above to match the Elizabethan side opposite. Then the Elizabethan prototype was taken down and rebuilt to match more exactly the rebuilt south side. Today the only courtyard front that has not been totally altered by Wyatville is the east (Fig. 118). Even so only the upper storey with pedimented windows remains quite untouched. Watson's splendid trophies (Fig. 119) were deprived of their original knotted drapery and raised between the windows of the middle storey.

Behind this east courtyard wall is the two-storey Painted Hall (Fig. 123), where the Elizabethan Great Hall formerly stood. Ceiling and walls were decorated between 1692 and 1694 by Laguerre and his partner Ricard with scenes from the life of Julius Caesar. The stone screen, with 'two boys upon the arch', was carved by Watson, but the stairs and gallery were added in 1911–12. The lower openings lead to the Grotto with carvings by Watson, and the steps to the Great Staircase on the floor above. Here the iron balustrade is the work of Tijou. During two short visits to Chatsworth in 1688 and 1691 Tijou taught a local smith, John Gardom, who in 1705 was to make the balustrade of the west staircase. The figures of Apollo and Lucrece within niches are carved by Caius Gabriel Cibber (Fig. 125) and the wreaths and swags suspended from rings under the cornice by Watson. The spirited *Triumph of Cybele* within an oval wreath on the ceiling was painted by Verrio who came from Burghley in 1691.

Verrio's contribution to Chatsworth is not as extensive as was once supposed. Apart from the canvas of *St Thomas's Incredulity* over the chapel altar and the ceiling roundels in the Great Gallery—now the Library—his only other work is the ceiling of the Great Chamber (Fig. 126). This, the first of the state rooms on the south front, is entered through a vast alabaster doorway from the Great Staircase landing. The state rooms were the first at Chatsworth to be decorated, being ready for the joiners in July 1689. Leading one into another they were treated as a unit. Floors and walls were of oak fetched from Hull. By September 1691 the wainscot, inclusive of cornices and conventional mouldings, of all the rooms except the Great Chamber was in place and only the applied carving was lacking. Between September 1692 and March 1694—an incredibly short time—the overmantels, door-cases, window-heads and wall panels were enriched with naturalistic flowers and foliage, trophies of arms and musical instruments, and swags of netted birds, fish and

122 *The original stairs in the Painted Hall, from a water-colour by William Hunt.*

123 *(right) The Painted Hall, decorated by Laguerre and Ricard, 1692–4. The staircase and gallery were rebuilt by Romaine-Walker in 1912–13.*

game, mostly in limewood (Fig. 132). These rich and delicate carvings were the work of Joel Lobb, William Davis, Samuel Watson and a team of apprentices.

All the ceilings of the state rooms are painted with mythological subjects. Verrio, the most sought after among the foreign artists then in England, could only be spared from Burghley to paint the Great Chamber ceiling. This he did with a mixed assembly of what Walpole called 'heathen gods, goddesses, Christian virtues, and allegoric gentlefolks'. The remaining state room ceilings were painted by Laguerre and Ricard and are wholly French in composition and colour. Laguerre, not surprisingly since he was brought up at Versailles, was inspired by the work in the palace by his first teacher, Charles Le Brun. *Phaeton Driving the Chariot of the Sun* (in the Music Room), and *The Triumph of Diana* (in the State Bedroom, Fig. 129) are composed with forethought, though the brushwork is hasty and somewhat flaccid. The lively figures of youths and nymphs in monochrome and gold in the coves of the Drawing Room and Bedroom (Fig. 128) are greatly superior.

Many of the contents of the state rooms were acquired by the 1st Duke, among them the Mortlake 'Apostle' tapestries

124 (right) The Great Staircase beyond the screen of the Painted Hall.

125 (opposite above) Decoration at the head of the Great Staircase: sculpture by Cibber, carving by Watson and painting by Verrio.

126 (opposite below) The State Dining Room or Great Chamber.

in the Drawing Room, and the superb pair of mirrors surmounted by the ducal arms in the Bedroom, which were supplied by John Gumley in 1703 for £100 each. The silver chandelier (Fig. 36) in the Closet Room, made about 1694 in Holland, as well as some of the finer pieces of delftware, may have been gifts from William III. Among furniture bought in Paris are the stalwart Boulle candelabra stands (c. 1695).

If the state rooms achieve a happy union of the decorative arts, the Chapel (Fig. 130), situated on the ground floor and occupying two storeys of the west corner of the south front, is triumphantly successful in this respect. Here the twenty-six-year-old Laguerre and Ricard excelled themselves. The ceiling oval and the upper stages of the walls are painted with the Ascension and scenes from the life of Christ. The altarpiece of white marble, Midlands

blackstone and alabaster, though unrelated to the decorative paintings, provides a magnificent complement. It was designed by Cibber who carved the standing figures of Faith and Justice. The rest of the architectural detail was worked by Watson, who under Thomas Young, Joel Lobb and William Davis had been engaged upon the cedar wainscot and pearwood wall panels.

Lastly we come, in the west wing, to the contribution of yet another young protégé of the Duke who was to acquire national fame. James Thornhill appeared at Chatsworth in 1706. He painted the ceilings of the Entrance Hall and West Staircase. In the latter he depicted The Fall of Phaeton with brilliant effects of foreshortening and perspective. But his greatest achievement is the Sabine Room (Figs. 133 and 134), one of the most important decorative interiors of the English Baroque. Ceiling and walls are

127 (above)
The State
Drawing Room.

128 (right)
Detail of the
decoration in the
State Bedroom.

129 (opposite)
The State
Bedroom.

130 *(left) The Chapel, decorated by Laguerre and Ricard; altarpiece designed by Cibber, the woodwork by Watson.*

131 *(above) Detail of the carving in the Chapel gallery.*

132 *(right) Carving in the State Dining Room.*

given over to one unbroken theme. *The Rape of the Sabine Women*, the groups of figures beside a statue of Hercules and, in the sky, Hersilia presented to Romulus, are viewed, as it were, through the arcades and open roof of a pavilion. The feigned architecture and sculpture, and the cool colours of Thornhill's palette make the Sabine Room far and away the least hackneyed and most accomplished of the decorated rooms at Chatsworth.

At his death in 1707 the 1st Duke of Devonshire had more or less completed the rebuilding of the Elizabethan house and the layout of the gardens. The 2nd Duke had merely to let the artists and craftsmen put the finishing touches to decoration inaugurated by his father. The 4th Duke between 1755 and 1764, transformed the grounds and surrounding country into the *picturesque* landscape which exists today. Through his wife Lady Charlotte Boyle he inherited the estates and possessions of her father, the architect Earl of Burlington. The 6th or Bachelor Duke made distinctive alterations and additions to both house and gardens between 1811 and 1858.

133 & 134 (above) Two views of the Sabine Room decorated by Thornhill after 1706.

135 (right) The Cascade House.

136 *The east entrance front.*

DYRHAM PARK, GLOUCESTERSHIRE

William Blathwayt, Secretary at War under William III, engaged Samuel Hauduroy to build the west front in 1692–4 and William Talman the east front in 1700–3 (A property of the National Trust.)

William Blathwayt had an eye to the main chance; and fortune favoured him. Yet whatever he earned—and it was considerable—was as much the reward of hard work as of intrigue. 'His knowledge in modern languages, his early and steady application to business', wrote the Gloucestershire historian, Robert Atkyns before 1712, 'advanced him to several publick and profitable employments: he was secretary at war, and also secretary of state to King William during his abode in Holland and Flanders: he was one of the commissioners for trade and plantations, and clerk of the privy council in the reigns of King Charles, King James, King William and Queen Anne.' This son of a

137 *Kip's view of the house from the west (1712).*

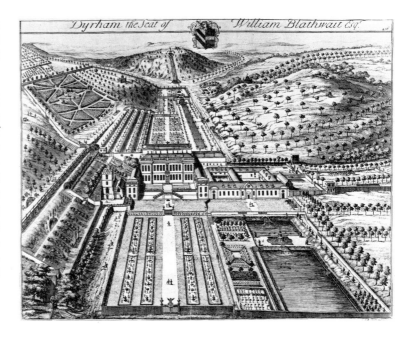

138 *Hauduroy's west front of 1692, flanked by the church and the later stable block.*

139 *The terrace in front of the west façade.*

140 *The stable block adjoining the west front.*

141 *Talman's east front of 1700.*

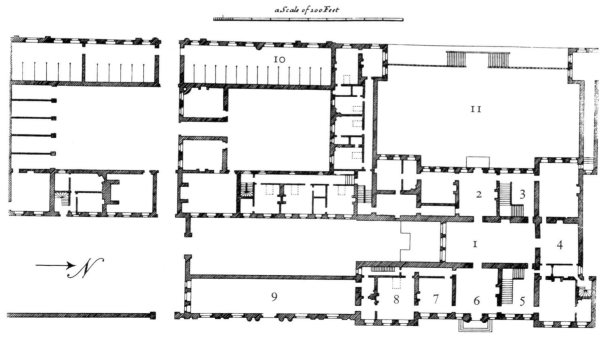

a Scale of 100 Feet

Plan of the principal Story of Dyrham house.

N

142 *The Orangery on the east front.*

143 *Plan of the ground floor from* Vitruvius Britannicus.
1 *Great Hall*
2 *West Hall (Balcony Room over)*
3 *Walnut Staircase*
4 *Dining Room*
5 *Cedar Staircase*
6 *East Hall*
7 *Diogenes Room*
8 *Queen Anne Bedroom and Closet*
9 *Orangery*
10 *Stable*
11 *Terrace*

144 *(opposite) The West or Ante Hall behind Hauduroy's façade.*

City lawyer was in fact a highly successful civil servant, intelligent, efficient, ruthless, unimaginative and unromantic, but with a sincere if conventional love of architecture and pictures. He owed his start in life to a maternal uncle, Thomas Povey, himself a senior civil servant and acquaintance of Pepys and Evelyn, who made some figure in society and was a man of taste.

When Blathwayt was about thirty-seven, in 1686, he married Mary, daughter of John Wynter, whose great-grandfather had purchased the Dyrham estates from the Denys family in 1571. Mary was no more than a year younger than her bridegroom and had just become heiress to Dyrham on the sudden death of her brother in 1685. The marriage was certainly not a love match. Regarded as a business venture it proved as successful as any ambitious man verging on middle age could wish for. Within two years William's father-in-law was dead and in November 1691 a kind, or unkind, fate removed both his mother-in-law and his wife. Blathwayt found himself in sole undisputed possession of a respectable property and with a son and heir to carry on the dynasty which he had founded with singularly little effort and trouble.

Either to console himself or do justice to his new terri-

torial status, Secretary Blathwayt promptly began building on the grand scale. In the first year of his marriage he had expressed the need for doing so. On the site there was an existing Wynter house, Tudor portions of which (notably the hall) have been incorporated in the present Dyrham. Blathwayt was however an extremely busy man. He was obliged to spend practically every summer of William III's reign with his monarch campaigning overseas. Consequently building operations, which could only be carried out in the summer months, were conducted by the Secretary through correspondence with his agent. For this reason there is a great deal of written data from which to piece together the story of the new Dyrham. Probably for the same reason, too, Dyrham was not built according to an overall plan, but in two separate stages. As work proceeded so the old house was demolished. The strange and rather uncomfortable outcome is, as it were, two houses, of totally different scale and style joined back to back by one large hall, or saloon, and one dining room (Fig. 143).

The way the odd juxtaposition came about was this. In only the third month of his widowhood, namely February 1692, Blathwayt before leaving for Holland with the King, engaged a Frenchman, one Samuel Hauduroy, to add a two-storey building to the old house. This is the existing front facing west. It is tucked under the hill and joined to the mediaeval church, which is carried on a bastion of rough wall, buttressed by yews (Fig. 138). No other building by Samuel Hauduroy is known, although other Hauduroys, presumably of the same family, did decorative painting, at Culverthorpe, Lincolnshire, Wrest, Bedfordshire, and elsewhere about this time. Our Hauduroy is recorded as marbling and graining the wainscot at Dyrham in 1694, and so may himself have been primarily a painter. The Hauduroy clan were probably Huguenots who came to England after the Revocation of the Edict of Nantes in 1685.

The shell of Hauduroy's west front (Fig. 139) was finished within the year. It is a pleasing front with two projecting wings to break the monotony of its fifteen bays. In 1693–4 corridors at right angles to the wings and ending in pavilions were added. The *cour d'honneur* thus formed and the *œil-de-bœuf* panels of the corridors gave a distinctly French flavour to what was intended for the entrance to the new Dyrham. Hauduroy's craftsmen however were mostly English: the principal mason, Philip West, came from nearby Corsham and worked the freestone which was supplied by Richard Broad from Box; John Harvey of Bath was paid for carving the central balcony enrichments and the urns adorning the balustrade. Most of the stone came from Tolldown, one and a half miles away.

Blathwayt was a relentless taskmaster who withheld payment until he had exacted the last ounce of labour from his employees. Hauduroy complained that on his return from Holland in the winter of 1692–3 he was made to get up two hours before dawn and draw plans until two o'clock the following morning. For this slavery all he had so far received was 10 guineas, without even travelling expenses. By 1694 the rooms behind the west front and the rebuilt Great Hall and adjoining Dining Room were fitted up.

Since the west and east fronts of Dyrham were built in two distinct stages, it is as well to treat the interior and the exterior of each independently.

The room entered by the door under 'Mr. Harvey's' carved balcony was called the Ante Hall (Fig. 144). It is paved with stone flags and small squares of black touch. The oak wainscot, swept up to meet the great door-head opposite, was the work of the joiners Nathaniel Power and William Banderlast, whose charges were 1s. 4d. a yard. In the adjacent Great Hall to the east (Fig. 145) the same craftsmen charged 2s. 4d. a yard for the wainscot in deal, then a more precious wood than native oak. At the same time they laid the floor of this long, high and slightly awkward room, lit by one vast window at the south end— with 'flemish oaken boards' fetched overland from Lechlade. The simple plaster ceilings in both rooms were worked by Thomas Porter from London. That of the Ante Hall is one of the few original ceilings to survive; the painted canvas panels by Andrea Casali in the Hall ceiling came from William Beckford's Fonthill and are nineteenth-century insertions. The marble for the twin bolection-moulded fireplaces was carved by Thomas Humphries of Lansdown, Bath. Both the Dining Room, originally called the Slope Room on account of the steeply rising

145 *(above) The Great Hall in the middle of the house.*

146 *(right) The Balcony Room over the West Hall (1693); the grained panelling is picked out in gold.*

ground seen through the window, and the Drawing Room which complete Hauduroy's ground-floor plan on the north have been largely 'Georgianized'. His staircase of Virginia walnut, now regrettably painted white, rises from the west front and leads to the Balcony Room upstairs.

The Balcony Room (Fig. 146) occupies the centre of the west front first floor. It is the most richly decorated of all the rooms at Dyrham, and was carved by Robert Barker of St Martin-in-the-Fields in 1693, the year before he executed the lavish Corinthian screen for University College Chapel, Oxford. Barker divided the wide pine panels with Ionic pilasters, which he made to support a correctly moulded entablature. Hauduroy himself gilded the moulds and painted the wainscot in 'marble', or rather walnut grain, which has toned to a dark treacle brown. The overmantel painting is by Hondecoeter. There still remain in this room a pair of kneeling blackamoors supporting shells and some of Blathwayt's blue and white delftware tulip vases, which are mentioned in the inventory of 1703. The blackamoors were bought with a quantity of furniture from Blathwayt's uncle, Povey. The splendid brass door furniture (Fig. 147) was supplied

by Henry Walton of St Martin's Lane. In the bedroom beyond hang Flemish *verdure* tapestries bought by Blathwayt.

After 1694 there was a four-year pause in building activity at Dyrham. The west front was now complete, tacked on to the old Wynter house. Whereupon Hauduroy disappeared from the scene as suddenly and mysteriously as he arrived. Meanwhile Mr Blathwayt's career was proceeding from strength to strength, while his income increased in salary and vails. By 1698 he turned his attention once more to improving Dyrham. First of all he concentrated on a new stable block (Fig. 140) which he joined to the south end of the west front.

A measure of Blathwayt's advance in status and wealth was his ability to engage the services of the Comptroller of the Board of Works, William Talman. Talman is credited with a preliminary design for the stables, which were supervised by a master-carpenter, Edward Wilcox. It is difficult to believe that the engaging but extremely un-

147 *Brass door furniture in the Balcony Room, the work of Henry Walton.*

148 *Hoogstraaten's perspec-*
tive in the Vestibule or East
Hall; the walls are covered
with stamped Dutch leather.

tutored design, in which the Tuscan order used is totally
deprived of entablature, and the columns of entasis, could
have met with more than Talman's qualified and distant
approbation.

In February 1700 the great east front (Fig. 141) was
begun. Colen Campbell in giving a plate of it in volume
II of *Vitruvius Britannicus*, ascribes the design to 'the
ingenious Mr Talman' whose letters to Blathwayt and
bills corroborate the attribution. Campbell furthermore
dates the design 1698, which is probably correct, although
the foundations were not laid until two years later. We
may well wonder how far the conservative Secretary of
State dictated the old-fashioned design. There is about this
staid, three-storey front under a flat, balustraded skyline, a
taste of Talman's Thoresby front (*c.* 1683) rather than his
later Chatsworth south front (1687–8). The conception
harks back to the type adopted by the Caroline architects
from Rubens's *Palazzi di Genova* and does not look
forward to the lively Baroque façades of Archer and Van-

brugh. The window-heads and pediments are dispropor-
tionately heavy, and the strapwork cartouches and swags
of flowers between first floor and attic storey are thoroughly
Mannerist. Both devices were probably taken straight
out of Vingboon's *Gronden en Afbeeldsels* (plates 18 and
34), which was in Blathwayt's library. Mr Kerry Downes[1]
has detected in some of the detail, notably the three-
quarter pilasters flanking the central window, influences
from J. H. Mansart's drawings for Versailles, brought
over by the British Ambassador in 1699 for Talman's
guidance in his projected 'Trianon' at Hampton Court.
He sees, too, in the curiously top-heavy entablature of the
Orangery joined to the east front (Fig. 142), and of the
loggia running into the slope on the north, a reflection
of Mansart's 'Orangerie' at Versailles. But top-heavy
entablatures are peculiar to Talman, and one is a conspicuous feature of the south front of Chatsworth. The only
apparent French influence is in the horizontal rustication

[1] *English Baroque Architecture*, 1966.

149 *The velvet-hung state bed in the Queen Anne Room.*

of the ground floor and the banded angles of the front.

The east front was not carried out exactly as depicted by Campbell. The richly carved shield and cornucopias under the central eagle, Blathwayt's crest, were omitted; and blind balustrades were put below the centrepiece and windows of the first floor instead of under those with segmental pediments. This solecism was surely committed by the builders when windows were substituted for doors on the ground floor below them. It is easy to appreciate how the local masons were perplexed where to put these balustrades after what must have been a last-minute departure from the architect's design. The same team of builders which worked under Hauduroy was engaged by Talman, or possibly by his mason-contractor, Benjamin Jackson. The east front is staid and rather gaunt when seen close at hand. Viewed from the twisting drive on the high ground it looks distinguished (Fig. 136). Whereas Hauduroy's west elevation is low and welcoming, Talman's is tall and somewhat rebarbative.

The eagle which John Harvey carved was hauled into its dominant position in July 1703. By now Blathwayt's fortunes were on the ebb; with King William's death he had been dismissed from the Secretaryship at War and one by one he lost his other lucrative posts. The moderate Tories under Queen Anne had less and less use for the superannuated civil servant. It was, Mr Mark Girouard[1] surmises, a growing sense of insecurity which accounted for Blathwayt's prudent, not lavish decoration of the rooms within Talman's block.

The entrance hall, called the Vestibule, was in 1702 hung with Dutch leather (Fig. 148), stamped with putti, fruit and flowers, painted and gilded. A memorandum addressed in Blathwayt's hand to Mr Williams, the upholsterer, calls 'the gilt leather in the Great Parlor [now drawing room] very ill putt up and must be stretcht which can be done only in wett weather'. Blathwayt was never satisfied with his workmen. 'These people', he wrote

[1] *Country Life*, 22 Feb. 1962.

150 *The Diogenes Room, wainscoted in Virginian walnut and hung with Mortlake tapestries.*

in 1701, 'want stirring up roundly and not to be overfed with money.' He was always urging speed. The Queen, he wrote in 1702, 'may be expected in August at the Bath'. If Anne did in fact take the waters there, she never honoured Dyrham or the man whom her ministers now held in little esteem. The Diogenes Room (Fig. 150), called after the two panels of Mortlake tapestry, was wainscoted in Virginian walnut by Alexander Hunter of the Angel, Piccadilly who had made sashbars for Hauduroy's wing ten years previously. So, too, was the bedroom to which Blathwayt's sumptuous bed, sold from the house in 1912, has been returned on loan by the Lady Lever Art Gallery. Made for the house about 1704, its hangings are of crimson and yellow velvet, and the tester of sprigged satin.

Hunter was also responsible for the cedar and walnut staircase which rises in three flights to the attic storey. The stairwell cornice is the work of Porter who was here allowed some freedom of stucco invention. But the flat of the ceiling was altered when another Casali canvas was inserted in the mid nineteenth century. The walls are surprisingly economical. Instead of mythological scenes by Verrio or Laguerre Blathwayt had the walls roughly

marbled in sienna paint which has now faded to a bilious green. Thomas Highmore, the Queen's sergeant-painter was responsible for both wall marbling and graining of the stair dado. The suite of bedrooms on the first floor, although of imposing size, was very simply panelled. They are now converted into flats.

If the state rooms at Dyrham were not remarkable for their decoration, the furnishings were rich and rare. Two household inventories of 1703 and 1710 record the silk damask hangings, crimson and gold velvets, Flemish tapestries and wide range of paintings of which a few, like the Hoogstraaten perspective in the entrance hall, survive.[1]

William Blathwayt died in 1717, if not in disgrace then certainly in eclipse. Dyrham passed in male descent from one squire to another. Mr Justin Robert Wynter Blathwayt sold the house in 1956 to the Treasury, but still retains the estate. The house, some of the contents and George London's garden (Fig. 137)—which in Secretary Blathwayt's time was renowned for its terraces, cascades and parterres—were transferred to the National Trust in 1961.

[1] J. A. Kenworthy-Browne—*Dyrham Park*, 1967.

151 *The house from the south.*

DRAYTON HOUSE, NORTHAMPTONSHIRE

Drayton came through marriage to the Mordaunts in 1499. Lady Mary Mordaunt (Duchess of Norfolk), married to Sir John Germain, employed Talman in 1702–4 to make alterations and build the frontispiece. From Lady Betty Germain it was inherited by the Sackvilles. (The seat of Colonel N. V. Stopford Sackville.)

No stranger passing the gates of Drayton would for a moment suspect that here was a house with claims to Baroque architecture. Certainly only a fraction of this vast pile was built within our period. Nevertheless it is so significant a fraction that it even communicates a Baroque flavour to that greater part dating from mediaeval and Elizabethan times.

152 *The gateway at the entrance to the forecourt.*

153 *The house as it appears from the east.*

154 *The door-case added to the east front by Talman.*

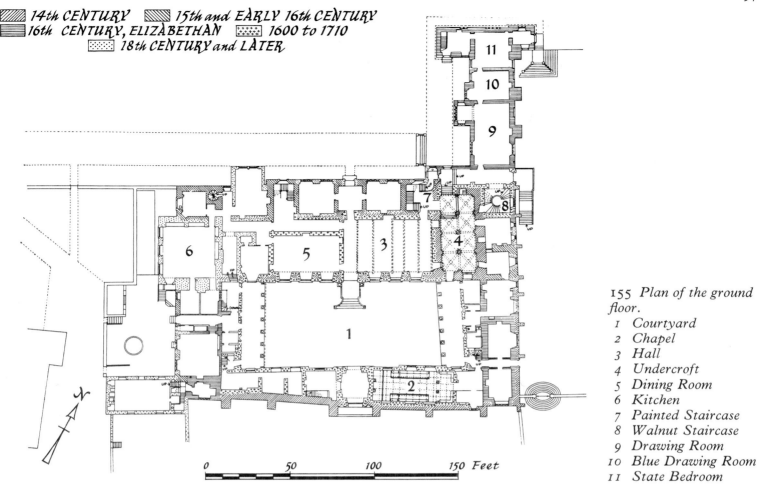

14th CENTURY   15th and EARLY 16th CENTURY
16th CENTURY, ELIZABETHAN   1600 to 1710
18th CENTURY and LATER

155 *Plan of the ground floor.*
1 *Courtyard*
2 *Chapel*
3 *Hall*
4 *Undercroft*
5 *Dining Room*
6 *Kitchen*
7 *Painted Staircase*
8 *Walnut Staircase*
9 *Drawing Room*
10 *Blue Drawing Room*
11 *State Bedroom*

The approaches to Drayton are unspectacular. You cover some flat, uneventful Midlands pasture which somehow serves to insulate the great house, which comes into view suddenly and unexpectedly. The first oblique vision of crenellated walls, buttresses, tall chimney-breasts, towers and turrets (Fig. 151), recalls Knole, or Hoghton Tower, rather than Petworth or Dyrham Park. Drayton, too, shares with the first two houses that peculiar timelessness and isolation from the twentieth century which make such enormous appeal to lovers of the past. It lies spread out in fields, almost like an Italian town in the plain of Lombardy, brooding, gentle, homely, yet palatial.

Drayton came to the de Vere family at the Conquest, and was in due course inherited by a cadet branch which adopted the territorial surname. In 1328 Sir Simon de Drayton obtained a licence to crenellate a defensive structure already begun in the late thirteenth century. From the start the house assumed what was unusual in mediaeval times, a rough symmetry, which no subsequent alterations and additions have blurred. From Sir Simon's descendants the property passed by the marriage of a de Drayton heiress in 1499 to the son of her astute family attorney, Sir John Mordaunt. The Mordaunts, remaining papists, prudently lay low after the Reformation. But towards the end of Elizabeth's reign the 3rd Lord Mordaunt, who preferred country retirement to court life, ventured to enlarge his ancestral seat considerably. The next Mordaunt owner to make substantial alterations was his great-grandson, the

2nd Earl of Peterborough, who reigned at Drayton from 1643 to 1697. He got John Webb in 1653 to provide chimney-pieces and overmantels, and in the 1670s and early 1680s one of his own servants, Isaac Rowe, to carry out further improvements, including the stable block, an entrance arch and a whole garden layout of terraces, portals and gazebos. All these things were done before our period opens with the accession of James II.

Lord Peterborough's heir was an only child, Mary, married to the 7th Duke of Norfolk. This lady caused great scandal by openly living with Sir John Germain, Bart., a mysterious soldier of fortune and financier, who never disclosed his origins and was probably an illegitimate son of Prince William II of Orange. On this account the Duke of Norfolk in 1700 divorced his wife who married her paramour the following year. In spite of her declared detestation of her first spouse the Duchess clung to his title and dignities long after her marriage to the baronet, and fairly plastered her old home with coronets and strawberry leaves.

One of the earliest displays of her ducal status is found upon the imposing gate-piers and ironwork at the entrance to the south forecourt (Fig. 152). Mr Cornforth[1] has attributed the piers to William Winde for two very sound reasons. Firstly, in a letter to Lady Bridgeman Winde revealed that he was about to wait upon the Duchess of Norfolk at Drayton in the spring of 1698, by which date

[1] *Country Life*, 13 May 1965.

156 (right) The centre-piece of the north side of the courtyard.

157 (opposite above) Talman's façade and Doric colonnade inside the courtyard.

158 (opposite below) Inside the Doric colonnade.

she had long been separated from the Duke. Secondly, the piers with their shell-headed niches and swags of carved stone closely resemble those well-known gateways at Hamstead Marshall, near Newbury, which Winde had put up for Lord Craven. Here cartouches on the piers display the arms of Mordaunt under a coronet and those of Germain, which the royal bastard purloined from the de Draytons, merely varying the tinctures and imposing a sinister hand, without any reference to the College of Heralds. A Mordaunt supporter, an eagle, perches upon the finials and urns. Upon the massive iron overthrow a ducal coronet

glimmers. The thick scrolls of foliage are worthy of the ironwork at Hampton Court by Tijou, to whom and to his pupil Robert Bakewell they have been ascribed.

Sir John Germain, as soon as he was firmly in the saddle so to speak, took over the reins. The architect whom he chose to carry out the next embellishments at Drayton was a far more flamboyant personality than Winde. Germain may have met William Talman through his royal half-brother. At any rate very soon after William III's death in March 1702 Talman was dismissed from the Comptroller-ship of the Royal Works. By the following August Germain

had signed a contract with Talman for certain jobs to be undertaken by his principal mason Benjamin Jackson who, as we have seen, had been in charge at Chatsworth and was at this very time finishing at Dyrham. Briefly, the programme amounted to rebuilding one of the Elizabethan twin towers and providing a new cupola to both; adding a door-case of pronounced Borrominesque character (Fig. 154) on the east front; building the frontispiece (Fig. 156) within the courtyard; transforming the Great Hall; and constructing a new staircase besides several servants' rooms and offices. These jobs were to be done 'in all points according to ye draft or designe by Mr Talman. . . .'

By walking southwards away from Winde's gates and then veering round again one gets an extraordinary impression of Drayton's combined symmetry and romance (Fig. 153). What one sees is a deliberate recession of masses. First, Sir Simon de Drayton's solid curtain wall with central archway added by the 2nd Earl of Peterborough in the 1670s; peering above it the attic of Talman's frontispiece; and stepped to right and left the twin towers, their elegant turrets capped by Talman's attenuated hexagonal cupolas. These are the offspring of a happy marriage

159 *The Tudor Hall as refitted by Talman and redecorated in the 19th century.*

between Baroque empiricism and Gothic accident. They are also a surprising tribute to a sensibility and humility rarely shown by Talman, whose architecture like his personality was often assertive and usually uncompromising.

In passing through the 2nd Earl of Peterborough's arch one is precipitated into the narrow courtyard. Straight ahead is the front (Fig. 157) imposed by Talman upon the Great Hall and Dining Room, with the old screens passage in between. It is hardly surprising that Horace Walpole dismissed the front as 'not in good taste'. Certainly it can in no sense be described as 'chaste'. It is strangely dramatic

and un-English, and quite unlike the sober Classicism of Chatsworth or the *cinquecento*-town-palace Mannerism of the Dyrham east front. Mannerist it undoubtedly is, but more Dutch than Italian. How much was this due to Germain's insistence? He may well have pressed for a design to remind him of the sort of architecture that was current in his native land at the time of his youth.

To enhance contrast with the grim, grey, mediaeval outer wall Talman and Jackson chose a different yellow stone for this spectacular façade. The treatment of the surface is most uneven and restless, for the scale of the

160 *The Stone Staircase decorated by Gerard Lanscroon, c. 1712.*

outer and inner window surrounds is totally unrelated. The outer windows have large alternating pediments balanced upon triple keystones, whereas the two inner have fussy little swan-neck lintels which merely reach the lower members of the pediments of the outer windows. The immoderately deep attic, the rows of busts on brackets, the carved trophy (Fig. 157) over the entrance, the capitals of the door columns composed of Germain hawks, and the raised gable-like centrepiece supported by caryatids, resembling that which crowns Rubens's garden house in Antwerp, are invitations to much speculation. Mr John Harris's explanation is that the whole unconventional assortment derives from a design made before 1702 by Talman's son John of a river front to William III's projected 'Trianon' at Hampton Court (Fig. 11).[1] The Roman Doric colonnades (Fig. 158) flanking the courtyard echo —only in a minor key—Wren's colonnade of the Clock Court at Hampton Court, which was well known to Talman. They were added after the Duchess's death in 1705.

While she was yet alive Talman transformed the Great Hall (Fig. 159). He gave it a barrel ceiling and panelled walls treated with the Ionic order like the Balcony Room at Dyrham. The marbling of the wainscot and the painting

[1] 'Hampton Court Trianon Designs of William and John Talman', *Journal of Warburg and Courtauld Institute*, vol. XXIII, nos. 1–2, 1960.

of the ceiling were, however, done about 1850. Around the room portraits of royal benefactors of the Mordaunts were hung. The Duchess's father-in-law, the 6th Duke of Norfolk, was even included in the august galaxy. The Stone Staircase (Fig. 160), entered from the north-east corner of the Hall, was not finished at the Duchess's death. One may conjecture that Tijou was responsible for the splendid wrought-iron balustrade, in which the geometrical scrolls reflect that more elaborate version on the Great Staircase at Hampton Court. Germain had evidently approached Thornhill, but in 1712 settled for Gerard Lanscroon to paint the walls and ceiling. Lanscroon was specially patronized by supporters of William III, and had in 1705 done a striking apotheosis of that monarch for Lord Rochford at Powis Castle.

The dimensions of the stairwell at Drayton were limited, but none the less Lanscroon's achievement is creditable. The allegory of the ceiling is perplexing: gods and goddesses fairly tumble over each other; upon one wall Hercules and Justice strike down Envy, Hatred and Malice, and upon another Minerva and the arts are glorified. The military achievement and superior prowess and virtues of King William can be read into these attributes. The way in which the ceiling subject spills down the walls is very spirited and the body of one of the vices, which is being made to fall to perdition over the edge of the plinth, is in a typically Baroque attitude.

The Duchess, much to the chagrin of her cousin, the 3rd Earl of Peterborough, left the Drayton estate to her widower. Sir John Germain wasted little time in choosing a second wife in Lady Betty Berkeley, a daughter of the 2nd Earl of Berkeley. The bridegroom was fifty-six, the bride twenty-six years old. She bore him three children, all of whom died in infancy. Then the soldier of fortune departed life in 1718, leaving to his second wife the immense possessions and riches of his first.

Lady Betty Germain lived for another fifty-one years. Thus from 1697, when the Duchess of Norfolk inherited Drayton, until the demise of her successor in 1769 Drayton remained in the ownership of one generation. It is true that Lady Betty spent most of her widowhood with her devoted friends the Duke and Duchess of Dorset at Knole. Horace Walpole recorded that, 'From the Drayton-estate she has scarce ever carried a shilling to London, except to make purchases or repairs for the place, spending the whole income in the neighbourhood, tho' she has seldom lived there above six weeks in the year. The old furniture and customs she has kept up most religiously, & maintained the house in the most perfect order & preservation. There is scarce a house in England so entire in the old fashioned manner. . . .'

Lady Betty, having no children of her own, bequeathed Drayton to the Dorsets' third son, Lord George Sackville, soldier and statesman, who assumed the Germain surname. Apart from decorating two fine rooms Lord George spent little of his life there. He was raised to the peerage in 1782 as Viscount Sackville of Drayton. The house and estate passed to his granddaughter, who in 1837 married William Bruce Stopford. Drayton is today the property of her grandson, Colonel Nigel Stopford Sackville.

KIMBOLTON CASTLE, HUNTINGDONSHIRE

Purchased c. 1620 by Sir Henry Montagu. Charles Montagu, 4th Earl and 1st Duke of Manchester, began reconstructing the Castle 1691–6, possibly employing Henry Bell. In 1707–10 he engaged Vanbrugh. The portico was added by Alessandro Galilei in 1719. Pellegrini painted the staircase. (The Governors of Kimbolton School.)

There is little enough of a castle in this regular but ponderous exterior (Fig. 163). The crenellated roof-line suggests nothing mediaeval to our sophisticated eyes. Still less castle-like is the soft red-brick courtyard within, or the civilized apartments entered from it. Yet the actual structure of Kimbolton preserves much of the core and follows the plan of a stronghold of indeterminate antiquity which had belonged to the Mandeville and Wingfield families. It was acquired from the last family in 1533 for Henry VIII's discarded wife, Katherine of Aragon, who eked out a miserable existence, to die here three years later.

The history of Kimbolton Castle thereafter is obscure

until it was purchased by Sir Henry Montagu, Lord Treasurer of England, towards the end of James I's reign. A scion of the Montagus of Boughton he was created Earl of Manchester by Charles I. His great-grandson Charles, the 4th Earl who inherited in 1683, was to become the most conspicuous member of his line and the creator of the Kimbolton we know today.

At his accession the 4th Earl was a handsome, cultivated young Whig of twenty-two or twenty-three. His interest in the arts outstripped his manners, for when accredited in later years to the court of Louis XIV the French complained 'that his Excellency blows his nose in the napkins, spits in the middle of the room, and laughs so loud and like an ordinary body that he [is] not thought fit for an Ambassador'. Very soon after James II came to the throne the Earl, disgusted by the new King's unconstitutional methods, quitted England and aligned himself with William of Orange. He fought for the Dutch prince in Ireland and did not settle in his own country until the Battle of the Boyne, in which he took part, had eventually firmly

161 Aerial view of Kimbolton showing the situation of the castle in relation to the town.

established William of Orange on the English throne.

The question arises when did the 4th Earl begin transforming his Huntingdonshire seat? Was it immediately after his inheritance in 1683 during the ensuring two years' comparative political lull? Or was it after the Boyne, and indeed his marriage, both of which events took place within six months of each other in 1690–1, and before his appointment as Ambassador Extraordinary to the Venetian Republic in 1696? Until documentary proof to the contrary is forthcoming, the evidence will point to the later period.

The Earl's initial work amounted to total reconstruction of the rectangular quadrangle (Fig. 165), transformation of the mediaeval hall into the White Hall, and the apartment adjoining it at the south-east corner into the Red Drawing Room, and the formation of the principal staircase on the south side. For the time being he left the exterior of the castle unaltered.

Unfortunately no building accounts for this initial work have so far come to light. Mr Avray Tipping[1] attributed it to one William Coleman on the grounds that Coleman was to be asked by the Earl in 1707 to submit a design for the south front. As we shall see, it was turned down.

[1] *English Homes*, Period IV, vol. I, *Late Stuart*, 1920.

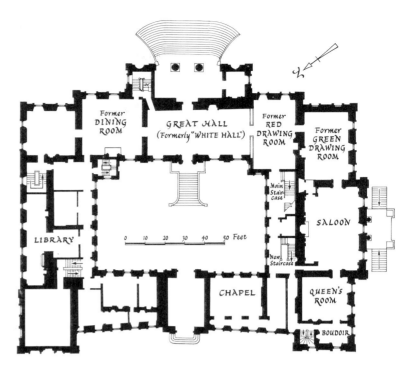

163 *The entrance front facing west towards the town.*   162 *Plan of the ground floor.*

Although a highly skilled craftsman—he was a joiner by profession—Coleman was presumably no better qualified a decade previously to design a quadrangle of unusual accomplishment. On the other hand Mr Martin Archdale's[1] claim that Henry Bell of Lynn was the Earl's architect on this occasion seems more acceptable. Mr Archdale points out a number of similarities in the Kimbolton quadrangle to known work by Bell in the vicinity. The first is the predominant use of finely gauged brick, with only the dressings in stone. The combination appears in the house Bell built in King's Lynn for Sir John Turner in 1685 (now the Duke's Head and stuccoed over), Clifton House, also in Lynn, and Stanhoe Hall for Sir Thomas Archdale in Norfolk. Another similarity is the distinctive use of the Corinthian order, with its almost paper-thin pilasters carrying an entablature, slightly broken forward to emphasize the central feature and unadorned frieze. This treatment is very conspicuous upon the east screen of the Kimbolton quadrangle which lights the White Hall, as well as upon the Sessions House which Mr Archdale believes Bell built in 1678–88 after the disastrous fire in Northampton. Yet another emphatic similarity, although a detail, is the eccentric carved window-crest, consisting of a pair of involuted acanthus sprays flanking a grotesque head. These heads, deeply undercut in the Kimbolton quadrangle, appear on the Sessions House façade and over the blank doorways of the quadrant arms at Cottesbrooke Hall (Fig. 192).

How far Bell, or Coleman, if by chance he was architect, was responsible for the iron- and lead-work in the quadrangle is unknown. Certainly there are no parallels in any other of Bell's buildings to the thinly wrought iron balustrade of the steps, where the Earl's cipher and coronet are displayed, nor to the lead rainwater heads and downpipes embossed with acanthus leaves and fastened to the walls by strips displaying the Earl's supporters, an antelope and griffin (Figs. 166 and 168).

The next stage in the transformation of Kimbolton opens with a series of letters addressed by Sir John Vanbrugh to the Earl, then in Venice acting for a second time as Ambassador Extraordinary. The first dated July 1707 announces that the south front of the old castle had collapsed. Lady Manchester 'did me the honour to ask my advice in carrying it up again'. So he hurried down from London accompanied by Hawksmoor in the capacity of draughtsman. With the letter Vanbrugh encloses a design for a new front 'which', he adds, 'differs very much from what Coleman had drawn, and particularly in that he had not brought the door of the house into the middle of the front; many other great exceptions there were to it, both within and without'. This is in fact the very first mention of Coleman's name. The Earl readily agreed that Coleman's design must be scrapped in favour of one by his more famous friend. A subsequent letter from Vanbrugh in September mentioned that poor Coleman 'owned he began to discover a gusto in it that he had no notion of before'. The great architect himself saw 'a manly beauty in it', which would give 'something of the castle air, though at the same time . . . make it regular', and he quoted as his

[1] 'An East Anglian Original, Henry Bell', *Country Life*, 15 Sept. 1966.

164 *(above) The entrance to the Hall on the east side of the quadrangle.*

165 *(above right) General view of the quadrangle looking south. A remodelling of the early 1690s.*

166–168 *(below right) Details of the elaborate lead rainwater heads and downpipes, and carved window-crests in the quadrangle.*

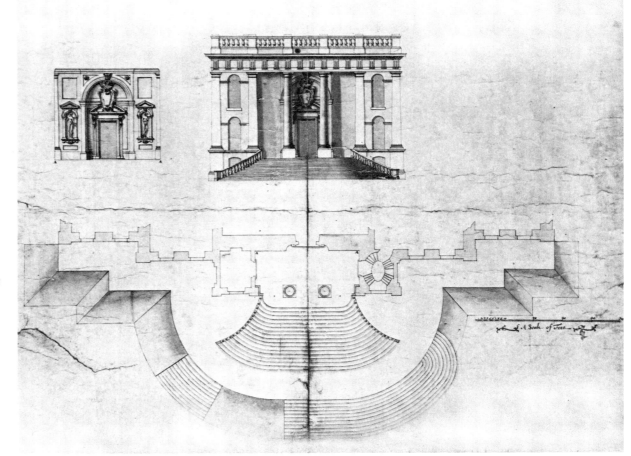

169 (right) Drawing by Alessandro Galilei showing his proposed treatment for the steps leading up to the Portico and the entrance to the Hall.

170 (opposite above) The east front with Galilei's Portico added c. 1719.

171 (opposite below) The south and east fronts, 1707–10.

precedent what Hugh May had done to Windsor Castle for Charles II. It is satisfactory to learn that Coleman's services as master-mason were retained and that Vanbrugh grew to appreciate them. 'I must do Coleman the justice', he recorded graciously, 'that he has manag'd the old materials to admirable advantage'; and again, 'I have a constant correspondence with Coleman, and am in most things very well satisfy'd with him: If we had such a man at Blenheim, he'd save us a thousand pounds a year.'

The old materials to which Vanbrugh referred disparagingly were the stones of the collapsed mediaeval front, to some extent re-used. The nine-bay south front (Fig. 171), with projecting centre, laced by stalwart rusticated angle piers, is not among the architect's most inspired compositions. But, he confided to his patron, 'to have built a front with pillasters and what the orders require, could never have been born with the rest of the Castle'. The rest of the mediaeval castle soon went the way of the south front. Once Vanbrugh got the bit between his teeth there was no holding him.[1] The west, then the north, and finally the east front were in turn rebuilt in more or less uniform fashion; and in order to make the 'castle air' convincing the skyline was provided with a genteel crenellation around all four fronts, or to be strictly accurate, all but the centre of the east front.

Avray Tipping, while admiring the Great Portico (Fig. 170) as a nobly proportioned conception, complained that

there was no apparent relation between its Classicism and the mock Gothicism of its background. In no sense did the Doric entablature and balustrade marry with the battlementing of the main structure. It looked like an independent monument instead of an integral part of the design. He could not understand what Vanbrugh was about. He did not know what has since come to light, that the portico was an afterthought, not of Vanbrugh, but of the Italian architect of the future St John Lateran façade in Rome, namely Alessandro Galilei, who was in England from 1714 to 1719. Vanbrugh's association with Kimbolton seems to have ended by 1710.

The portico may not have been imposed upon Sir John's incomplete east front before 1719 when the Duke of Manchester, which the Earl had this year become, was addressing letters to Galilei. It is true the Duke does not specifically state that the new portico is by Galilei, but on 29 June he writes to him as follows: 'I found one pair of stairs only in ye middle of ye colonnade [portico] would not doe well so have ordered two more on each side as you first proposed it. . . .' Of these stairs, or steps, three survive today. Their disposition is shown in a plan with elevation of the portico (Fig. 169) which document is distinctly signed with the initials A.G.[1] The elevation must be a prospective drawing because it includes an elaborate door-head which was not carried out, and puts windows where there are now niches. In other respects it is the same.

[1] Mr Marshall Sisson sees no reason to assume that Vanbrugh was responsible for the remaining fronts.

[1] In the Huntingdon County Record Office.

172 *The Staircase decorated by Antonio Pellegrini about 1711–12. The main scenes depict* The Triumph of Caesar.

173 *The Staircase built in 1709–10 but incorporating earlier carved woodwork.*

174 *The Staircase ceiling. Minerva points to a portrait of William III and Fame blows her trumpet.*

175 *The Musician on the upper flight of the Staircase.*

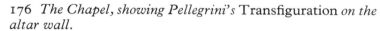

176 *The Chapel, showing Pellegrini's* Transfiguration *on the altar wall.*

177 *(above right)* The Children of the 1st Duke *by Pellegrini.*

The Duke had begun his letter to Galilei: 'I have been at Kimbolton where the front next ye town is finished & what you designed over ye gate looks very well.' This is a reference to the west front and a scroll-work cresting which Mr Marshall Sisson assures me Galilei designed and built. The feature disappeared long ago. The Duke ended his letter by exhorting Galilei to see that 'ye stone cutter' does the chimney-pieces 'well according to your design'.[1] On 10 July he again wrote lamenting that the Italian was about to depart for Tuscany.[2]

Manchester had not been responsible for Galilei's visit —largely abortive as it proved—to this country and also Ireland. On the other hand he did bring back with him from Venice in the autumn of 1708 the painters Giovanni Antonio Pellegrini and Marco Ricci. The former, having with Ricci designed the scenery at the Haymarket Theatre for Alessandro Scarlatti's opera *Pyrrhus and Demetrius*, proceeded to Kimbolton where he painted the staircase walls and ceiling in 1711–12 (Fig. 172). Pellegrini's *Triumph of Caesar* panels, 'a pastiche in Venetian terms of Mantegna's *Triumph* at Hampton Court',[3] unlike the feigned

architectural scenes of Verrio and Laguerre, are contained within compartments. His treatment of the separate themes, the introduction of turbaned figures playing flutes and trumpets, a monkey, parrot and dog upon the upper staircase, and his novel lightness of touch and gamut of delicate colours, mark a departure from the sombre Baroque to the gayer Rococo methods of decorative painting. Pellegrini was a far better artist than his countrymen who had lately preceded him to England; and his subjects and style foreshadowed the work of a still greater artist, Tiepolo. His charming group of the 1st Duke's family (Fig. 177) which hangs in the White Hall shows how elegant and spirited he could be as a portrait painter. Pellegrini likewise painted the Boudoir ceiling, and the *Transfiguration* and *Four Evangelists* of the Chapel in the west wing.

The 4th Duke of Manchester commissioned Robert Adam to design a number of ceilings for the house, and a dairy, orangery and other subsidiary buildings. Of his designs those for a pair of gate-piers on the St Neot's road and the entrance arch and screen are in Adam's most monumental manner. The deeply cut rustication of the Doric entrance and pavilions is evidence of his declared respect for Vanbrugh's robust style.

Kimbolton remained the principal seat of the Manchester family until sold by the 10th Duke in 1949. It is now Kimbolton School. Mr Marshall Sisson has been responsible for extensive and skilful reparations. He has also removed the plate glass and put back sashes and crown glass in the windows of the four elevations.

---

[1] One of these is probably that with shells and festoons in the Saloon.
[2] Ilaria Toesca—'Alessandro Galilei in Inghilterra', *English Miscellany*, 3, 1952.
[3] Whinney and Millar—*English Art 1625–1714*, 1957.

178 *Burley from the south; Neale's engraving of 1822.*

BURLEY-ON-THE-HILL, RUTLAND

Begun by Daniel Finch, 2nd Earl of Nottingham, in 1696. The architect has not been ascertained. A fire in 1908 practically gutted the interior, but spared Lanscroon's painted staircase of 1708. In 1939 Burley passed from the last Finch to a great-nephew. (The seat of Colonel J. R. Hanbury.)

In 1694 Daniel Finch, 2nd Earl of Nottingham, bought for £50,000 the Burley-on-the-Hill estate from the executors of the 2nd Duke of Buckingham. This spendthrift ornament of Charles II's court had died seven years previously overwhelmingly in debt. The house which the Duke's notorious father had 'built à la moderne', according to John Evelyn, was burnt down in the Civil War, and only the stables were left standing.

Lord Nottingham was a lukewarm supporter of William III, with whom, however, he managed to remain on good terms, without ever being a favourite. Queen Mary, who never relished his prudence and pessimism, referred to him as Don Dismallo. In 1689 Nottingham had sold his Kensington house, later to become Kensington Palace, to the King and in 1693 he thought fit to resign the Secretaryship of State for War, which he had held since 1688. He

was not to receive office again until the next reign.

For some time before his actual purchase of Burley Lord Nottingham had been negotiating for the property. In November 1693 he wrote from London, 'I am resolved to go into the country, though I live in the stables at Burleigh.' This he evidently did for a number of years while his new house was building. Work did not begin until 1696. Once in hand it proceeded apace. Lord Nottingham kept records and accounts in abundant detail. A voluminous scrapbook, into which with numerous letters and sketches they were pasted, remains at Burley to this day. The names of craftsmen, paid by task work, and artisans are noted with meticulous precision. Over fifty masons were employed; they were mostly local men from Clipsham and Ketton, where the stone also came from; a few were from London. To Edward Chapman of Bedford Row Lord Nottingham writes with a charming familiarity, even signing himself 'your affectionate friend'. The bricklayers were mainly from Nottingham, and some from London. Most of the joiners, glaziers, painters, plasterers and chimney-piece-makers were London men who had worked at other well-known buildings. Henry Dormer—he had rebuilt the Chapel of St Mary in Arden

179 *The south front.* 180 *The centrepiece of the south front.*

near Market Harborough—acted as supervisor at the start. In 1697 his place was taken by John Lumley of Northampton, a man of more proven architectural ability.[1]

Alas, there is no specific mention of who provided a design for Lord Nottingham's house. Mr Hussey's surmise[2] made as long ago as 1923 that the Earl was his own architect is perhaps correct. In a letter to his brothers concerning his wishes should he die before completion of the building the Earl wrote: 'You will find among my papers my designe of an house and gardens at Burley. . . .' Study of the elevations, however, compels us to infer that at least he got ideas from some professional source.

Lord Nottingham's correspondence reveals that he was for several years discussing his project with other landowners. In a letter to his father-in-law he refers to a talk with Sir Christopher Wren who advised him that for floor-boards fir was better than oak, which was apt to warp through weight—an odd piece of advice conflicting with normal experience. In 1695 he obtained building hints

[1] John Lumley wrote that in April 1697 he first 'weighted' on Nottingham. At his lordship's instigation he designed Ampthill Park in 1704–7 for Lord Ashburnham.

[2] *Country Life*, 10 Feb. 1923.

181 *(opposite above) An old aerial view, showing the extent of the colonnades and forecourt.*

182 *(opposite below) The north front from the eastern end of the 'Piazza Walk'.*

183 *(above) The north-west quadrant linking the house to the west wing.*

184 *(left) The entrance gates to the forecourt, by Joshua Lord.*

from the Surveyor of the Ordnance, Sir Henry Sheeres, and he also had a model for the house made by one Thomas Poulteney, a carver who worked on several City churches. In a letter of 1700 he mentions having seen a model made by 'Mr Pforth [Alexander Fort] the King's joiner . . .' for his friend, the 1st Viscount Lonsdale. Now Lord Lonsdale's new house, Lowther Hall in Westmorland, may possibly have been designed by Robert Hooke, who certainly built Ragley Hall for Lord Conway, Nottingham's uncle.

Mr Kerry Downes,[1] in the light of these connections, has surmised that Hooke had a hand in the design of Burley. He sees in the exaggeratedly spread H-plan (Fig. 181) a resemblance to Ragley, and in the great transverse room on the first floor to the original Montagu House, Bloomsbury. There is also a similarity in the rusticated, astylar ground floor (Fig. 179), the hexastyle pilaster centrepiece and the balustraded skyline to the front of Lowther Hall, illustrated in *Vitruvius Britannicus*, vol. II.

By 1700 Burley was structurally complete. In fact the Nottingham family had moved in for Christmas 1699, but for a time they endured great discomfort owing to the large numbers of decorators still inside the house.

The situation of Burley could hardly be bettered. The house stands on a plateau (Fig. 178), facing south over the Catmose Vale with Hambleton Hill in the left foreground. Until Repton swept them away in 1795 a series of terraces descended the hill to the fish-ponds beside the Oakham to Stamford road. Daniel Defoe in 1724 was so struck by the incomparable view that he was inspired to declaim in verse,

> The under-lying vale shews with delight
> A thousand beauties, *at one* charming sight;

He was no less enthusiastic about the house. 'I say there may be some that excell in this or that particular, but I do not know a house in Britain, which excels all the rest in so many particulars, or that goes so near to excelling them all in every thing.'

Indeed the approach to Burley from the north reveals a composition of quite extraordinary majesty (Fig. 182). The lane sweeping past the church suddenly precipitates you into—can it be?—the Vatican *piazza*. At first the illusion is permissible, and probably is what Lord Nottingham intended. At the age of eighteen he had spent a year in Italy at the very time, 1665, when Bernini was engaged upon his immense colonnades in front of St Peter's. Young Daniel Finch must have witnessed the stupendous construction and never forgotten it. Here at Burley the design bears no more than a general relation to St Peter's open, aisled colonnades. Short quadrant arms of Doric columns (Fig. 183) link the main block to a pair of seven-bay pavilions set confronting each other. From them closed colonnades, lower than the quadrant arms and called in the accounts the 'Cloysters', or 'Piazza Walk', inscribe two vast arcs, joined to yet another pair of pavilions, of which the eastern is the 1st Duke of Buckingham's stables. These were transformed after a serious fire in 1704 which destroyed, so Evelyn noted in a second diary entry about Burley precisely fifty years after his first, much good

[1] *English Baroque Architecture*, p. 64.

185 *The vaulted stalls in the eastern pavilion.*

186 *(right) The Great Staircase, decorated by Gerard Lanscroon.*

furniture stored there at the time. W. Thomson and Nat. Halliday were the masons in charge, and to them no doubt are due the robust vaulting and columns (Fig. 185) seen through the loose boxes. The forecourt provided is of immense size. Its northern boundary, originally a wall and pair of square, high-domed lodges, was replaced with railings by Repton. The extremely fine entrance gates, side wickets and crestings (Fig. 184) were wrought in 1700–4 by Joshua Lord, an anonymous but highly skilled smith. The spreading and horseshoe balustrade of the north perron leading to the front door was fashioned by Mr Philpott of Oakham 'according to the pattern he brought

this day', i.e. 22 November 1700. A pencil sketch of the iron bars and rails accompanies the estimate. Mr Philpott may therefore have made the perron on the south, or garden side, as well.

By the addition of the north forecourt Lord Nottingham certainly created a *tour de force*. The scheme was undeniably ambitious; the result extraordinarily impressive. Nothing quite like it was built in Baroque England, and the forecourt is what one rather expects to find gracing the palace of a Continental Grand Duke. Yet upon analysis both façade and forecourt at Burley prove to be a trifle thin, a trifle provincial. In the first place the projecting wings are too narrow for the fifteen-bay length of the centre block. The central pediment—for the carving of the fine armorial achievement Salvator Musco was paid £10 in 1698—is too slight. The finished front lacks balance and solidity. It has just a slightly cardboard look, which the recent sad deprivation of Mr Miles Pomeroy's urns over the colonnades has done nothing to mitigate.

In 1908 during a house party, at which Sir Winston Churchill was a guest, a disastrous fire broke out. Except for the Great Staircase practically every contemporary room was gutted. By good fortune the painted ceiling and walls of the Staircase by Lanscroon were spared, though

187 *Lanscroon's painting at the head
of the Great Staircase.*

blackened. Those of the first-floor Great Room, representing scenes from the life of Julius Caesar, were totally destroyed. The stair balusters, three to a tread, are twisted, and the strings, moulded into brackets, delicately carved (Fig. 186). Allowing for the rather forlorn condition of the paintings (Fig. 187) we cannot allocate Lanscroon the same high praise for their execution as for their composition. Perhaps he did not consider total payment of £163. 16s. 3d. enough for so much labour, which he brought to a finish around 1708. Feigned marbled columns frame scenes of Perseus' story as though they were tapestry panels. Musical maidens and winged figures with trumpets trespass from the ceiling on to the walls where they are supported by clouds over the cornices. In the lesser spaces between the columns bronze figures in niches and lapis lazuli busts are disposed with grace and imagination.

A letter dated 1701 from George London, the famous Brompton gardener, suggests that he and his partner Henry Wise were then busy with the gardens. Lord Nottingham had already begun, in 1696, levelling and constructing terrace walks on the south side and building walls of brick and stone. Although the terraces were replaced by a parkland slope at the instance of Repton, long avenues still stretch from the east and south fronts into the distance.

Professor H. J. Habakkuk[1] has estimated that Lord Nottingham spent £30,000 on building, furnishing and landscaping Burley, which was double his original estimate. One half of this enormous cost was paid out of the emoluments of office, the other from the sale of surplus lands. Lord Nottingham, who succeeded to the senior Earldom of Winchilsea in 1729 at the age of seventy-two, died less than a year later. Burley passed to his son, the 8th Earl of Winchilsea and 3rd Earl of Nottingham. In 1826 it was inherited by Mr George Finch, an illegitimate son of the 9th Lord Winchilsea. On the death in 1939 of Mr W. H. M. Finch the house and estate passed to his great-nephew, Colonel James R. Hanbury, the present possessor.

[1] 'English Landownership 1680–1740', essay in the *Economic History Review*, vol. X, 1939–40.

188 *The original entrance front flanked by pavilions, from the south.*

COTTESBROOKE HALL, NORTHAMPTONSHIRE

The property was bought by Sir John Langham, 1st Bart., in 1637. The present house, begun c. 1702, was finished by 1712. The names of William Talman and William Smith have been suggested for designer and builder. (The home of Sir Reginald and the Hon. Lady Macdonald-Buchanan.)

'The mansion is a handsome modern structure, consisting of a centre and two detached wings; it stands in a small park, from whence the prospects are pleasing.' This succinct account of Cottesbrooke is given in *Paterson's Road Book* of the 1820s. The faintly disparaging, distinctly condescending undertone is reminiscent of words spoken about another smallish property by Lady Catherine de Bourgh. Now Jane Austen is said to have had Cottesbrooke in mind when writing *Mansfield Park*. What is more probable, therefore, than that, had Lady Catherine visited Mansfield Park after patronizing the Bennets' domain at Longbourn in *Pride and Prejudice*, she would have expressed herself in terms very like those used by Paterson?

Cottesbrooke is surely an idealized picture of a well-to-do baronet's seat in Queen Anne's reign. In size it comes midway between the lesser gentleman's and the grand nobleman's. It is compact, trim and dignified. In spite of two rather drastic alterations in 1779 and 1937 the house keeps its original plan and elevations (Fig. 188). They are remarkably sophisticated for the time of building. We know that the house was finished by 1712 because a reference in John Morton's *Natural History of Northamptonshire*, published in that year, implies it; we also now know that the house was begun in 1702 or soon after.

In 1699 Cottesbrooke was inherited by Sir John Langham, 4th Baronet, then aged twenty-eight. His grandfather Sir John Langham, 1st Baronet, who was born in 1584, had been a poor yeoman farmer's son from Guilsborough, a nearby village. Unkindly treated in infancy he left home for London where he made a huge fortune in the City as a Turkey merchant. He returned to Northamptonshire before the outbreak of the Civil War and bought the Cottesbrooke property for £17,000. A devoted

189 *The south front from the forecourt (in 1936).*

190 *The west pavilion and the quadrant arm linking it to the house, as it was in 1936.*

191 *The north front.*

192 *Detail of the blind Ionic arcade applied to the east quadrant.*

royalist he was twice imprisoned in the Tower. He advanced money to Charles II in exile and was one of those sent in 1660 to petition the King to return. He was rewarded at the Restoration with a baronetcy.

The Turkey merchant's grandson Sir John, the 4th Baronet, was rich and already connected through various family marriages, including his own, with other territorial, mostly baroneted families. But he did not exactly belong to the aristocracy, nor did he play any part in national affairs. Instead he spent all his long life quietly at Cottesbrooke, a country squire among his own people.

Sir John's new house consisted of a rectangular block of two storeys raised over a basement (Fig. 189). The main floors were punctuated on both long fronts by four giant pilasters of the Composite order, two at the angles and two defining the slightly projecting centre of three bays. The pilasters of the south front, which until 1937 was the entrance front, support a continuous pulvinated frieze and modillion cornice; those of the north front (Fig. 191) merely their own entablatures. The original front door has a bold swan-neck pediment, embracing a cartouche, over Corinthian columns. But there is no pediment crowning either front, and the flat roof-line is formed by a parapet of alternating balustered and blank panels. The walls are of unusually small red bricks, laid in Flemish bond and very finely pointed. The basement is of orange Duston ironstone, the dressings of grey Ketton limestone. The contrasting materials were obviously chosen with deliberation. One does not know which to admire more, the glowing red brickwork or the exquisite carved stonework.

Quadrant arms of the Ionic order link the south front to a pair of single-storey pavilions with hipped roofs (Fig. 190). The high doorways[1] with broken elliptical pediments facing each other across the forecourt, and the central windows enclosed within a tabernacle of rusticated bands and pediment, which overlook the park, give liveliness to an otherwise orthodox design.

We may well ask from what sources the Northamptonshire Baronet derived this fairly novel disposition of a centre block using the giant order and connected by curved walls to balancing pavilions. Was Sir John's architect reverting to Inigo Jones's, or rather following the Wren–Hawksmoor rendering of a Palladian motif? In other words was his project influenced by Stoke Bruerne Park (begun in the 1630s) or by Easton Neston (1700–2), both of which houses are in Northamptonshire? We can only be sure that Sir John's architect was bound to have known both these important and local houses. Alternatively, Cottesbrooke might even have been inspired by Buckingham House in London, which is held to be the prototype of several Midland houses. Buckingham House, although built by William Winde, was probably designed by Talman, who was engaged by the Duke of Chandos around 1712 to design Cannons Park in the same formula (it was eventually perfected by Gibbs). Now the Cannons property came to the Duke through his first wife, Mary Lake, who was first cousin to Sir John Langham. They were married in 1696,

and the Duke's journal relates how the Langhams were constantly in and out of his house. Is it therefore too speculative to suggest that Talman provided the overall project for Cottesbrooke?

Mr Arthur Oswald[1] long ago ascribed Cottesbrooke to Henry Jones, to whom All Saints church and the Sessions House in Northampton, as well as Haselbech Hall in the next parish, were then attributed without documentary proof. Whoever was the architect of these buildings, all of which date from as far back as the 1670s, there is a certain treatment common to them[2] and to Cottesbrooke which Mr Oswald has spotted. This is a curious and very distinctive architrave interrupted by a boldly carved keystone, flanked by sprays of acanthus cresting. It is conspicuous over the Sessions House windows and over the blind doorways (Fig. 194) in the quadrant arms at Cottesbrooke. But these strange architraves also appear in the courtyard screens of Kimbolton and Drayton. They do not, therefore, provide sufficient ground for proving a common architect, and may merely have been a regional device adopted by several local builders. Nevertheless, Henry Jones, who is described in his will as a carpenter from Lamport, three miles from Cottesbrooke, could well have worked for Sir John Langham as one of his masterbuilders.

As it happens, Sir Gyles Isham and Mr Bruce Bailey

---

[1] An engraving in Bridges' *Northamptonshire* (compiled *c.* 1721 but published 1762–91) does not show these doorways. Possibly they were part of Robert Mitchell's 'Baroque' improvements.

[1] *Country Life*, 15 Feb. 1936.

[2] The 1677 Haselbech Hall disappeared long ago.

193 (opposite) The staircase with its original wrought-iron balustrade. The plasterwork was added c. 1740 by John Woolston of Northampton.

194 The Northampton Sessions House, attributed to Henry Jones. The window decoration bears a strong resemblance to the treatment of the aedicules in the quadrants at Cottesbrooke.

have lately come across a letter written by Sir Roger Cave, 2nd Baronet of Stanford Hall (q.v.) to Sir John Langham, whose first wife was his first cousin once removed. It is dated 'Ye 12 of Jan 1701/2', and runs:

Sr
According to my promise heave sent you over the Beror who undertooke my House, I doe really belive him as Honest a dealor as ye kingdom has and as retionable I wish he may please you then I have what I desire Sr . . .
Your sarvaent & Kingsman
Rr Cave

The architect of Stanford Hall, begun in 1697, was William Smith of Tettenhall, the elder brother by eleven years of the better-known Francis, or Smith of Warwick. There is nothing to prove or disprove that William Smith was engaged by Sir John Langham or that the younger brother worked with him at Cottesbrooke. Certainly the style accords less with William's conservative Stanford elevations than Francis's Calke Abbey and Chicheley Hall with their Baroque use of the giant order.

The 4th Baronet lived until 1747. His second son, also Sir John, the 6th Baronet, a philanthropist who founded in the City of London a society for distressed soldiers and sailors, redecorated the ceilings and walls of the staircase and the ceilings of hall and saloon in a restrained Rococo style. Sir James, 7th Baronet, employed Robert Mitchell (architect of Moor Place, Much Hadham) to carry out

more extensive alterations in 1775–9. His Neo-Classical decoration of the present drawing room and dining room involved throwing out an extra bay with wide bow at the west and east ends of the north front (Fig. 191). Mitchell, who adopted the Adam–Wyatt style of his generation, was remarkably respectful of the Baroque character of the exterior. His treatment, notably in duplicating the giant pilasters of the front and continuing the parapet, is a model of propriety.

Although the disposition of the rooms inside has changed little, hardly any of the Queen Anne decoration has survived. The Pine Room, formerly the entrance hall, has kept its bolection-moulded panelling, now stripped of paint. The robust wrought-iron balustrade of the staircase (Fig. 193)—William Marshall, who worked for Talman at Chatsworth, was paid £224 for unspecified ironwork—and the wide but shallow treads in dark, polished slate, are original. At landing level the monogram of the 4th Baronet appears in the balustrade.

In 1911 Sir Charles Langham, 13th Baronet, sold Cottesbrooke to Captain R. B. Brassey. In 1937 house and estate were bought by the present owners, Sir Reginald and the Hon. Lady Macdonald-Buchanan. That year they converted the north front into the entrance and the south forecourt into a formal garden. They transformed the old kitchen into a ballroom, and made a number of other alterations. They also moved to a different site and restored Mitchell's gates and sentry-box lodges, which had fallen into sad disrepair.

195 *The house at the end of the avenue.*

HANBURY HALL, WORCESTERSHIRE

In 1701 the house was finished for Thomas Vernon, whose grandfather bought the estate in about 1620. In 1710 Thornhill decorated the staircase and ceilings of the hall and two other rooms. (A property of the National Trust.)

Thomas Vernon, whose grandfather Edward bought the Hanbury estate in the early seventeenth century, practised for forty years as a barrister in the Court of Chancery. He also sat in Parliament as Whig Member for Worcester City from 1715 until his death in 1721, and although not a

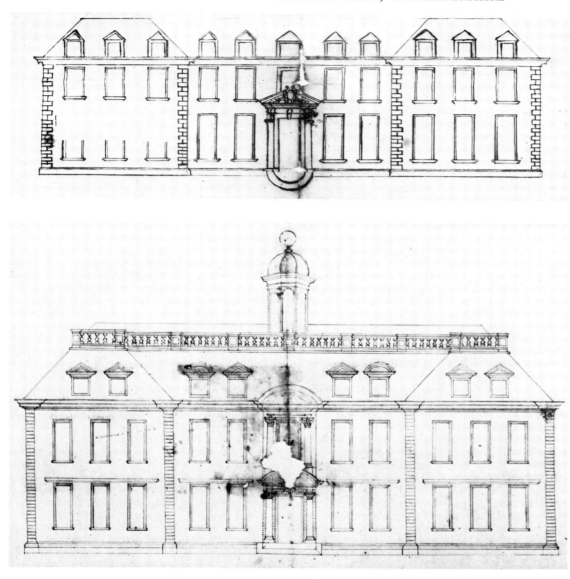

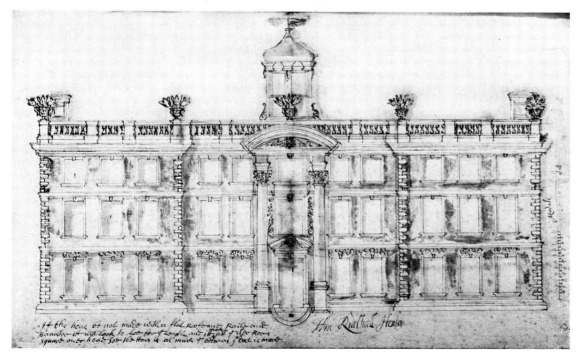

196 *(far left) The east front.*

197 & 198 *(above) Proposals for the east front by 'Mr. Withenbury' and 'Jon Chatterton'.*

199 *(left) William Rudhall's proposed design for the east front.*

great national figure Vernon nevertheless amassed a large
fortune. He is remembered by some voluminous notes on
Chancery cases posthumously published, a life-size reclining monument between impressive images of Justice
and Learning by Christopher Horsnaile in Hanbury
Church and, what is our concern, Hanbury Hall.

Vernon's arms and the date 1701 are displayed over the
front door for all to see. The house is a complete specimen

200 (above) The centrepiece of the east front; the porch was
added in the Regency period.

201 (above right) The Hall. The trompe l'œil painting of
the ceiling is probably by Thornhill's assistants.

202 (right) The bust of Thomas Vernon, the builder, in the
Hall.

of its date, for it was neither an addition to an older building, nor has it suffered extensive alterations since. It remains much as it was when Thornhill took a sketch of the house 'from ye bowlingreen' soon after it was finished. The chief changes are the disappearance of the stable block and tall cupolaed building to the north of the forecourt and, of course, the substitution of the original forecourt by a Victorian version with gazebos, piers and rather coarse ironwork.

Approached by a winding drive through a well-wooded park the house looks from a distance conventional enough. Mature red brickwork with buff stone dressings, hipped roof, dormers, central wooden lantern and wide modillion cornice are gradually revealed through branches of oak and elm. But on closer inspection the plan and the centrepiece (Fig. 200) of the east front turn out to be more sophisticated than at first they seemed.

Three prospective drawings for this east front, all by different hands, have survived. Each shows a front of eleven bays with three-bay projecting wings. The most detailed of the drawings (Fig. 199) which is signed 'William Rudhall, Henley', bears some resemblance to Talman's

Thoresby Hall (Fig. 8), Nottinghamshire, after an upper storey and balustrade had been added to that great house following a disastrous fire about 1685. In Rudhall's design for Hanbury the centrepiece consists of a pair of giant Corinthian columns, or half-columns, supporting an elliptical pediment and embracing one bay only throughout the three storeys. It is not surprising that Mr Vernon rejected this clumsy arrangement notwithstanding Rudhall's written recommendation that no expense ought to be spared. Rudhall also warned his client against doing what in fact he did do, which was to abandon 'a flat Roofe and Raile and Banister', without which 'itt will look to loe for ye Length'. The Hanbury front as carried out has no upper storey, but a hipped roof and dormers. It is in fact a compromise between the two other Hanbury designs I have mentioned. They are endorsed respectively, 'Mr. Withenbury's Draught for a Best ffront', and 'Draught of building Jon Chatterton's of a Best front'.

Nothing so far has come to light about Chatterton, and little about James Withenbury, who was the sculptor of a marble monument in Fladbury church to Bishop Lloyd of Worcester in 1718. William Rudhall is no less anonymous. He was probably a member of a well-known family of bell-founders, and a number of his children by his wife, Mary, were buried at Henley-in-Arden and Wotton Wawen. He may well have worked at Ragley Hall—a mere eight miles from Henley and in Warwickshire—when Robert Hooke was building it for the Earl of Conway in the early 1680s. Indeed Hanbury bears distinct resemblances to Hooke's Ragley, not only in the roof treatment but in the Thoresby-type centrepiece (with the addition of a pediment), and furthermore in the wings. There were no wings at Thoresby; Ragley had them, but at Hanbury the wings are considerably advanced and in the side elevations considerably returned, so as to form distinct pavilions in that French manner which Hooke is known to have favoured. Ragley, therefore, rather than Thoresby appears to be Hanbury's immediate prototype.

The Hall (Fig. 201) is entered straight from the porch, which is a Regency addition to the east front. It is a long, low room, occupying the whole ground floor of the five-bay centre. A bust of Thomas Vernon in wig and bands stares from a niche over the fireplace at whosoever enters the front door. A staircase of turned oak balusters descends into the Hall. The arrangement is similar to that of Talman's Fetcham Park, Surrey, where the stairwell is painted by Laguerre. Here the artist whom Thomas Vernon engaged to paint his stair walls and ceiling was no less a master than the Englishman, James Thornhill.

203 (left) The Staircase, decorated by Thornhill with scenes from the life of Achilles.

204 (above right) A preparatory drawing by Thornhill for the ceiling and main wall of the staircase (in the Cooper-Hewitt Museum of Design, the Smithsonian Institution, Washington, D.C.).

205 (right) The figure of Mercury, a detail of the decoration on the south wall.

The walls of the staircase illustrate scenes in the life of Achilles. They are contained within architectural settings against feigned rustication (Fig. 203). The scene on the main wall facing the Hall represents Achilles choosing a spear and shield while the daughters of Lycomedes seize upon the jewellery which Ulysses, disguised as a pedlar, has thrown among them: that on the wall facing the windows depicts the Cyclops forging the armour for Thetis who watches from a cloud. The staircase ceiling contains an assembly of the classical deities, while Mercury flying across the cornice points to the notorious Dr Sacheverell's portrait about to be set alight by the Furies. The incident dates the ceiling after February 1710, in which month the Tory doctor was impeached for seditious treason much to the delight of the jubilant Whigs. Thornhill's signature appears on a scroll carried by a boy directly below Mercury.

The Hall is painted in monochrome with emblems of the seasons and may be by an assistant of Thornhill. The long room on the north front was made out of a small breakfast room and a passage, or vestibule, leading from the Hall to the north garden. Hence the dissimilar shapes of two ceiling paintings on plaster, the larger in full colours, and the lesser in brown and blue. The first is of *Apollo in his Sun-chariot*, the second of *The Rape of Orithyia by Boreas the North Wind*. Thornhill's original sketches for both panels are now in the Courtauld Institute. The elaborate plaster frames of oak and olive branches are a skilful parody of William and Mary work, actually done when the two rooms were thrown into one, probably at the beginning of the last century.

The formal gardens by George London on the south side of the house disappeared long ago. The red-brick Orangery in hair-thin pointing, with a basket of fruit and trailing foliage in the pediment, parapet urns and pineapple finials all in carved stone, is a little later than the house.

Thomas Vernon dying without issue left his Worcestershire estates to his first cousin once removed, Bowater Vernon. Hanbury passed by inheritance to Sir George Bowater Vernon, 2nd and last Baronet who died in 1940. Under his will the house and garden came to the National Trust in 1953. His widow lived there until 1962.

206 *The upper part of the staircase hall.*

COUND HALL, SHROPSHIRE

Dated 1704 Cound was built for Richard Cressett. An early elevation drawing is signed by John Prince. The design is a prototype of several later Shropshire houses. (The property of Mr James Morris.)

Were it not for the date 1704 carved clear as day upon the north front we might suppose that Cound Hall was built in the 1720s or even early 1730s. It belongs to a well-defined Midlands group of houses, of which Buntingsdale (1721) (Fig. 427), Hardwick (1720–30) and Mawley (1730), (Fig. 24), all in Shropshire and all possibly by Francis Smith, are comparable specimens. The most distinctive features shared by the four are giant pilasters embracing two floors, emphatic entablatures and cornice, a third storey or attic, sharp breaks in the elevations, and the use of red brick with stone dressings. Height, not to say gauntness, is the first impression they convey; quirkiness and eccentricity prevail to a marked degree. In short this

particular group of English country houses is as Baroque in its way as any domestic architecture of the Continent.

Close study reveals that the Cound elevations are more unorthodox and outrageous than those of the later houses mentioned, which belong to the reigns of George I and II. Obviously the architect here was experimenting with a formula which Francis Smith—if it were he—was to resolve in the others with greater expertise, and caution. The formula had first been expounded by Hawksmoor upon the King William Court (finished in 1704) at Greenwich Hospital, the design for which the architect must surely have seen. He was quick to transpose Hawksmoor's highly sophisticated design for part of a palace to a small country-house entity in distant Shropshire. Rash though his adaptation of this Baroque formula may have been, his craftsmanship was of a superior order. The small bricks laid at Cound are in Flemish bond and finely pointed. A beautiful gauged brick is used for the window-lintels.

207 *The south front.*

As for the stonework the carving of virgated pilasters, swags of window-aprons, *amorini* and cipher over the front door of the north front is of outstanding delicacy.

There exists a skilful drawing (Fig. 208) of the north front with a small-scale plan inset in the top right-hand corner, signed 'Prince, architect, Salop'. The drawing shows the front much as it is today (Fig. 209). Whereas Smith at Buntingsdale and Mawley stopped his Corinthian order at least short of the attic storey, which he put above the cornice, the architect of Cound has dragged up his pilasters so that the capitals and entablature are on a level with the top-floor windows. The oversailing cornice is heavily enriched, down to the pendent pine-cone at each angle. It sits like a wide-brimmed hat over a countenance which expresses a somewhat pained surprise.

Mr Avray Tipping concluded that Prince was the architect of Cound. Mr Kerry Downes[1] on the other hand suggests that the drawing was not an architectural design but a later illustration, or record, by that John Prince who was to become surveyor of the Harley estates in Marylebone around 1719.[2] John Prince was a bricklayer by trade who turned speculative builder.

Whether John Prince was or was not the architect of Cound Hall, the owner was a Shropshire squire of no more than county standing, albeit ancient lineage. Richard Cressett who was High Sheriff of Shropshire in 1702 had his crest, a demi-lion holding a cresset, or beacon, carved upon the friezes above the central pilasters of the

entrance front. He was descended from the Cressetts of Upton Cressett near Bridgnorth, one of whom came into Cound by marriage with a Townshend heiress in 1603.

Richard Cressett had chosen for his new house a flat, open site close to the little river Cound which flows north to join the Severn. The towering bulk of the building was, and still is, visible on all sides from afar. The two long fronts are identical except for the crowning feature of each centrepiece; that of the south (Fig. 207) is a pediment broken in the centre (it was repeated by Smith over the end bays at Buntingsdale) whereas that of the north was a raised parapet with panelled swags. The swags have now gone and instead the roof-line of the north front has been given a continuous parapet without a coping, and rendered in cement—an unsightly thing which effectively conceals the pitch of the roof at either end. The short sides facing east and west are of five bays, the three central bays considerably advanced.

Cound passed from the Cressetts to the Pelhams in the reign of George III. In 1878 it was inherited by James Thursby Pelham who sold it to Mr A. C. McCorquodale. The interior underwent a good deal of alteration by the Pelhams towards the end of the eighteenth century, when the present flying staircase was built into the hall, and again at the hands of Mr McCorquodale. It is now divided into separate tenements. The ground-floor plan inserted in Prince's drawing shows the original disposition of deep entrance hall and shallow saloon, axial corridor running the length of the house, and staircase occupying the north-west corner—a plan closely followed at Buntingsdale.

[1] *English Baroque Architecture*, 1966.
[2] C. H. Collins and M. I. Baker—*Life of James Brydges, 1st Duke of Chandos*, 1949.

208 (opposite) A drawing for, or after, the north front, by John Prince.

209 (above) The north front.

210 (left) Part of the centrepiece on the north front.

HINWICK HOUSE, BEDFORDSHIRE

Acquired by the Orlebar family through marriage in the 1640s, the house was built in 1709–13 by Richard Orlebar. (The seat of Mr Richard Orlebar.)

There is at Hinwick a prospect of the house painted soon after it was completed (Fig. 213). The house appears exactly as it appears today—if we discount the 1860 addition to the north; and even in 1715 there was in that quarter a minor extension which the Victorian wing has replaced. True, the iron gates and *clairvoie* before the east front do not now exist (they may never have been more than artistic licence), but the crescents, hugely exaggerated, of young lime trees are still *in situ*. The gangling youngsters have become wide-spreading veterans, towering above the house which once overshadowed them.

The great charm of Hinwick House lies in its unchanged state and purpose. It was built by Richard (III) Orlebar between 1709 and 1713; it is lived in by Richard (IX) Orlebar today. The family originally came from Orlingbury, nine miles north across the Northamptonshire border, and the present spelling of the territorial surname is a corruption. Hinwick was part of a large settlement made shortly before his death in 1647 by Richard Child upon his daughter Margaret, wife of George Orlebar. Their great-grandson Richard (III) was actually obliged to buy back the Hinwick part of the property from a female cousin upon whom it had devolved, before he could start building in 1709. The previous year he had married Diana, daughter and coheiress of Sir Samuel Astry. Unfortunately the devoted couple were not destined to have children. Diana was delicate—her portrait next to her husband's in the Dining Room confirms it—and she died in 1716. Her widower is described on their joint monument in Podington church as 'elegant, facetious and polite', virtues which his genial countenance does not belie (Fig. 218).

Richard Orlebar chose a site for his new house slightly to the east of an old farmhouse—now known as the Turret (Fig. 212)—to which he added a square tower and cupola. The house, facing east, presents a front in that familiar formula propounded by Winde's Buckingham House, that is to say a rectangle of two storeys contained within a giant order of pilasters (Fig. 9). Over the entablature comes an attic storey crowned by a flat balustrade. Hinwick is a much modified version of the Buckingham House formula, being not a palace but a squire's home. Instead of brick, stone was the material used, local Hinwick laid in narrow courses for the wall surface, and Ketton for the carved features. The house presents other digressions from the formula; it has no quadrant corridors and

211 *The entrance front from the east.*

pavilions, and the west, or rear portion has a deep recess. Its two arms are of unequal width and the windows asymmetrically set. The recess contains a splendidly robust downpipe with the Orlebar crest and the date 1710 upon the rainwater head (Fig. 215).

Richard III's building accounts begin in February

1709 and end in 1714. By the end of 1710 the structure was finished; whereupon the fitting up of the rooms proceeded rather more leisurely. Detailed payments are recorded and the names of masons, glaziers, joiners, plasterers and smiths employed are all noted down. Unfortunately no name of a specific architect appears, but two names

212 *The south front and the Turret lying to the west.*

213 *A painting showing the house after its completion.*

214 *The relief showing* Diana in her Chariot, *carved by John Hunt, in the middle of the south front.*

215 *A rainwater head dated 1710 and bearing the Orlebar crest.*

216 *The oak staircase.*

feature prominently. They are those of the principal freestone mason, Richard Knight, and the carver 'Mr John Hunt'. Knight, who often charged £5 at a time, was clearly in control of operations. Hunt—he is invariably given the prefix 'Mr'—was possibly the designer.

John Hunt was a sculptor and statuary of some note. A native of Northampton, he became a pupil of Grinling Gibbons and in his own city he made the statue of King Charles II now standing above the portico of All Saints church. That was in 1712; two years previously he did his most spectacular carving, which is the large relief (Fig. 214) within the triangle on the attic of the south front of Hinwick House.

The relief depicts the goddess Diana, supposedly in compliment to Mrs Orlebar, in her Roman chariot drawn by a pair of deer with three hounds (representing the absorbing pursuit of Mr Orlebar) running in the rear. It was an ambitious undertaking and gives an eccentric accent to the elevation (Fig. 212). The carving of the relief seems less professional than that of the pilaster capitals and swan-neck pediment of the entrance door on the east front, which Mr Arthur Oswald[1] assumes were likewise Hunt's work.

Nothing in the accounts proves that Hunt was architect of the house, but Mr Oswald very plausibly suggests that as the relief is so prominent a part of the south front its creator may have designed the whole setting. And indeed the two groups of niches, rather clumsily introduced below, must have been related deliberately to the relief above them. Although many monumental masons in the provinces turned their hand to architecting a house or two, not all could do so by any means. It is therefore not impossible that the architect of All Saints church or Cottesbrooke Hall[2]—Henry Jones, Henry Bell or William Smith?—provided the overall design. The affinities be-

[1] *Country Life*, 22 Sept. 1960.
[2] See section of Cottesbrooke Hall, p. 119.

217 *The landing at the head of the staircase.*

218 *Portrait of Richard (III) Orlebar, the builder.*

tween Cottesbrooke and Hinwick are too obvious to need elaborating.

Behind the three central bays of the east front lies a shallow Entrance Hall. The fan over the front door is carved out of a solid piece of oak. The two plain stone fireplaces were probably supplied by Richard Knight, and on their either side are doorways within semi-domed recesses. The panelling is contemporary. West of the hall the staircase (Fig. 216) rises within a very generous space. The turned oak balusters, three to a tread, are evenly graduated as they ascend and on the landing they form a spacious gallery (Fig. 217). Daniel Wyman was the joiner responsible. The two English tapestries on the landing are part of a set of five illustrating the history of Ulysses and date from the early eighteenth century. The portraits here and throughout the house are mostly of late Stuart and Georgian Orlebars.

Little was done to Hinwick for the first century and a half of its existence. With the building of the north wing in 1859–66 the then owner, Richard (VI) Longuet Orlebar, changed the use of certain downstairs rooms in the Queen Anne block, and so to some extent their character. None the less Hinwick House is redolent of the spirit of family continuity which to many visitors is more precious than decorative purism without it.

219 *The entrance front from the west.*

EASTON NESTON, NORTHAMPTONSHIRE

Acquired by the Fermor family in 1535. Sir William Fermor, 2nd Baronet and later 1st Lord Lempster, consulted Sir Christopher Wren and finally commissioned Nicholas Hawksmoor to build the present house, 1699–1702. (The seat of the Lord Hesketh.)

'A great, staring, unpleasant dwelling, of neither comfort or content; surrounded by great offices, adorn'd by statues, and commanding an offensive view' is the pejorative description of Easton Neston given by John Byng in 1789. It is not likely to be endorsed by the connoisseurs of today, and yet, like most grossly exaggerated and some bad-tempered remarks, contains minute elements of truth. We shall touch upon them in due course.

The first of the Fermor family to become possessed of the estate was Richard, grocer of London and rich merchant of the staple of Calais, in 1535. His descendants have held it ever since. William Fermor's loyalty to Charles I

was rewarded in 1641 with a baronetcy to which his son, likewise William, succeeded in 1661 at the age of twelve. This Sir William was the builder of the present house. He married three times, each with indirect or direct benefit to his fame and fortune.

His first wife, Jane Barker, a squire's daughter of Fairford Park, Gloucestershire, had the distinction of being closely related to Sir Christopher Wren. Although her married life was cut very short it did achieve the effect of introducing the great architect into the Fermor family. Two letters from Wren to Sir William, undated but probably written in the 1670s, survive. One contains the phrase, 'if you ask me any questions wee can resolve by letter, I shall readily serve you till I can find opportunity to wait on you'; the other gives advice about garden walls and floorboards for his cousin's proposed 'great house', one storey of which he hopes will be up by the following year.

From this correspondence there is no evidence that

220 (*above*) *The brick wing on the north side of the forecourt, built c. 1682.*

221 & 222 (*left and below left*) *Views of Hawksmoor's preparatory wooden model for the house.*

223 (*below right*) *The ground plan from* Vitruvius Britannicus.

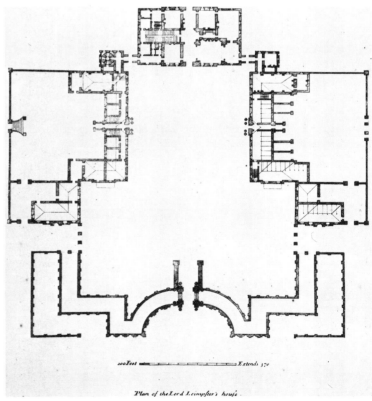

224 (above) The vermiculated gate piers standing to the west of the entrance front.

225 The south façade.

226 (above) A view of the north façade showing the use of mezzanine floors and a fenestration pattern comparable with that in Fig. 227.

227 Engraving of Ammanati's Collegio Romano in Rome.

Wren designed Fermor's 'great house', proposals for which were abandoned at an early stage. On the other hand Bridges, the Northamptonshire historian, left a note before his death in 1724 that 'The wings [of Easton Neston] are of brick, and were built by Sir Christopher Wren', adding that the house was 'finished 1702, about 20 yrs after Erection of wings. It was built by Hawkesmore who hath very much departed from the first design.'
Of the pair of red-brick wings or pavilions the northern remains (Fig. 220), the other having disappeared early in the last century. The survivor consists of a single storey with eight tall windows of double transoms, roundel openings over end doorways and a pedimented centre-piece and portal in ashlar. There is every reason to believe that this pavilion dates from about 1682, and if it was to Wren's design, he certainly had nothing to be ashamed of. It precedes in date and design the north pavilions added to Chelsea Hospital later in the decade.

In the very year 1682 Sir William married a second time. His new wife was Catherine, daughter of the 3rd Lord Poulett. By now the Baronet must have been more strongly of opinion than ever that the old house below the church in which he was still living was unbecoming to his enhanced status in the county. His second marriage may have determined the building of the pavilions, whether or not

a matching house got further than paper. All we know is that by 1686 Hawksmoor was giving sketches for ground levels. He was at the time Wren's 'domestic clerk' in the Board of Works, a young man of twenty-five, and rapidly becoming his indispensable 'gentleman'. The master, busy and important, would have sent down the pupil to his Northamptonshire kinsman while he supervised the building's progress from afar, but work proceeded slowly.

The year 1692 brought matters to a head. In March the Baronet married his third wife, Sophia, a widowed daughter of the 1st Duke of Leeds. This ducal alliance could permit no further delays. Moreover in the following month Sir William himself was raised to the barony of Lempster (or Leominster). Hawksmoor was given the signal to steam ahead. A wooden model (Fig. 221) was presumably the first result. It represents more or less the rectangular shape and plan of the house as executed, but the actual elevations greatly differ from the model's which are of two superimposed orders, with a projecting centre of five bays distinctly in the Wren manner. The entrance bay is given a segmental head, in which Mr Kenworthy-Browne[1] detects a French derivation. Unfortunately, of the ninety-five drawings of the house known to have been

[1] 'Easton Neston I', *Connoisseur*, Oct. 1964. He cites S. de Brosse's crowning façade feature of St Gervais, Paris (1616–21) as prototype.

228 *(opposite) The east front which faces the garden.*

229 *(left) The Great Hall as it is today.*

230 *(below) The Great Hall before the late 19th-century alterations.*

made by Hawksmoor, only three survive. We are left then with little beyond our knowledge of Hawksmoor's meeting in 1699 with Vanbrugh, from which to deduce the abrupt departure (noted by Bridges) from the style of the model to that of the actual building finished in 1702. This date is clearly carved on the entablature of the garden front.

Since the pavilions already existed Hawksmoor was obliged to keep his house within the prescribed limit of the 125 feet between them. This would have been all very well for a modest squire's dwelling like, for example, Fairford Park, the first Lady Fermor's home, and indeed for Sir William Fermor's original intention. But for the new Lord Lempster's palace it presented distinct handicaps. Hawksmoor overcame them with ingenuity; and the result is a noticeable constriction in the planning. It is reflected in a certain cramped look about the elevations, and perhaps in the lack of comfort and content observed by that cross-patch, John Byng.

On the other hand the merits of the west (Fig. 219) and east (Fig. 228) fronts are astonishing. A fine, pale-silvery stone from Helmdon was the material chosen—'the finest stone I have yet seen in England', John Morton[1] declared. With this beautiful and tractable material Hawksmoor composed fronts of great virtuosity and movement. Various prototypes have been put forward—the King's Pavilion at Marly, the south front of Chatsworth, and the east front of the King William block at Greenwich (almost surely designed by Hawksmoor contemporane-

[1] *Natural History of Northamptonshire*, 1712.

231 *(left) The Great Staircase looking south from the half-landing.*

232 *(above) Lord Lempster's cipher incorporated in the wrought-iron balustrade at the head of the staircase.*

ously). All three may well have provided inspiration for the treatment of giant Corinthian pilasters on the west and east fronts. But Hawksmoor introduced to Easton Neston a new element, more subtle, and distinctly Baroque, in the alternating projection and recession of the bays between the pilasters, culminating on the west front in a single jutting bay between two advancing columns. On the west front the entablature of the centrepiece carries a segmental panel bearing Lord Lempster's arms, supporters and coronet in heavy relief. The fine horseshoe-shaped perron on this front was wrought by a highly skilled smith. It provoked unstinted admiration in John Lumley, Lord Nottingham's overseer, who on 9 September 1708 wrote to his client at Burley-on-the-Hill: 'The ston stairs at ye Lord Lemsters are but 6ft 4 ins, projecting out of ye wall and ye iron raile takes 2 ins of it. These are called noble staires by reason which Sir Christopher Renn and Mr Hawksmoore designed them. . . .' The inclusion of the first name is surely significant.

The south end (Fig. 225) transgresses Hawksmoor's dictum delivered to Lord Carlisle that an abrupt change of fenestration in one front to another is inadmissible if both fronts can be viewed 'from the diagonal', which is certainly the case here. The mezzanine floor taking the place of the architrave, and the central pediment rising from the

cornice, are, to say the least, incorrect by classical standards. The north end (Fig. 226) with its multiplicity of mezzanine windows jostling inordinately long windows, is still less orthodox. It was perhaps suggested by Ammanati's Mannerist Collegio Romano (1578) in Rome (Fig. 227), which Hawksmoor must have known from textbooks. It is the only front which exactly follows the model, so evidently the architect saw no reason to alter this early design with which he remained satisfied.

Lord Lempster died in 1711 and his son, still a minor, called a halt to further operations. This explains why Hawksmoor's grandiose intentions to transform the pavilions into a distinctly Vanbrughian guise, to provide a forecourt and entrance—cunningly broadened so as to suggest immensity—and to add a cupola to the house, all outlined in *Vitruvius Britannicus*, vol. I, 1715, were postponed and then abandoned. We need not regret them. But Hawksmoor's very proposal to tamper with the 1682 pavilions as well as his assurance to Lord Carlisle in 1731 that they were 'good for nothing' suggests that Wren, to whom his pupil was consistently loyal, was not, in spite of Bridges's statement, wholly responsible for them. If the pair of collared and vermiculated gate-piers (Fig. 224) now standing 350 yards from the front door are on their original site, they strongly suggest that Hawksmoor may have entertained plans for future ambitious outworks beyond the forecourt. Even by 1731 Easton Neston was in Hawksmoor's words 'not quite finish'd'. As for the park it was 'capable of much improvement, and it is much wanted and I am affrayed will continue so'. Presumably the distant canal to the east on a line with

the garden door was already dug. No doubt when John Byng took a walk in the park the flat, outdated landscape seemed to his 'Capability'-trained eyes, uninviting. The formal pool and parterres close to this front were laid out by the 1st Lord Hesketh early this century. He also rectified the asymmetry caused by the disappearance of the south pavilion by building a low wall, which he returned with a balustrade to join the north wing.

The plan (Fig. 223) of the house is curiously old-fashioned in that an axial corridor, or screens passage gave entry from the front door straight into the Great Hall, which extended as far as the south end of the house. Such an arrangement was still in the mediaeval tradition. The Hall of three sections, the central one rising into the floor above, is shown in the model, but was done away with before 1900, no doubt on account of draughts. A dining room was then formed by walling in the passage and lowering the ceiling of the central section (Fig. 229). At the

233 *(left) The Gallery.*

234 *(above) The semi-circular apse opposite the entrance in the middle of the Gallery.*

same time the wall on the opposite side of the passage was taken down and the little dining room behind it thrown into the present hall. The new hall contains part of an important set of early Mortlake tapestries, depicting Solomon and the Queen of Sheba, woven for the first Villiers, Duke of Buckingham, whose arms appear on the border. They were acquired by the 1st Lord Lempster.

The remaining downstairs rooms which are narrow and very deep have been little altered since the time when the 2nd Lord Lempster, who in 1721 was created Earl of Pomfret (or Pontefract), decorated them between 1730 and 1740. The cornices had been set up by Hawksmoor, but the ceilings of the Smoking Room and present Dining Room (originally the Drawing Room), and the walls of the last, belong to a later period altogether. The stucco picture-frames, beautiful in themselves and teeming with trophies, ribbon and scrolls, may, according to Geoffrey Beard,[1] be

[1] *Georgian Craftsmen*, 1966.

the work of the Northampton stuccoist, John Woolston. They have been applied to the walls, however, with no regard to proportions or available space. The noble chimney-piece of Carrara and 'black and gold' marble is a Palladian design, and the ceiling oval, taken from Titian's *Venus and Adonis*, is most sensitively modelled.

Occupying a central section from corridor to north end of the house and lit by a broad, high window is Hawksmoor's monumental staircase (Fig. 231). Again our first impression of constriction here must quickly give place to admiration. The architect has within a comparatively narrow tunnel achieved sublimity. True, the two dog-leg flights are immensely long. But what a pleasure to mount those wide and shallow stone treads and to grasp the gilded rail of the wrought-iron balustrade, which is clearly the work of one inspired by Tijou, if not actually of the master himself. (As Clerk of the Works at Kensington Hawksmoor was intimately acquainted with Tijou's Great Staircase in the royal residence.) In several prominent panels (Fig. 232) appear the cipher and coronet of the 1st Lord Lempster, the double Ls being a deliberate crib of Louis XIV's monogram found all about Versailles. The cipher reappears in stucco among the shells, flowers and leaves upon the barrel ceiling which Mr Beard tentatively ascribes to Edward Goudge. The superb craftsmanship of the Staircase is matched by the grisaille panels of scenes in the life of King Cyrus, painted by Thornhill between 1702 and 1713. The shell-headed niches were designed to contain some of the Arundel Marbles which Lord Lempster had purchased in 1691 and which the first Lord Pomfret's widow bought from her bankrupt son and bestowed upon Oxford University in 1753.

In stepping through the doorway at the head of the Staircase we at once understand the climax of Hawksmoor's ceremonial approach: for we are brought straight into the middle of the Gallery (Fig. 233) which runs from east to west. This impressive apartment cuts the first floor into two halves. It is lit at either end by great arched windows reaching practically from floor level up to the frieze, and it has a barrel-vaulted, but undecorated, ceiling. The semi-circular theme is repeated in the apse (Fig. 234) facing the doorway through which we entered. Fluted pilasters, broken forward, flank it, and Mr Kerry Downes[1] has noticed an affinity between the alcove and the rotundas at the ends of the Kensington orangery. The wainscot of the gallery, crisply carved, is painted white and gold.

When the 1st Earl of Pomfret died in 1753 his successor, harassed by gambling debts, was obliged to sell many of the contents collected by his father and grandfather. Happily a rich heiress whom he married eleven years later helped him retrieve a well-nigh hopeless situation. With the death in 1867 of the 5th Earl the titles of Pomfret and Lempster became extinct, and Easton Neston passed to his sister, wife of Sir Thomas Hesketh, 5th Baronet of Rufford Hall, Lancashire, who prefixed the Fermor surname to his own. Sir Thomas Fermor-Hesketh, 8th Baronet, who re-created the gardens around the house, was made Lord Hesketh in 1935. His grandson, the 3rd Lord Hesketh, is the present owner.

[1] *English Baroque Architecture*, 1966.

CASTLE HOWARD, YORKSHIRE

Henderskelfe Castle came to the Howards with the marriage of Lord William Howard to a Dacre heiress in 1571. Charles Howard, 3rd Earl of Carlisle, commissioned Sir John Vanbrugh to build on a new site a palace (1699–1726) which he called Castle Howard. Hawksmoor was also employed from start to finish. (The seat of Mr George Howard.)

Charles Howard, 3rd Earl of Carlisle, was twenty-three when in 1692 he inherited his father's honours and large estates. These, which included the Castle of Henderskelfe in the North Riding, had come to the family by the marriage of Lord William Howard, Walter Scott's 'Belted Will', a younger son of the 4th Duke of Norfolk, with the Dacre heiress in 1571. Charles Howard who had 'a very good understanding; with very grand deportment', was absorbed in politics and architecture. He also liked gossip and conviviality. It is hardly surprising, therefore, that on all these counts the young nobleman soon swam into John Vanbrugh's orbit. Besides, they were fellow members of the Kit Cat Club. Carlisle became perhaps the architect's closest friend, and certainly his most consistent patron.

In 1702 he got Vanbrugh made Comptroller of Works in place of Talman and, in his capacity as acting Earl Marshal, appointed him two years later Clarenceux King of Arms. Friendship could scarcely go further. The building of the Earl's house covered Vanbrugh's entire architectural career until his death in 1726.

It appears that Carlisle had in the summer of 1698 commissioned Talman, then Comptroller of Works, to draw up plans for a new house on the site of Henderskelfe Castle, to face east and west. Talman was socially pretentious and exorbitant in his charges. Trouble ensued almost immediately, to end eventually in a lawsuit between the two men in 1703. Much to everyone's surprise the Earl

235 *(below) The main pile of the north front.*

236 *(right) The central block and the east half of Vanbrugh's composition.*

237 *(below right) Campbell's vision of the house from the north, as published in* Vitruvius Britannicus, *vol. III.*

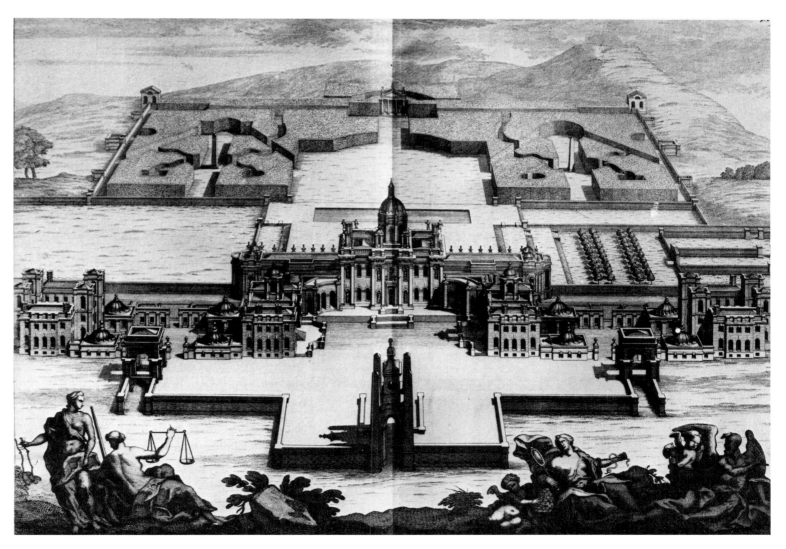

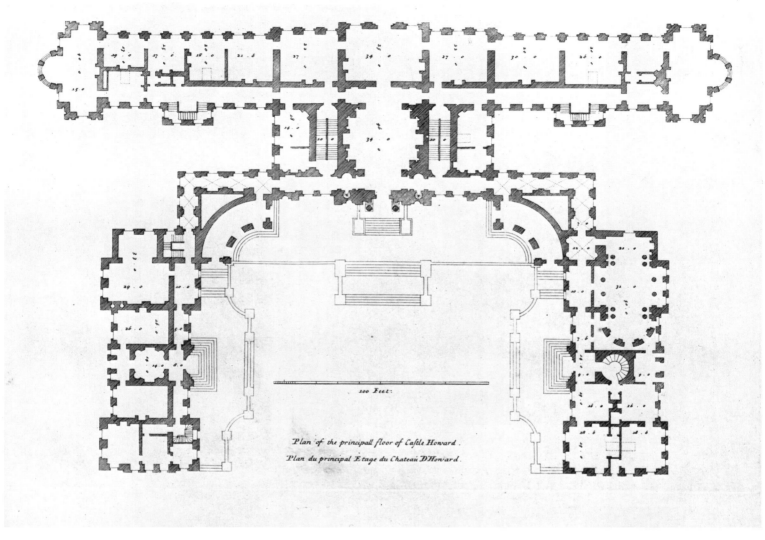

Plan of the principall floor of Castle Howard.

Plan du principal Etage du Chateau D'Howard.

238 *(above left) Detail of the centrepiece of the north front.*

239 *(left) The dramatic build-up of the house from the north-east. Robinson's west wing (1753–9) is on the right.*

240 *(above right) The proposed ground plan from* Vitruvius Britannicus.

in 1699 commissioned Vanbrugh, the boon companion and ex-playwright who had not yet built a thing, to undertake one of the largest and most ambitious palaces in England. Had the Earl, who was to become First Lord of the Treasury in 1701, consulted the Surveyor of Works, Sir Christopher Wren? It may account for the long association with Castle Howard of Nicholas Hawksmoor, who for twenty years had been clerk and close assistant to Wren. The influence of Wren's St Paul's upon the hall at Castle Howard and of Hawksmoor's contemporary Easton Neston upon the north front (Fig. 235) is evident. Sir Nikolaus Pevsner also sees in Wren's first design (1694) for Hampton Court the unquestionable source of the long south front (Fig. 241). In any event Hawksmoor worked closely with Vanbrugh at Castle Howard—he even drew up

the first designs—from start to finish. His position was that of indispensable coadjutant. Without his impeccable scholarship and sound sense the other's genius and drive would have got him nowhere. How much of the actual house was to Hawksmoor's design we have no means of telling.

In a letter of Christmas Day 1699 Vanbrugh writes to the Earl of Manchester that his designs for Castle Howard have been commended by the Duke of Devonshire and other noblemen, and a wooden model of the house was being sent to Kensington, 'where the King's thoughts upon't are to be had'. The designs were subsequently altered and very soon approved by Lord Carlisle, and in 1700 the terms of Hawksmoor's engagement were settled. Negotiations with London master-masons having broken down, three local men, William Smith, John Ellsworth and Manger Smith were selected by the Earl himself. They were employed off and on until 1719 when William Shutt became master-mason of the outworks. In 1721 William Etty, member of a distinguished York family of builders, was made clerk of the works and general overseer on the spot. The regular craftsmen in the early days appear to have been 'Mr Sabyn, joyner, and Sam[l] Carpenter',

241 *The south front.*

242 *The south front in perspective, showing the treatment of Vanbrugh's east end.*

243 *The centrepiece of the south front.*

244 *The Hall and the corridor to the east wing.*

245 *(opposite) The west side of the Hall showing the recession of planes.*

who worked in wood and stone and whose names crop up repeatedly. The names of other important craftsmen arise in the various account books in connection with special carved features.

Three little volumes entitled '*Book of Disbursements relating to my Building*', kept exclusively in Lord Carlisle's neat handwriting, give a comprehensive view of the building operations from 1701 until a year before the Earl's death in 1738. The last entry in a sadly shaky script, records that a total of £78,240.2s.10d. was spent 'on my buildings, gardens, plantations, & out works to Mids 1737'.

Vanbrugh, unlike Talman, chose a site slightly to the east of Henderskelfe Castle for his new house, which he turned to face due north and south. The old castle in which the family still lodged was suffered to remain until 1724 when it was totally demolished. Work began almost certainly in 1700. All the creamy ashlar used came from quarries in the park. By 1703 nearly 200 men were employed and the grand central pile was well in hand; the east wing (Fig. 236) for the family's occupation was even further advanced, and by 1706 the rooms were ready for decorating. The west wing never got further than the foundations and herein lies the tragedy of Castle Howard.

The rather misleading plate given in *Vitruvius Britannicus*, vol. I, shows the house as Vanbrugh (or even Colen Campbell) would have liked to see it, with balancing wings and curtilages to east and west—an immensely noble frontage of 667 feet. Linked to the central pile by quadrant arms the east wing, the base court with two out of four

shallow ogee domes at the corners, and the outer domestic ranges conspicuous by their tall square towers, were duly carried out. Not so the corresponding west ranges. Lord Carlisle became more interested in embellishing the park and gardens as the years went by. Only a week before his death Vanbrugh begged him in vain to complete the house. It was left to Sir Thomas Robinson, brother-in-law of the 4th Earl, to add in 1753–9 the west wing (Fig. 239), which he did in the prevailing Palladian style, and with total disregard for Vanbrugh's symmetry. In consequence the west wing, which in itself is unexceptionable architecture —it was given steps and an entrance to conform with those opposite in, surprisingly enough, the late 1870s[1]—throws the north front into confusion and the south out of balance. Robinson cannot be excused for the wilful havoc he caused to one of the noblest Baroque compositions of this country. Since the curtilages on the west side were entirely omitted, Carr of York was called upon in 1771 to build the present stable block further westwards towards the great obelisk.

A bird's-eye view (Fig. 237) in vol. III of *Vitruvius Britannicus* shows the imposing forecourt which Vanbrugh intended for the north front. The fanciful gatehouse, with its clustered obelisks, facing the front door, was not built; but a visitor in 1732 mentions entering the court 'through 2 large heavy stone arches with a monstrous quantity of stone pil'd up to a great height without any beauty'.[2] They

[1] An attic storey was removed from the west wing at the same time. For many detailed particulars the author is indebted to Mr George Howard.

[2] *Iter Boreale*, 1732. Unpublished MSS, probably by John Tracy of Stanway. Quoted with kind permission of the owner, Mr Paul Grinke.

246 *The west side of the Hall with one of the staircases visible through the arch.*

may refer to the side entrances shown in the plate. Today the visitor approaches the house from the west, and, before he knows what has happened, is plunged into the forecourt.

In spite of the 3rd Earl's procrastination and Sir Thomas Robinson's mischief, what confronts us is certainly monumental, 'not festive, indeed rather sombre'.[1] On this vast front (Fig. 236) no more than five bays are fenestrated. Four are occupied by niches holding urns and statues. If we can discount the niches, as well as the arched heads and the deep-channelled rustication, we must, I think, be struck by a resemblance to the Easton Neston fronts. For although here the order is Doric, not Corinthian,

[1] N. Pevsner—*Yorkshire, The North Riding*, 1966.

the same unmistakable theme is repeated—that is to say groups of giant pilasters embracing a single bay, and treated in marked recessions and projections.

The four figures flanking the front door are carved by the Huguenot, Nadauld, who had been working at Chatsworth under Talman. This highly skilled artist was also paid for the stone trophies, lions and tritons on the south front, of which the last have their exact counterparts on the west front of Chatsworth. If Nadauld was not also responsible for the frieze, pediment and garlands on the north front, Samuel Carpenter and Daniel Harvey were no less capable of executing them. The whole entablature is topped by a balustrade bearing figures, and crowned by an octagonal drum and dome. Nothing like this assemblage of classical

247 *The vista from west to east across the Hall.*

components had been seen in England before. Vanbrugh's inspiration of a dome came as early as 1700, at which date Wren's dome of St Paul's had not yet been raised, nor had his twin domes at Greenwich been completed.

The south front is altogether gayer. Although the great length of twenty-seven arched windows on the ground floor, if we include the single-storey pavilions, makes the house look like a Continental palace, the units of this front are strikingly unforeign. To begin with, only the basement is channelled. The giant order—this time Corinthian—is used on the grand pile, but in a regular articulation. The three-bay centre under a pediment projects in a fashion by no means un-English. The west front of Chatsworth, with the tall basement omitted, however, is at once suggested.

From the distant high ground the dome appears to better advantage than from the falling ground on the north. Even so Vanbrugh has placed the dome nearer to the north than the south front. Consequently, whereas it is never lost to view if one approaches the front door from the great lake, its height is correspondingly and suitably diminished when viewed from the flat terrain on the garden side. The south-east corner of this front is finished with a pavilion (Fig. 242) of only one bay which, it must be confessed, seems a less adequate termination than Robinson's (Fig. 241) at the west end. His pavilion is wider, and furnished with a Venetian window. But the little dome of the south-east pavilion is missing; so too is its twin over the delightful returned elevation. Both, which were over the Little

248 (right) The roof of the Hall (after the fire). The spandrels retain Pellegrini's original paintings; the dome was redecorated in 1962 by Scott Medd.

249 (below) The Lute Player: decoration by Pellegrini over the arch to the north-west corridor.

250 (below right) The 3rd Earl of Carlisle, with Castle Howard in the background.

251 *A vista of arches. The view along the north corridor with a glimpse of the Hall.*

Gallery, were victims of the fire of 1940 and have not yet been replaced. On this disastrous occasion the great dome fell in, and the centre block and all to the east of it were gutted. The house was at the time occupied by a girls' school 'evacuated' from Scarborough.

Vanbrugh carefully arranged for the north front door to be approached up three flights of steps. The visitor, already impressed by this stately ascent, was, once he had entered the portals, straightway dumbfounded by the magnificence within. To left and right of him stretched long stone-vaulted corridors (Fig. 244)—that on the right to be extended appreciably by Robinson into the west wing—and both lined with statuary collected by the 4th Earl, who

had lived much in Rome. Vanbrugh so planned the house that no state rooms faced north except the entrance side of the Hall which merely served as a link with the corridors. Even so he boasted that 'those passages would be so far gathering & drawing wind', as Lord Carlisle once feared, 'that a candle would not flare in them, of this he has lately had the proof, by bitter stormy nights in which not one candle wanted to be put into a lanthorn, not even in the Hall which is as high . . . as that at Blenheim'.

The Hall (Fig. 245) was, when finished, the most original apartment yet to be seen in a country house. In plan it is a Greek cross, more like the transept of a Baroque cathedral than a room in a private dwelling. Four open

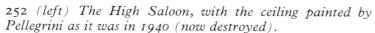

252 *(left) The High Saloon, with the ceiling painted by Pellegrini as it was in 1940 (now destroyed).*

253 *(above) The doorway of the High Saloon (destroyed).*

254 *(above right) An old photograph of a corner of the High Saloon, showing Pellegrini's wall paintings before they were covered as in Fig. 252.*

arches on clustered piers allow vistas through to the pair of staircases to east (Fig. 247) and west. Verticality is forcibly accented by the scagliola niche (Fig. 246) with its ogival head and the plaster chimney-piece (Fig. 245) opposite, each crowned with a statue and busts,[1] and of course overhead by the soaring gallery and distant dome. Geoffrey Beard attributes niche and chimney-piece to the Italian stuccatori Giovanni Bagutti and 'Mr Plura', and the York plasterer Isaac Mansfield; and the wrought-iron galleries to John Gardom of Baslow, a pupil of Tijou, who in 1708 was paid for the 'iron gates for ye garding'. But the decorator of the dome, spandrels and other surfaces of hall and stairs was an even greater artist than these. From 1709 to 1712 Giovanni Antonio Pellegrini, who had been brought to England from Venice by Lord Manchester, was working at Castle Howard. His masterpiece, which

---

[1] Originally the chimney-piece carried 'three large urns upon the top. Two of a red, the middle of a blew and white colour.' *Iter Boreale*, unpublished MSS.

was the representation of Phaeton and his horses hurtling from the dome, and his Rococo ceilings and walls of the Garden Hall beyond, and of the High Saloon (Fig. 252) over it, were totally destroyed in the fire of 1940. The allegorical figures on the dome spandrels and the stairs survived the fire after a fashion; but they were not his most successful paintings. The priming on the stone walls was somewhat thin and the brush-work desultory. Yet the figure of a boy wearing a feathered cap and playing a lute over the north-west corridor (Fig. 249) has the lightness and insouciance of Tintoretto.

As though to mitigate the feeling of being at the bottom of a deep narrow well, Vanbrugh planned another corridor to run straight across the further end of the hall and the entire length of both wings on the south front. By this means he also gave the state rooms a privacy not enjoyed by any contemporary Continental palace. The fire of 1940, as we have said, made grave inroads upon Vanbrugh's south front. Only three of his state rooms have survived. Although the destruction of William Thornton's extremely fanciful overdoors (Fig. 253) in the High Saloon is deplorable, yet Nadauld and Carpenter's carved entablature of the Music Room (Fig. 256), with its paired trusses painted white and gold, and the frieze of lions and foliage in the Tapestry Room (Fig. 255), have mercifully been spared us. For the last room a splendid series of tapestries of *The Seasons* after Teniers was supplied by John Vander-

255 (left) The Tapestry Room as it was in 1940. The tapestries were woven by Vanderbank after Teniers.

256 (below left) A detail of the entablature in the Music Room.

257 (above) Vanbrugh's Temple of the Four Winds and Hawksmoor's Mausoleum in the distance.

bank of Soho. These and panels of 'Chinese men and women in variety of postures, all sorts of birds, beasts and fish'[1] woven for a room in the south-east wing, now hang elsewhere. In a letter of 1706 to the 3rd Earl, Hawksmoor meticulously advised on which particular wall each panel should be put—'the light striking in from ye left hand as you look upon ye sayd hangings', and so forth.

Early and mid Georgian visitors like Sir John Clerk of Penicuik and Mrs Lybbe Powys criticized the state rooms for being too small, 'though in the wing now building', the latter writes in 1757, 'there seems by the plan some fine apartments to be intended'. This is a reference to Robinson's west wing which in being brought up to the south front was to involve the sacrifice of Vanbrugh's bow-windowed Grand Cabinet, 'a very elegant room, there are two domes in it',[2] a ceiling painting of Endymion and Diana, and doors and windows of Derbyshire alabaster. The comparative smallness of the state rooms was doubt-

less deliberate. 'He', Vanbrugh wrote of his patron, 'finds that all his rooms, with moderate fires are ovens'—a consoling discovery during the rigours of North Riding winters. Besides, Vanbrugh's object was to provide an enfilade of several audience chambers for the important public figure which Lord Carlisle had become. In 1701 and again in 1715 he was First Lord of the Treasury, a post shortly to be identified with that of Prime Minister. Carlisle received at Castle Howard a constant stream of official visitors and petitioners to whom he gave audiences in the ceremonial manner of his time. Upstairs in the grand pile there were no more than four bedrooms because of the height and space occupied by the hall, staircases and reception rooms.

The east wing (Fig. 236), termed the hunting apartment and dominated by a square cupola, was where the Earl and his family retreated for their private comfort. It was attached to the grand pile by a quadrant arm and closed passage. Sir Thomas Robinson was only prevented from altering this wing by the death of his brother-in-law, the 4th Earl, in 1758.

A description of the gardens and immense park at Castle Howard does not come within the province of this book.[1] Strictly speaking, it is wrong to divorce from Vanbrugh's stupendous palace the surroundings which took shape simultaneously. The two are essentially interdependent. It happened that Lord Carlisle towards the end of his life concentrated upon the landscape to the detriment

[1] Iter Boreale, unpublished MSS.
[2] Ibid.

[1] See Christopher Hussey—English Gardens and Landscapes, 1967.

of the house, which his architect could not persuade him to complete. Many of the garden and park buildings were even begun after Vanbrugh's death, including the Temple of the Four Winds (Fig. 257), which is to his design, only slightly modified by Hawksmoor. The Mausoleum is wholly Hawksmoor's. For size and cost, not to mention importance, these buildings can be compared with Wren's City churches rather than with ordinary landscape adornments.

The Temple's setting is miraculously right, at an oblique angle to the house, on a knoll at the south-east corner of Ray Wood. Vanbrugh called it the Belvidere in his letters to Lord Carlisle. Such it truly is, for it commands views of the park in all directions. From its windows the house is seen in a perspective vista down the winding terrace, grass-mown and lined with statues on plinths. Infinite pains were taken over the design and several alternative 'scizzas', or sketches, were submitted by Vanbrugh and Hawksmoor. Finally, a model basically on the plan of the Villa Rotonda was chosen, Indeed, the Ionic temple, with its four porticoes, dome and lantern, is Palladian, 'being of the more delicate kind', as Vanbrugh described it. The delicacy does not altogether marry with Vanbrugh's sense of the colossal. The porticoes are not large enough and the four corner vases are too large for the cella. After Vanbrugh's death Hawksmoor continued as architect-in-chief with William Etty in charge of the Temple. Dan Harvey carved the stone door-heads and shell-headed niches. The date 1739 appears on a window-

sill of the enchanting interior. The black- and yellow-veined scagliola of door columns and wall pilasters is the work of Francesco Vassalli. So too is the exquisite plasterwork of roundels, cornice and dome, in spite of Hawksmoor's advice to his patron to 'stick to Hannibal Carrats [sic] in the manner of the painting' of the interior.

Nowhere do we get a clearer picture of the decisive role Lord Carlisle played in the shaping of Castle Howard projects than in Hawksmoor's correspondence with him over the Mausoleum. The architect deferentially submitted scholarly ideas which the Earl often politely and firmly parried, retaliating with others of his own. One was that there should be a colonnade, the feature which actually gives the Mausoleum (Fig. 258) its overriding character. In 1731 building began upon another knoll south-east of the Temple's. Work was only completed in 1742 when both men were dead. The vast cylindrical structure, initially inspired by the tomb of Cecilia Metella, is raised on a square base, and surrounded by a bastion wall—successfully added by Daniel Garrett. The composition is strong, noble and sublime. Walpole's dictum that its beauty might tempt one to be buried alive is only just an overstatement. Lord Burlington's criticism that the columns were too narrowly spaced to be virile seems academic. On the contrary his protégé Garrett's double staircase, modelled upon that of Chiswick House, far from being 'monstrous', as John Adam called it in 1759, is rather too feminine.

The crypt in which the 3rd Earl found his ultimate

258 *(opposite) The Mausoleum. The bastion and double staircase were added by Daniel Garrett after Hawksmoor's death.*

259 *The Mortuary Chapel inside the Mausoleum.*

resting-place has a groined vault, the ribs of which meet in a central boss. It is straightforward, utilitarian Gothic. The Mortuary Chapel (Fig. 259) is the perfection of monumental architecture. Corinthian columns on high plinths are recessed in the thick stone walls which are treated very simply. The carving of entablature and dome panels, for which Charles Mitley received £81. 11s. 8d. in 1738, is crisp and bold. The floor echoes the pattern of the dome in marble and brass inlay.

After the 3rd Earl of Carlisle's death in 1738 his son, the 4th Earl, reigned for twenty years. As Lord Morpeth he had shared and encouraged his father's interest in the creation of Castle Howard, and he was a travelled and cultivated man. He commissioned Robinson's west wing in 1753. The 5th Earl, having sowed his wild oats to some tune, turned to politics, and became Lord Lieutenant of Ireland in 1780. On the death of the 9th Earl's widow, Rosalind, in 1921 the family estates were divided. Naworth Castle in Cumberland having been inherited by the holder of the earldom, Castle Howard passed to her fifth and only surviving son, the Hon. Geoffrey Howard, M.P. His only surviving son, George, is the present owner. Mr Howard, through his knowledge, indefatigable efforts and the help of the Historic Buildings Council, has succeeded in largely repairing the ravages brought upon Castle Howard during the last war.

260 *The palace from the north-west.*

BLENHEIM PALACE, OXFORDSHIRE

In 1705 Vanbrugh began the great palace in celebration of the victory of Blenheim over the French and Bavarians by John Churchill, 1st Duke of Marlborough. Hawksmoor was his partner. An army of illustrious artists was employed to decorate the palace until the death of Duchess Sarah in 1744. (The seat of the Duke of Marlborough.)

In spite of the vexations and flaming rows which accompanied its prolonged building Blenheim remains the most complete of Vanbrugh's great houses. It is the boldest, grandest and I dare to suggest most imaginative Baroque palace in Europe. Pints of ink have been spilt over the differences between its wilful, improvident creator and its autocratic, parsimonious chatelaine. Both Sir John Vanbrugh and Sarah Jennings, Duchess of Marlborough had genius of different sorts. The inevitable clashes of temperament have been recorded objectively by Blenheim's chief chronicler, Mr David Green.[1]

No English country house is more copiously documented. There are in its archives 30,000 manuscripts relating to the house and its occupants. Blenheim's origin

[1] *Blenheim Palace*, 1951.

is well known. On 13 August 1704 was fought and won by John Churchill, 1st Duke of Marlborough, a smashing victory near a small village on the left bank of the Danube, over the French and Bavarians. Thus the Holy Roman Empire was saved from the aggressions of Louis XIV. In February 1705 Queen Anne signified her intention, which Parliament immediately ratified, of presenting the handsome hero and the nation's darling with the royal honour of Woodstock[1] and of raising for him a residence to immortalize his achievement. The only return stipulated was the annual presentation to the Sovereign by the Duke and his heirs of a standard emblazoned with three fleurs-de-lis on a field argent. At the time both Duke and Duchess were so high in favour with the Queen that no one questioned whether the necessary funds would in the future be forthcoming from the Exchequer. Lack of any

[1] The old manor house and Rosamund's Bower stood until 1723 on the north bank of the river Glyme.

261 *(above right) The north forecourt and one of the flanking colonnades.*

262 *(right) The north front, from* Vitruvius Britannicus.

The generall Front of Blenheim Castle is most humbly Inscrib'd to his Grace Iohn Duke of Marlborough, Prince of the Holy Empire Cap' Generall of all his Majesty's forces and Knight of the most Noble Order of the Garter &c.   Design'd by S'. Iohn Vanbrugh K'.

Elevation general du Chateau de Blenheim.

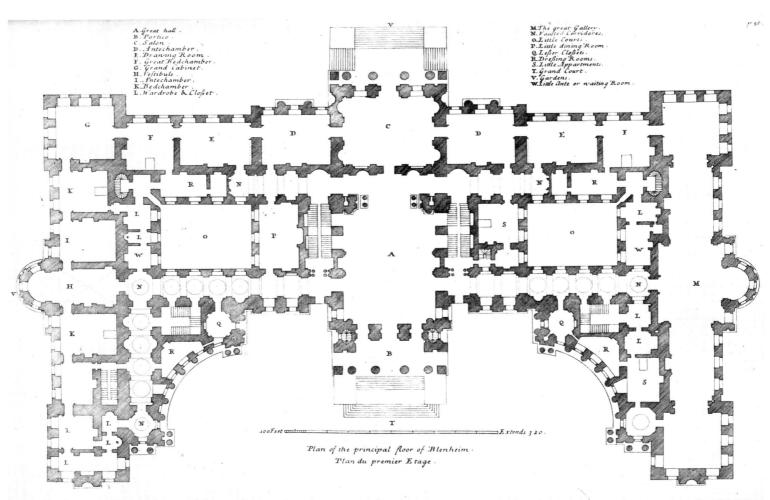

A . Great hall .
B . Portico .
C . Salon .
D . Antechamber .
E . Drawing Room .
F . Great Bedchamber .
G . Grand Cabinet .
H . Vestibule .
I . Antechamber .
K . Bedchamber .
L . Wardrobe & Closet .

M . The great Gallery .
N . Vaulted Corridores .
O . Little Courts .
P . Little dining Room .
Q . Lesser Closets .
R . Dressing Rooms .
S . Little Appartments .
T . Grand Court .
V . Gardens .
W . Little Ante or waiting Room .

Plan of the principal floor of Blenheim .
Plan du premier Etage .

263 *(above left)* *The west side of the Grand Court or forecourt.*

264 *(left)* *Plan of the ground floor, from* Vitruvius Britannicus.

265 *(above)* *The clock tower in the Base or Kitchen Court, on the east side of the forecourt.*

proper agreement with the Crown and of acceptance of estimates from the architect was the principal cause of future troubles.

It appears that the Duke himself invited Vanbrugh, a fellow Whig and member of the exclusive Kit Cat Club, to be the architect. Vanbrugh was then Comptroller of the Queen's Works under the Tory Wren, who agreed to act as unofficial consultant. At a later date the Lord Treasurer Godolphin formally appointed Vanbrugh surveyor to the Duke, a strangely inconsequential arrangement. Vanbrugh did not let the grass grow under his feet. In no time he prepared designs and a model which were generally approved by the Queen, the Government and the Marlboroughs. Comparison of Vanbrugh's original project (Fig. 267) for the south front with what was carried out (Fig. 268) shows how little the design was basically altered. A portico was added as an afterthought, and instead of an equestrian figure of the Duke trampling his enemies underfoot a 30-ton bust, captured at Tournai, of his arch-foe Louis XIV was hoisted upon the parapet like a head upon a pike. The Corinthian order was substituted for the Doric; and upon the corner towers, arcaded and grenaded gazebos, which give the house its most distinc-

tive quality, took the place of squat mansard domes.

Vanbrugh's immediate action was to engage Hawksmoor to collaborate with him, as he had already done at Castle Howard. The equivocal partnership lasted until Vanbrugh resigned in 1716. Deeply though the Duchess disliked Sir John and all his works, she respected his more deferential coadjutor, whose services she re-enlisted in 1722 long after Vanbrugh's dismissal. Throughout Vanbrugh's association with Blenheim Hawksmoor was responsible for most of the detail. But owing to an immense amount of engagements in London and elsewhere the partners could only visit Woodstock at infrequent intervals. Accordingly they appointed as resident overseer Henry Joynes from the Board of Works, then aged twenty-one. 'Honest Harry', for whom Hawksmoor had a fatherly affection, became a skilled designer. His post was a responsible and unenviable one. For a pitiful salary of £200 a year—in 1748 he was still claiming arrears due to him—he was obliged to work with a joint Comptroller, the Duchess's disagreeable 'creature', William Boulter, and after his death another, Tilleman Bobart, as well as to supervise an army of masons and workmen. The master-masons were men of national reputation: the Edward Strongs father and son, fresh from St Paul's Cathedral, responsible for the most important stonework of the main pile; John Townesend and Bartholomew Peisley, both of Oxford, responsible for the Clock Tower, Grand Bridge and east front; and Henry Banckes of Guiting, who built the colonnades of the Great Court. In addition, several illustrious artists were engaged: Grinling Gibbons (1708–12), who received more than £4,000 for carving the principal trophies, statues and urns in stone, some fireplaces and the Saloon door-cases in marble, and four Corinthian capitals of the Bow Window Room in wood; Sir James Thornhill and Laguerre for painting the Hall and Saloon; Isaac Mansfield for stuccoing and plastering the Gallery ceiling; besides a number of specialists in clocks, sundials, locks and ironwork. Moreover Henry Wise designed avenues, plantations, walled gardens and formal parterres at the very start.

On 18 June 1705 the foundation stone of Blenheim Palace was laid, and by August 1,500 men were digging, rigging up scaffolds and protective sheds, and hauling timber and stone. Since stone from the park and near-by Glympton proved unsatisfactory, relays of waggons fetched it from Taynton and Barrington quarries under contract with the Strongs who owned them, and from Guiting quarry which belonged to Banckes.

The Duke of Marlborough had been greatly taken with Vanbrugh's model of Castle Howard. He was in full agreement with his architect that Blenheim must be a national monument rather than a simple home, which is what the Duchess pretended to require. Her frugal and philistine soul hated the extravagance and the art with which Vanbrugh loaded the whole project. Certainly the plan (Fig. 264) of Blenheim is a development from that of Castle Howard. The disposition of apartments and corridors in the main pile is the same. The dependencies round the Grand Court, Base Court and Stable Court are, however, kept at a more appreciable distance from the main pile.

As at Castle Howard entrance is from the north (Fig. 260). But the flat Oxfordshire terrain did not present the architect with the same problems as in Yorkshire where the ground rises steeply to the front door. Instead the chief obstacle was the wide cleft formed by the little river Glyme which cut a course from east to west right in front of the new house, thus prohibiting a straight, ceremonial approach. This is just what Vanbrugh was determined to have. There was only one thing he could do. At the cost of a great deal of money from the Treasury and bad temper from the Duchess, Vanbrugh turned the river into three canals, which he crossed with a bridge of gargantuan proportions. The stupendous structure with windows in the piers, inspired by Michelangelo's attic windows of St Peter's, roused the Duchess to fury. There were thirty-three rooms in it, she averred caustically, 'but that which makes it so much prettier than London Bridge, is that you may sit in six rooms and look out at window into the high arch while the coaches are driving over your head'. Even so the arcaded superstructure which Vanbrugh intended was never carried out. Later in the century Capability Brown, by turning the straight canals into a lake gave a little more point to the Grand Bridge, although in the process he raised the water level up to the imposts of the side arches. In spite of Vanbrugh's expensive ceremonial route two shorter drives to Blenheim are habitually used. One is from the Hensington Gate (Fig. 288) on the Oxford road leading direct to the Base Court; the other from the Triumphal Arch built by Hawksmoor in 1723 at the western end of Woodstock town. The bridge has merely served an aesthetic purpose in being one of the most pretentious park features in England. It carries the

266 (above) East Gate (Vanbrugh's 'Cistern Tower') with additional ornament by Chambers. The clock tower is visible through the arch.

267 (above right) Vanbrugh's projected design for the south front in the Doric order (1704–5).

268 (centre right) The south front as executed, except for statuary and trophies (published 1715).

269 (below right) The south and west fronts.

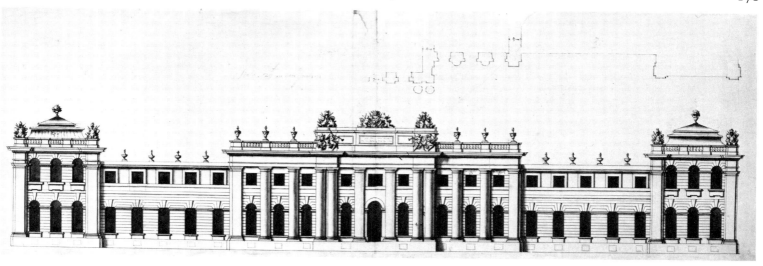

The Elevation of BLENHEIM Castle towards the Gardens, Is most humbly Inscrib'd to his grace IOHN Duke of MARLBOROUGH Prince of the Holy EMPIRE, Capt. General of all his MAJESTYES Forces, and Knight of the most Noble Order of the Garter &c. Invented by Sʳ Io. Vanbrugh Kᵗ.

Elevation Du Chateau de BLENHEIM du Costé des Jardins. Inventée par Mʳ Le Chevalier Vanbrugh.

270 (left) The portico on the south front surmounted by the great busto of Louis XIV.

271 (above) The east front, with the parterre restored by the 9th Duke.

272 (below) Vanbrugh's roofscape: the finials carved by Grinling Gibbons and his assistants.

273 (right) The Lion and Cock—'The Savaging of France'—one of the two identical groups by Gibbons on the clock tower.

274 *(above) The Great Hall, looking south.*

275 *(left)* The Glorification of the Duke of Marlborough. *The ceiling, painted by Thornhill (1716).*

276 *(above right) The corridor across the south end of the Hall.*

277 *(far right) The staircase on the east side of the Hall.*

eye of the visitor standing in the forecourt of the palace to the great fluted Column of Victory which bears the 1st Duke's leaden effigy, and was raised by the architect Earl of Pembroke in 1730.

Let us then approach the palace by the Hensington Gate with its great perforated stone piers set diagonally, each carrying a 'flower-bason' carved by Grinling Gibbons. A straight elm avenue leads to the eastern gateway (Fig. 266) of the Base Court. This massive arch of splayed Tuscan pilasters resting on stone cannon-balls fulfils a dual function, in commemorating on a large tablet Queen Anne's munificence to the Marlborough family, and by accommodating within the attic a water cistern. The masked and flaming finials are from Grinling Gibbons's hand. The Base Court (Fig. 265) within, 'regular, decent and clean', in Vanbrugh's words, 'which is all it pretends to', has open colonnades on either side, Ahead rises Townesend's Clock Tower, its base of horizontal rustication, its middle stage bearing the dial under a segmental

pediment. Through the arch below we are plunged into the north forecourt or Grand Court.

The Grand Court, owing to the generous plateau on which the palace is built, is more spacious and noble than its Castle Howard counterpart. Its long sides are occupied by the fronts and twin towers of the Base and Stable Courts. From the far end Banckes's long colonnades stretch northwards from the main pile towers (Fig. 263). These with their Borrominesque gazebos and astonishing grenades, capped by a ducal crown over reversed fleur-de-lis—evolved long after the towers were built to receive them—are nearly as high as the centrepiece of the main pile, to which they are joined by solid quadrant arms. The main pile elevation (Fig. 261) does not instantly explain itself. On analysis it discloses five sections, that is to say, a background variant of the Easton Neston theme, the Corinthian giant order in recessions and projections, but interrupted here by the vast hall nave. This section not only towers above the pile, as the dome at Castle Howard does, but advances by three bays into a portico crowned by Britannia with her trident. The pediment is crammed with Gibbons's masterpiece of carving, namely the Marlborough arms borne upon the imperial eagle under a crown, and supporters emerging from martial trophies.

The Hall clerestory was one of those features which Vanbrugh took from the Smythson school of Elizabethan builders. Had he perhaps visited Wollaton Hall during that summer tour of 1699 when he told a correspondent that he had 'seen most of the great houses in the north'?

He was to reproduce the same arrangement years later at Seaton Delaval but at Blenheim the treatment was fantastically novel. Over the portico pediment are raised the sliced ends of another, the central apex portion being pushed deeply back. This apex is made to carry a copper ball, against which a pair of captives lean precariously. No bolder example of Baroque movement can be found in any other building of this country.

Three flights of steps lead to the floor level of the Hall. The long sides of the church-like interior, 67 feet high, are divided into two storeys of arcades (allowing Vanbrugh's favourite vista into the staircase) and a third of clerestory windows. At each corner stands an enormous fluted column. Beyond the great arch at the south end a gallery (Fig. 274) at first-floor level is supported by scrolled acanthus brackets. 'Cutt extrordingry rich and sunk very deep' was Gibbons's description of his enrichments here. The flat ceiling was ready in 1716 for Thornhill (Fig. 275), who depicted the Duke in classical garb pointing to a plan of the Battle of Blenheim while Britannia proffers him a laurel crown. Thornhill next proposed to decorate the Saloon at 25s. the yard, which the Duchess declined ('not worth half a crown a yard') because of the expense. 'Painters, poets and builders', she wrote testily, 'have very high flights, but they must be kept down.' Instead she commissioned Laguerre, who was cheaper.

The Saloon (1719–20) occupies the space behind the Hall in the centre of the south front (Fig. 278). Vanbrugh and Hawksmoor had originally designed walls of high-

278 *(opposite above) The Saloon with murals by Laguerre.*

279 *(opposite below) Laguerre's portraits of himself and Dean Jones: a detail of the decoration in the Saloon.*

280 *(left) One of Gibbons's marble door-cases in the Saloon.*

standing Corinthian columns and two rows of niches to be filled with statues. Nothing came of this. Instead Laguerre substituted in paint a peristyle of feigned columns with numerous figures representing the Four Continents looking out into the room. He quite deliberately copied Le Brun's theme for the Escalier des Ambassadeurs at Versailles, the palace of the great Duke's vanquished foe.[1] He made the columns rest on a deep base painted in imitation marble, with swags in the panels. The rusticated dado is of real marble, veined red and white. Over the attic, painted by Laguerre with caryatids and flags, the ceiling is ablaze with an apotheosis of the Duke of Marlborough. The three marble door-cases (Fig. 280) with rounded heads topped

[1] M. Whinney and O. Millar—*English Art, 1625–1714*, 1957.

with shells are superb specimens of Hawksmoor's designing and Gibbons's carving. The latter at the age of sixty-four was working in person with eight assistants when all work on the palace was suspended in 1712, at which date only the west door had been set in place. In quality of fresco and marble decoration the Blenheim Saloon can vie with the most splendid palace rooms in Europe.

On either side of the Saloon extend the state rooms, or 'ceremonies' as Hawksmoor styled them, allowing a total vista of 300 feet. They 'were planned in two suites of ante-room, drawing room and bedroom,' Mr Green tells us, 'the bedrooms being next to the Long Library, on the west, and the Grand Cabinet (Fig. 283), in the south-eastern tower. The scheme of decoration has for the most part been altered

281 *The Green Writing Room showing Judocus de Vos's tapestry of Marshal Tallard, commander of the French forces, surrendering to Marlborough.*

282 *The Second State Room – further Brussels tapestries by de Vos, depicting the march to Bouchain and its siege in 1711.*

283 *The Grand Cabinet. Romney's portrait of Caroline, wife of the 4th Duke, hangs over the fireplace.*

since Vanbrugh's time, but the chief glory is unchanged: the tapestries (Figs. 281 and 282), ordered by Marlborough in Brussels from Judocus de Vos and still, as his Duchess described them in 1740, "as fresh as new".' De Vos was given the most explicit directions how to depict the battles each tapestry represented, the position of troops, and the exact figures of the chief participants down to General Cadogan's favourite dog. The groups are full of animation and rich colouring against backgrounds of pearly tones.

The east front (Fig. 271) was intended and still is reserved for the family's private use. Its walls were the first part of the palace to be completed by Townesend in 1709. By 1712, when Queen Anne finally broke with the Duchess and the Tories dismissed the Duke from all his offices, nearly the whole house was roofed, though the east front was not ready for occupation until 1719. Three years previously Vanbrugh had left for good and Joynes with him. On 8 November 1716 provoked beyond all further endurance, he sent the Duchess his famous letter of resignation. 'You have your end, Madam,' he concluded, 'for I will never trouble you more unless the Duke of Marlborough recovers so far, to shelter me from such intolerable treatment.' The break was complete. Years later she had the satisfaction of refusing him entry to the palace while admitting the friends who were with him. 'That B.B.B.B. old B the Dutches of Marlbh:' were his parting words of impotent rage against her.

284 *(opposite) The Gallery or Long Library.*

285 *The door-case in the centre of the north side of the Gallery.*

After Vanbrugh's dismissal Marlborough had but a few years to enjoy his new possession. That summer he suffered a severe stroke. There are accounts of him sitting in the Bow Window Room in front of Gibbons's marble chimney-piece playing cribbage with his chaplain Dean Jones ('like a sort of domestic', the Duchess described him), or watching his grandchildren acting *All for Love* under the arch of the wide bow, of which the Corinthian columns are Gibbons's sole wood carving at Blenheim.

The last of the state rooms takes us into the south end of the Gallery (Fig. 284), which occupies two storeys of the whole west front and is 180 feet long. The room was intended for the Duke's picture collection. Soon after its

decoration (1725) it received the famous Sunderland library, which was sold in 1872. Hawksmoor was certainly responsible for the design of fluted Doric pilasters carrying an attic (the present bookshelves were inserted by the 9th Duke) and the ceiling compartments, of which the end ovals have false domes. Isaac Mansfield was the stuccoist employed. William Townesend and Bartholomew Peisley junior put up the scroll-headed doorways within vast tabernacles, all in marble (Fig. 285). The central portion of the Gallery is widened by the great two-storeyed bow (Fig. 269), on the outside of which caryatids are conspicuously ranged. White on black marble is profusely used for pilasters, skirting and doorways. At the southern

286 *Rysbrack's statue of Queen Anne in the Gallery.*

end Queen Anne's statue (Fig. 286) by Rysbrack gazes down the long vista. When ordering it the Duchess wrote in a surprisingly generous vein: 'I have a satisfaction in showing this respect to her, because her kindness to me was real.'

The last of all the apartments at Blenheim to have been finished and the last to be visited is the Chapel. It is reached from the north end of the Gallery, behind the 9th Duke's organ, by walking down steps into the west colonnade of the Grand Court. We have the Duchess's word that the Chapel was finished in 1732, 'and considering how many wonderful figures and whirligigs I have seen architects finish a chappel withal that are of no manner of use but to laugh at', she was well satisfied with the result. In spite of her wish to keep it 'plain and clean' the Chapel strikes us as sumptuous enough in its marble and stucco walls and ceiling. It is dominated by the 1st Duke's

colossal monument by Rysbrack (Fig. 287). At this late stage Hawksmoor was overlooked in favour of the Burlingtonian Kent who supplied the design. Kent may have claimed to be a strict Palladian but the group of mourning figures around the sarcophagus and the background obelisk are obviously inspired by the High Baroque tombs of Bernini and his followers in St Peter's, Rome.

When the 1st Duke of Marlborough died in 1722 he was succeeded in the dukedom by his eldest daughter Henrietta, married to the 2nd Earl Godolphin. The 2nd Duchess died in 1733 without living issue and the title went to her eldest surviving nephew, Charles Spencer, 5th Earl of Sunderland. As 3rd Duke of Marlborough he did not come into Blenheim until the death of his grandmother, Duchess Sarah, in 1744. She had been left the entire estate for her life, a vast jointure and £10,000 a year with which, as Vanbrugh put it, 'to spoil Blenheim her own way'. In

287 *The Chapel monument to the Great Duke. Designed by Kent and executed by Rysbrack.*

288 *(below) Hensington Gate. The piers were originally part of the layout of the east parterre.*

fact she completed the house and outbuildings after quarrelling right and left and being involved in lawsuits with 401 persons concerned with the building of Blenheim. For the architecture she called upon Hawksmoor whenever it suited her. For decoration she relied upon her own taste and that of her 'oracle', the cabinet-maker James Moore. By the end of her life Blenheim had cost £300,000, which was three times the estimate given by Vanbrugh. About one-fifth of the total was paid out of Marlborough money.

George, 4th Duke of Marlborough (succeeded 1758 and died 1817), employed Capability Brown to sweep away Wise's and Vanbrugh's formal layout and substitute the natural landscape which survives to this day. Charles, the 9th Duke (succeeded 1892 and died 1934) carried out considerable restorations to palace and gardens (including the east and west parterres under Achille Duchêne). His son, the 10th Duke of Marlborough, is the present possessor.

289 *The entrance front and forecourt from the north.*

SEATON DELAVAL, NORTHUMBERLAND

**Owned by the Delavals since Norman times. In 1720
Admiral George Delaval got Vanbrugh to build him
a new house with large forecourt. The house was
gutted by fire in 1822. (The seat of Lord Hastings.)**

So romantic is Seaton Delaval on account of its semi-
ruinous condition, its semi-industrial yet wild situation,
and its association with the still wilder family which owned
it since Norman times that writers have found difficulty in
assessing the architecture of the house objectively.

Only ten miles north-east of Newcastle, Seaton Delaval
stands a mere mile from the inhospitable North Sea on a
flat, sandy, windswept tract of land. From the front door
Lindisfarne and the Cheviots are distantly visible. The
great house can only be approached by land through a
blasted area of derelict pits, disused railway sidings and
miners' dwellings. The 'gay Delavals' who lived here
were, in Lawrence Whistler's words, 'the most charming,
mischievous, spendthrift people in the North of England,
utterly without morals, loved by the people of the country-
side and damned from birth'. Their long history is one of
inebriation, elaborate practical jokes and, alas, violence,
since the occasion when a Plantagenet Delaval slew a
monk for stealing his roast pork—'Oh! horrid dede! To
kill a manne for a pigge's hede!' the whole monastery

chanted in righteous indignation—down to that other when
the last of his race died from a kick in the groin delivered by
a laundry maid whom he was attempting to seduce. This
fateful event took place in 1775.

Admiral George Delaval, who in 1717 had bought the
Seaton property from the impoverished elder branch of his
family, wrote to his brother in February 1718: 'I intend to
persuade Sir John Vanbrugh to see Seton if possible & to
give me a plan of a house, or to alter the old one, which he is
most excellent at; and if he cannot come, he'll recommend
a man at York who understands these matters. So something may be done by degrees & be the entertainment of
our old age, or as long as we can live. I am much out of
order with the scurvy.'

The Admiral's health was not good. Nor at this time were
Vanbrugh's prospects. His services were not difficult to
enlist because this very year his allies in the Board of
Works, Wren and Hawksmoor, were ousted and he himself
narrowly escaped superannuation. Sir John visited Seaton,
if not before, then certainly in August 1721, a year after
work had begun on the new house. The weather was vile,
but just what Vanbrugh expected from the dramatic
north, so unlike 'the tame sneaking south of England', he
exclaimed not without relish. He paid another visit in
1724, but never saw the house finished. The man from

290 *The central block of the north front.*

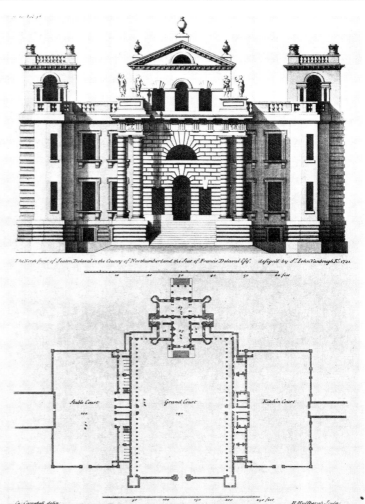

York, who acted throughout as his deputy, was William
Etty. Etty was necessarily absent a good deal—Vanbrugh
appointed him clerk of works at Castle Howard in 1721—
and the Admiral's agent Mr Mewburn was left to struggle
with the architectural instructions which he had much
difficulty in understanding. He kept the building accounts
in a beautiful copybook hand, and resented and loathed
William Etty.

Intensely individual though the house is, several features
at Eastbury, devised just before, and at Grimsthorpe a
few years later, are conspicuous at Seaton Delaval, where
they attain a consummation of excellence. By now we can
detect in Sir John's work a distinct whiff of the new
Palladianism emanating from the familiar Vanbrughian
diet. First of all we have the forecourt, or Grand Court as it
is called in the plan provided by *Vitruvius Britannicus*,
vol. III. It is immense, 180 feet long and over 152 feet
broad, with an open end sloping practically due north down
to Blyth harbour and the desolate ocean. The east and
west sides are composed of open arcades (Fig. 289) over
which are built long wings of fifteen bays each, far longer
than the central block to which they are connected at right

291 *The north elevation and ground plan from* Vitruvius
Britannicus.

292 *The eastern arm of the forecourt.*

293 *The open arcade on the west side of the forecourt.*

angles. The ends of the arcades are punctuated by square pavilions (Fig. 292) with high windows. Indeed, the Grand Court transcends in area that of Eastbury where, on the other hand, the central block was larger. Yet here comparative lack of bulk is cleverly obviated by Vanbrugh's masterly grouping of his masses.

As at Eastbury the house, compact and rectangular, has turrets at the four corners (Fig. 290). Instead of being square they are octagonal and almost freestanding. Avray Tipping was the first to see in them a derivation from Elizabethan domestic architecture, notably Smythson's angle turrets at Barlborough Hall. Whereas at Eastbury a pair of staircases were contained within square towers rising from the body of the plan, here staircase towers have been made to project from the middle of each side elevation.

These Claude-like features (Fig. 297) have been given Venetian windows on all four fronts of the upper stages, whereas the lower stages are banded in alternating courses. The treatment is best appreciated from the west flank. From this angle, too, the long clerestory is seen like a Greek temple sailing above the clutter of an acropolis. Arched chimney-stacks like great ears spring from the eaves.

The north front (Fig. 290) is an astonishing contradiction of styles. It fairly derides the laws of gravity. For if Smythsonian Mannerism is coupled with the new Palladianism, weight is imposed upon lightness. The over-slim angle turrets stagger under the massive staircase towers. The narrow entrance arch balances upon the keystone the sill of a wide lunette window. In its turn the lunette appears

294 *The kitchen court. The Venetian window in the bow lights the original kitchen.*

295 *The back of the north-west quadrant.*

to carry the dominant clerestory (another Smythsonian inspiration from the raised hall at Wollaton, a house which Hawksmoor actually believed to evince 'some true stroaks of architecture'). The pediment is filled with a massive escutcheon, trophies and mantling. All these top-heavy anomalies are only prevented from crashing to the ground by twin groups of three gigantic ringed Tuscan columns, standing upon stalwart plinths of cushioned rustication and bearing a well-defined entablature. Ringed columns are a favourite Vanbrughian device and are found at Blenheim and Grimsthorpe acting as buttresses. Vanbrugh intended the columns and the pediment here to carry colossal statues and urns, the presence of which would have given emphasis to the buttresses and mitigated the feeling of unease which the composition induces without them.

The south front (Fig. 296) bears a general resemblance to the garden front of Eastbury, but here the new Palladian spirit is already apparent. The fluted Ionic portico is almost too elegant, and on this sunnier front Vanbrugh has changed to an altogether gentler key. The wall surface is not deeply rusticated like a Florentine palace, but is made of unwrinkled ashlar, and the window-heads are adorned with graceful pediments, or Vitruvian entablatures.

Catastrophes dogged the Delavals and their home. Long before the house was finished the Admiral was thrown from his horse one evening after dinner and killed outright. His nephew Francis Blake Delaval took over. During his lifetime events proceeded smoothly enough until he fell in a drunken fit under the portico. He was succeeded in 1752 by Sir Francis, 'the gayest and most accomplished

296 (above) The south
front with its Ionic portico.

297 (right) The staircase
tower and polygonal corner
turrets, from the south-west.

298 (opposite) The stables
in the east wing.

Lothario of his age'. In his reign were staged the maddest, most hilarious entertainments conceivable—tournaments, rope dances and masquerades. Drunkenness, debauchery, extravagance and fun were the order of day after day. Delavals died of drink, strokes, sex and, as we have recorded, kicks. Finally on 3 January 1822 a terrible fire practically gutted the main block, which has never been rebuilt.

Wide steps lead straight from the front door into the longitudinal Hall (Fig. 299), now open to the roof, but originally two storeys high with a gallery across the southern end. Similar dispositions exist at Castle Howard and Blenheim, providing upstairs access from one side of the house to the other. On the east and west sides fireplaces, upheld by stucco torsos, interrupt in a clumsy way the blind arcades on the ground stage. The arcades are duplicated overhead where they enshrine stucco figures of the arts, still broken and calcined by the fire (Fig. 300). This wall treatment was repeated by Vanbrugh at Grimsthorpe. Openings under the Gallery reach through vaulted passages to the staircase towers. The stone stairs twist unsupported round an oval well.

Beyond the Hall the now gutted Saloon occupies the entire south front of the house. This great room, 75 feet long and 30 feet wide, was divided into three by semi-screens of square Corinthian piers.

Ever since 1822 the west wing has served as sole residence for the family. It was also seriously damaged by fire in 1752. Nevertheless much of the interior remains intact; the old kitchen has been converted into the family's drawing room. It has a groined vault and a Venetian window (Fig. 294) is set high in a large segmental bay. At the back of this wing there is a parterre garden in which fine lead figure groups, from the workshop of John Van Nost, stand on stone plinths. The Doric Orangery (Fig. 301) may be Etty's work to his own design. The east wing comprises the stables (Fig. 298).

The first and only Lord Delaval, father of the kicked youth, died suddenly while eating his breakfast in 1808. With this courtly, elegant and apparently enchanting peer the Delavals faded away. The property was eventually inherited by descendants of Lord Delaval's sister Rhoda, who had married Sir Edward Astley, 4th Baronet. The 6th baronet called out of abeyance the ancient barony of Hastings created by Edward I. The 22nd Lord Hastings is the present owner.

299 *(right) The Hall, which was gutted by fire in 1822.*

300 *(below) The double-storey blind arcade and fireplace on the east wall.*

301 *(below right) The Doric Orangery.*

GRIMSTHORPE CASTLE, LINCOLNSHIRE

In 1722 Vanbrugh began transforming Grims-thorpe Castle, an early sixteenth-century dwelling round a quadrangle. His clients were the 1st and 2nd Dukes of Ancaster. On Vanbrugh's death in 1726 only the forecourt, north front and the rooms behind it were finished. (The seat of the Earl of Ancaster.)

Through membership of the Kit Cat Club and a naturally engaging manner Vanbrugh had the widest social and political contacts. He never lost an opportunity of turning a casual acquaintance to professional advantage. Towards the end of 1718 he was sent by his friend the Duke of Newcastle as political agent to persuade the Duke of Ancaster to lend his influence in repealing the Occasional Conformity Bill. Vanbrugh stopped a night at Grimsthorpe Castle on his way to spend Christmas at Castle Howard. He cleverly ingratiated himself with the Duke, succeeded in his mission, and at the same time persuaded his rich and powerful host to rebuild his ancestral seat. Plans and designs were prepared during the winter of 1722. In July 1723 the Duke died. His son, the 2nd Duke—'for I don't take him to be of an ungratefull soyle', Vanbrugh wrote immediately to Newcastle—soon summoned the architect to press ahead with the scheme approved by his father.

Work began that very year before winter set in and proceeded until the architect's death in 1726. Grimsthorpe was Vanbrugh's last, albeit uncompleted, great country house. As far as we know he did not for once delegate the building to an experienced subordinate, such as Etty or Joynes.

Grimsthorpe's earliest association with Lord Ancaster's family dates from before the Reformation. When a Spanish cousin and lady-in-waiting to Queen Katherine of Aragon married the 10th Lord Willoughby de Eresby, Henry VIII bestowed the Lincolnshire manor upon the pair. After Lord Willoughby died in 1525 his daughter and heiress, Katherine, married the King's widowed brother-in-law, Charles Brandon, Duke of Suffolk. Their two sons having both died of the 'sweating sickness', the Duchess was succeeded in her own title by a son of her subsequent marriage with a successful upstart called Richard Bertie.

According to Leland, Grimsthorpe Castle was what 'I may call an extempore structure, got up on a sudden by Charles Brandon Duke of Suffolk to entertain King Henry VIII.' In other words, apart from the surviving south-east corner tower, known as King John's, and certainly dating from the thirteenth century, the four-square castle round a courtyard was built in the first half of the sixteenth century.

302 *Vanbrugh's great north front and forecourt.*

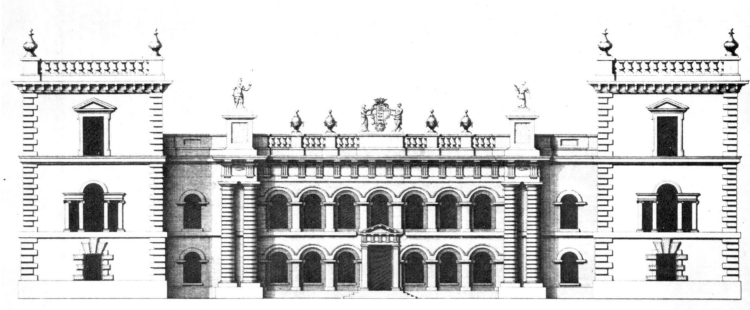

The North front of Grimsthorp in the County of Lincoln the Seat of his grace the Duke of Ancaster and Kesteven Hereditary Lord great Chamberlain of England. Designd by S.t John Vanbrugh K.t 1723.

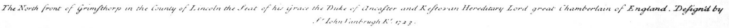

The Garden front of Grimsthorp in the County of Lincoln the Seat of his Grace the Duke of Ancaster and Kesteven Hereditary Lord great Chamberlain of England. Design'd by Sr John Vanbrugh Kt.
1723

303 *(above left) Elevation of the north front, as built (from* Vitruvius Britannicus*).*

304 *(left) The south front as it is today.*

305 *(above) Vanbrugh's Palladian proposal for the south front (from* Vitruvius Britannicus*).*

306 *(right) Plan of the ground floor from* Vitruvius Britannicus*, showing Vanbrugh's projected remodelling of all four fronts. The State Dining Room is in the north-east tower, the Chapel in the north-west.*

This structure, which had been given a new north front about 1685, was the house inherited by Peregrine Bertie, 2nd Duke of Ancaster and Kesteven and 17th Lord Willoughby de Eresby, in 1723.

Vanbrugh's overall scheme is fully recorded in *Vitruvius Britannicus*, vol. III, published in 1725. Not only is a plan (Fig. 306) given but a plate of the north, south (Figs 303 and 305) and west fronts respectively. Of these only the north or entrance front was carried out. After the architect's death the 2nd Duke either lacked interest or funds to complete the others. Vanbrugh's intentions were quite clear. He meant to pin down the Elizabethan house by four massive corner towers, projecting from the fronts, and to provide the interior quadrangle with a corridor round three sides, devoting the whole of the fourth front, then a riding school to a huge hall, which was duly constructed. The scheme was a development of what Vanbrugh had

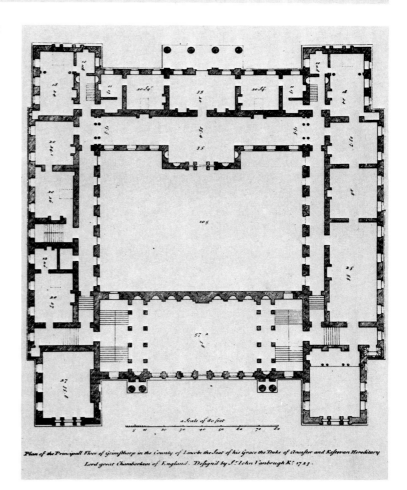

Plan of the Principall Floor of Grimsthorp in the County of Lincoln the Seat of his Grace the Duke of Ancaster and Kesteven Hereditary Lord great Chamberlain of England. Design'd by Sr John Vanbrugh Kt. 1723.

307 *(above) The north front from within the forecourt.*

308 *The Bertie arms and the Willoughby supporters in the overthrow of the gates to the forecourt.*

309 *(above) The east side of the house and forecourt, showing the earlier house and Vanbrugh's tower.*

310 *The original servants' hall, below the State Dining Room, on the ground floor of the east tower.*

done at Kimbolton and Lumley Castles. Indeed Laurence Whistler[1] terms Grimsthorpe 'a baroque version of Lumley'. Such the existing north front (Fig. 302) undoubtedly suggests, for quite gone are the mediaeval battlements and rugged little turrets of Lumley in favour of turned balusters and festooned urns. But there is also evidence, especially in the designs of the unexecuted fronts, of a move away from the Baroque towards the new Palladianism of George I's reign. It is interesting to speculate how far Vanbrugh might have veered in the strictly classical direction had he lived longer.

Avray Tipping[2] believed that the intended south and

west fronts may actually have been designed by Colen Campbell. Laurence Whistler, with whom I agree, disputes this. After all, the Corinthian portico of the south front has its somewhat feminine counterpart at Seaton Delaval. Also the classical windows of both south and west fronts are found on the towers (Fig. 303) of the north front, which unquestionably was built by Vanbrugh. As an early design[1] for this front shows, he thus altered them from his customary simple, arched type. Again the basement windows, with heavy surrounds, on both unexecuted fronts, are distinctly Vanbrughian. Moreover, Campbell, who was always ready to claim credit to himself, ascribed

[1] Sir John Vanbrugh, Architect and Dramatist, 1938.
[2] English Homes, Period IV, vol. II, Sir John Vanbrugh and His School.

[1] Published in Architectural Drawings in the Library at Elton Hall, ed. H. Colvin and M. Craig, Roxburghe Club, 1964. In this drawing the flat roof-line is unadorned.

311 *(opposite) The Stone Hall. The upper arcade on the south side is decorated with images of English monarchs by Thornhill.*

312 *(left) The double staircase seen through the central arch in the east arcade of the Hall.*

in *Vitruvius Britannicus* all the fronts to Vanbrugh.

The approach to Grimsthorpe is dramatic. Lincolnshire is not a hilly county, but the castle stands on the edge of a plateau, overlooking south and westwards a wide lake with gentle, undulating parkland beyond. Vanbrugh arranged for the approach to be long and straight. The wide triple-lined avenue leads like the nave and aisles of a vast cathedral to a culminating reredos, which is the north front. The sanctuary is, as it were, the forecourt. A wrought-iron screen and a pair of gates (Fig. 308), on which are displayed on the overthrow the Willoughby supporters (a friar and a savage), the Bertie arms and a ducal coronet, mark the boundary of the impressive enclosure. The smith responsible for the ironwork was Edward Nutt (1730). The east and west sides of the fore-court are walls treated with twenty-six blind arcades ending in a pair of square pavilions which flank the iron screen. The forecourt is a variant of Vanbrugh's entrance at Seaton, an outward-looking concept denied him at Kimbolton and Lumley Castles.

Unlike the majority of Vanbrugh's palatial designs which draw the eye involuntarily to a central percussion of movement, here the façade (Fig. 307) theme is centrifugal and almost quiescent. The emphasis is of course upon the angle towers and the advancing pair of ringed columns, which strike the only vertical accent. The two storeys of arched windows, reiterating the forecourt arcades, sug-gested to Avray Tipping a Roman amphitheatre. The Roman monumentality is certainly accentuated by the robust Doric frieze and cornice, the balustrade and the

313 *The ceiling of the State Dining Room painted by Francesco Sleter.*

314 *The State Dining Room.*

315 *The north end of the Chapel before the recent restoration. The reredos and the ceiling antedate Vanbrugh's alterations to the house.*

Bertie arms, the two statuary rape groups over the columns and the festooned finials of the towers. These skyline punctuations are truly strokes of genius. By contrast the astonishing casual manner in which the towers are tied to the façade is typical of Vanbrugh's indifference to correct finish when he had no experienced subordinate to attend to such a tiresome matter on his behalf. He unblushingly sacrificed all means to one end, which was a grand effect.

On this magnificent front Vanbrugh has achieved, in the words of Laurence Whistler, 'the grandeur that proceeds, not from violence, but from repose'. It is all the more successful in that it faithfully emphasizes the plan behind it. The front door leads straight into the hall (Fig. 311). Behind the two tiers of seven arched windows on the front are two tiers of seven blind arcades. Behind the coupled Doric columns run breadthwise arcaded screens; behind

the isolated end windows a pair of stairways. The hall disclosing the stairs through the screen openings is the noblest room Vanbrugh ever designed. It surpasses the halls at Blenheim and Seaton Delaval where he had adopted a like symphony of superimposed arches. The walls of creamy Ancaster stone are bare. Only the upper arcades facing the windows are filled with feigned statues in grisaille and gold of those Kings of England to whom the Bertie family were specially beholden. They were painted by Thornhill after 1722. The sharp Doric cornice is an echo of the one outside, and the chimney-piece, which resembles that in the Duchess's bedroom at Blenheim, has an heraldic overmantel unlike anything of the sort else-where. The domed and bordered ceiling is reflected on the floor in a rippling pattern of black marble and stone.

The double dividing staircases contained in the single

316 *The King James's Drawing Room in the east range, possibly by Vanbrugh but enriched later.*

end bays of the façade achieve monumentality in spite of their confined space. The delicate wrought-iron balustrades (Fig. 312) by one Bell of Sheffield are silhouetted against the stone background. The west ceiling panel, painted on canvas by Thornhill, is of Apollo and the Muses; the east one, probably by Sleter, is of Cybele or Rhea. The walls are hung with battle scenes of the Duke of Marlborough by Laguerre. A pair of imposing doorways, with narrowing pilaster jambs, has been traced to Michelangelo's entrance to the Capitoline Palace.[1] The eastern one leads into the State Dining Room, the western to the Chapel.

The State Dining Room (Fig. 314) occupies the first floor of Vanbrugh's east tower. The skeleton of the room is his, that is to say the high Venetian window and the arrangement of the ceiling panel framing a canvas by Francesco Sleter of the Muses, Arts and Sciences (Fig. 313). The doors are early examples of the use of mahogany, but inlaid and veneered with holly and walnut (*c.* 1725). The rest of the decoration is later than Vanbrugh's time. The tapestries were woven in Brussels around 1700. The room contains several pieces of furniture acquired on the death of monarchs as perquisites of the Lord Great Chamberlain, an office shared by Lord Ancaster with Lord Cholmondeley and inherited by the 13th Lord Willoughby through his mother who was heiress of the last de Vere Earl of Oxford. Below this room is the present Entrance Hall (Fig. 310), formerly the servants' hall, with a long, low-vaulted roof supported on square piers.

[1] F. Saxl and R. Wittkower—*British Art and the Mediterranean*, 1948, p. 66.

In the western tower the Chapel (Fig. 315), basically of the 1680s, fills both ground and first floors. It is lit from three sides, and occupied by a gallery on the fourth. The great Venetian window is over the altar; the other windows have broken triangular pediments. Neither the walls in the Corinthian order nor the thick plaster ceiling ribs are Vanbrugh's. It is just possible that Hawksmoor was called in to finish this sumptuous work after Vanbrugh's death, for in the sale catalogue of his belongings one lot consisted of drawings for 'the Duke of Ancaster's Chapel'.

A succession of state rooms lies within the east range of the castle. Of these only the King James's Drawing Room (Fig. 316) may have been reached by Vanbrugh, for the chimney-piece and Corinthian pilasters and entablature suggest his hand. The rest of the decoration is later.

Building entirely ceased in 1726. Except for the decoration during George II's reign of the remaining state rooms, wherein the superb contents vie with the best in English country houses, nothing further was done until 1811. Then the west front was rebuilt in Tudor fashion for Lord Gwydyr, who had married the elder daughter of the 4th Duke, the 1st Marquess of Cholmondeley having married the younger. The dukedom of Ancaster became extinct in 1809. The Gwydyrs' granddaughter Clementina, Baroness Willoughby in her own right, married in 1827 Sir Gilbert Heathcote, 5th Baronet, created Lord Aveland, and had a son, 24th Lord Willoughby and 2nd Lord Aveland. In 1892 he was created Earl of Ancaster. His grandson, the 26th Lord Willoughby de Eresby and 3rd Earl of Ancaster, is the owner of Grimsthorpe today.

317 *The gate piers at the entrance to the forecourt.*   318 *(below) The east, entrance front.*

BRAMHAM PARK, YORKSHIRE

Robert Benson, Chancellor of the Exchequer in 1711 and created Lord Bingley in 1713, was probably his own architect of Bramham Park house, having previously consulted Thomas Archer. The house was begun c. 1703 and finished c. 1710. The stable block was added by John Wood c. 1724. (The home of Colonel and the Hon. Mrs F. Lane Fox.)

Of the hundreds of visitors who annually pay tribute to the gardens at Bramham how many consider the house to be more than a decent Queen Anne appendage? The gardens are certainly the largest and least altered specimen of the formal layout to have survived in England. They are carved, as it were, out of 70 acres of moorland into straight vistas, *ronds-points*, intersecting rides, high clipped hedges, basins, a canal and cascade, and are dotted with temples, urns and an obelisk. A study in themselves they do not come within the purlieus of this book,[1] although strictly speaking both gardens and house, since they were de-

[1] See Christopher Hussey—*English Gardens and Landscapes*, 1967.

319 *The stable block on the south side of the forecourt, from one of the Tuscan loggias.*

320 *Elevation of the entrance front and plan of the main floor (from* Vitruvius Britannicus).

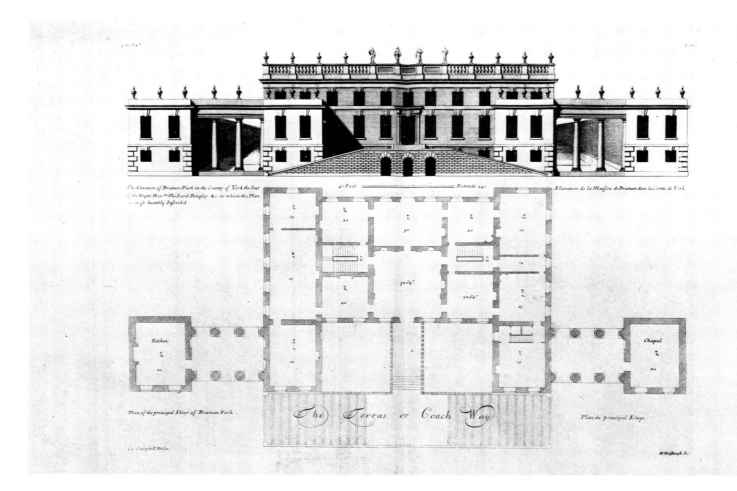

signed as an entity, ought to be taken together. Yet the house itself happens to be of extraordinary interest, and there is no other of a design quite like it.

There has been and still is speculation as to who was the architect of Bramham. Because J. P. Neale in his *Views of Seats*, vol. IV (1821) stated that the owner Robert Benson employed an Italian, Wyatt Papworth[1] jumped to the conclusion that he must have been Giacomo Leoni. But the Palladian Leoni did not arrive in England before 1715, long after the house was finished. Mr Marcus Whiffen[2] was the first to attribute Bramham to Thomas Archer on the grounds that Archer had been introduced by Benson to his neighbour Lord Strafford at Stainborough, and was to design a town house in Cavendish Square for Benson in 1720. The attribution has been strengthened by Mr Geoffrey Beard's discovery that in 1699 and 1700 Archer was paid by Benson £874. 7s. 6d. in all for unspecified services.[3]

The fact is that Bramham was finished in 1710 and its un-quirky elevations do not the least resemble those of any known building by Archer, including the Cavendish Square house which was definitely of bizarre design. The surfaces are almost of *cinquecento* austerity. Only the massing of the groups can be termed Baroque. The orders are not even used upon the fronts of Bramham if we except the Tuscan loggias which, linking wings to pavilions on the entrance front (Fig. 318) are in a fashion not found at any

321 *The west, garden front looking south along the Broad Walk, with one of Archer's piers in the foreground.*

322 *Another view of the pier shown in Fig. 321.*

other English country house. The single visible evidence of association with Archer is the pair of eccentric detached piers (Fig. 322) with inward-curved volutes standing opposite the garden front. These are indeed typical of Archerian detail based on Late Roman Baroque studies.

I believe Mr Arthur Oswald's conclusion to be the right one[1]: namely that Benson was his own architect, having possibly consulted Archer and even obtained from him preliminary designs which he subsequently modified. There was often, it seems, a time-lag between an owner getting plans from a well-known architect and his embarking upon the actual building. The interval usually resulted in a good deal of alteration of the scheme first submitted.[2]

From what we know of Robert Benson he was fully qualified to design his own house. Born in 1675 he visited Italy as a young man and made architecture his study. He advised the Duke of Chandos in the building of Cannons and he consented to 'look after' the building of Stainborough for Lord Strafford during his absence as Ambassador in Berlin. There is evidence that Benson's friends

---

[1] *Dictionary*, Architectural Publication Society, 1852–92.

[2] *Thomas Archer*, 1950.

[3] *Georgian Craftsmen*, 1966.

[1] *Country Life*, 20 Feb. 1958.

[2] The names of Gibbs and Talman have also been put forward. They are based on Benson's known friendship with Gibbs and his sister's marriage with Sir John Wodehouse of Kimberley, for which Talman made some undated (and unexecuted) plans.

323 (right) The Stone Hall. The original ceiling was destroyed in a fire of 1828.

324 (below) The south wall of the Stone Hall, with a full-length portrait of Queen Anne over the fireplace.

325 (opposite left) The chimney-piece in the Boudoir.

326 (opposite right) The early 19th-century staircase.

thought highly of his skill in this respect, and Lord Bute in correspondence refers to his 'consummated experience'.

Robert Benson inherited in babyhood a huge fortune from his father who had amassed it by dubious means. The father began life as an attorney's clerk and ended it as land speculator and money-raiser for Crown and Government. The son was frequently sneered at by contemporaries on account of his 'mean extraction', but he was handsome, affable, astute and very cultivated. In 1699 he bought the Bramham estate, on which there was then no house. How soon afterwards he started to build we do not know for sure. Possibly it was at the time of his marriage in 1703 to Elizabeth Finch, a daughter of the 1st Earl of Aylesford and niece of the 2nd Earl of Nottingham, then busily engaged upon Burley-on-the-Hill. Benson's duties as a Tory M.P. throughout the first decade of the century seem to have brought little interruption to his Yorkshire pastimes. But in 1710, when his house and gardens at Bramham were completed, he was made a Commissioner of the Treasury; and the following year Chancellor of the Exchequer. In 1713 he was created Lord Bingley.

The forecourt (Fig. 317) is entered through a pair of gates flanked by stone sphinxes on raised plinths and monumental piers. The piers consist of a cluster of Doric columns with vermiculated collars. On the jettying entablature of each a bear supports Lord Bingley's escutcheon. Immediately ahead is the east front of the house, while on the left the handsome stable is set at a right angle (Fig. 319). The long block with its portico and lantern clock was almost certainly built by John Wood

while at Bramham in 1724, whereas the end pavilions were probably added as afterthoughts by James Paine in the 1750s. With their Venetian windows and gables in the form of incomplete pediments the pavilions evince a different style and later period.

Campbell gives a plate (Fig. 320) of the entrance front in vol. II of *Vitruvius Britannicus*. 'Of an elegant tho' plain manner' is how he describes the front; and so it is. But the unusual thing about it is the composition. The low, two-storeyed centre is recessed behind flanking blocks imposed upon the end wings and then linked to duplicate pavilions. The most unusual feature is the ramped approach to the front door. Three arches pierce its rusticated base. Campbell makes the ramps—he calls them the coach way—straight, whereas in fact they are curved, and so give greater movement to the composition. It is a pity that the statues and urns which Campbell puts upon the roof balustrade are no longer in place. The design is straightforward yet dramatic, Palladian in its symmetry, Baroque in its plasticity. The garden front (Fig. 321) has end projections, not shown in Campbell's plan, and curved steps leading from the *piano nobile* down to the terrace. These steps were conjectural restorations by Detmar Blow.

A fire all but gutted the interior in 1828. Thereafter the house was left deserted until just before the First World War. The walls of the central stone hall (Fig. 323)—'an exact cube of 30 foot, and most artfully decorated' according to Campbell—were more or less intact, although the roof was gone. Giant Corinthian pilasters carry a finely carved entablature. Over the great doorway on the west

wall a stone panel displays the arms (without a coronet) of Robert Benson as he still was when the room was finished. A pair of niches flank the doorway. The fireplace (Fig. 324) of Gibbsian blocks is contained within a surround of bolection mould. Above it hangs a full-length portrait of Queen Anne said to have been given to Robert Benson after a royal visit to Bramham.

Some decoration survived the fire in rooms at the south end of the house, notably the chimney-piece and door-case in the Boudoir (Fig. 325). The basket of flowers in carved wood cresting the overdoor is particularly delicate. Similar French-style carving was carried out in neighbouring country houses by the York school of joiners, several members of which were in fact Huguenot craftsmen.

Robert Benson, Lord Bingley died in 1731 without a male heir. Three months after his death his daughter Harriot married George Fox. In 1751 George Fox inherited great estates in Ireland from his mother, Frances Lane, sister of the 2nd Viscount Lanesborough, and he added the Lane surname to his own. In 1762 he was created Lord Bingley, but in 1772 his title died with him. His heir was his nephew James Fox-Lane, son of his brother. A descendant, the late Colonel George Lane Fox was made Lord Bingley of the third creation in 1933. He too died without male issue in 1947. His eldest daughter Marcia and her husband Colonel F. Ward-Jackson, who changed his name to Lane Fox, are the present owners of Bramham.

327 *Chettle House. The entrance front, from the west.*

CHETTLE HOUSE, DORSET AND MARLOW PLACE, BUCKINGHAMSHIRE

Two houses, closely resembling one another in size, material and detail, and attributed to Thomas Archer. Chettle House was built for George Chafin c. 1710, and Marlow Place for John Wallop c. 1712–20. (Chettle House is the property of Mrs E. M. Bourke and Marlow Place of Mr J. W. Jackson.)

Even today Cranborne Chase and the Thames Valley are far apart in distance and regional characteristics. How much more so they must have seemed two hundred and fifty years ago. Yet they can boast two lesser country houses —Marlow Place at the time of building was on the fringe of a village—of the Baroque period remarkably alike in unconventional design and detail. Professor Geoffrey Webb[1] was the first to detect their strong and strange

[1] *Country Life*, 6 Oct. 1928.

resemblance and to ascribe them both to Thomas Archer, the gentleman-architect who alone among his countrymen had studied and sought to emulate some of the attributes of Borromini's style.

As far as we are aware there was no blood relationship between George Chafin, squire of Chettle, and John Wallop, squire of Farley Wallop in Hampshire and, through his mother Alicia, born Borlase, of the manor of Great Marlow in Buckinghamshire. The sole connection seems to be that Chafin and Wallop both sat in the House of Commons together, the one as Member for Dorset (1713–47); the other for Hampshire (1715–20). They were most probably friends in Westminster for there was no more than a year between them in age. Moreover, Chafin owned extensive properties in Hampshire as well as Dorset, which may also have brought them together in the country.

328 *The centrepiece of the entrance front.*

Geoffrey Webb's astute conjectures have been confirmed by subsequent evidence. In the first place a plan, dated 1712, and a design for a staircase by Archer for John Wallop's Hurstbourne Priors in his native Hampshire have lately come to light. The particular plan was not executed, but paintings of the house that was built suggest that Archer may have been the architect. If Archer designed for Wallop in Hampshire it is quite likely—style apart—that he designed for him at Marlow. In the second place Mr John Harris has lately unearthed, among the Colen Campbell papers from Newby Hall, a plan almost certainly in Archer's hand of Chettle House exactly as carried out.

The next question to arise is when were Chettle House and Marlow Place built? Professor Webb thought 1730 a likely date for both houses, making Chettle's possibly the earlier because he found its planning more Baroque and

that of Marlow less 'movemented'. Mr Kerry Downes retards the date of their commencement by five years or more. Actually he attributes Chettle to 1720–5 and Marlow presumably to the same time, although he does not specifically say so.

On the other hand Hutchins, Dorset's county historian (1774), states that George Chafin built Chettle in 1710. This date seems nearer the mark for two reasons. Firstly, George Chafin, whose father had died when he was two, was then a young man of twenty-one, an age when someone just come into a large acreage and accumulated income was more likely to build anew than in his mature forties. Besides it happens that this squire spent his fortune so extravagantly on sport that in his middle years he was obliged to sell several of his estates. Secondly, Archer, who unlike his improvident client grew rich with age, is

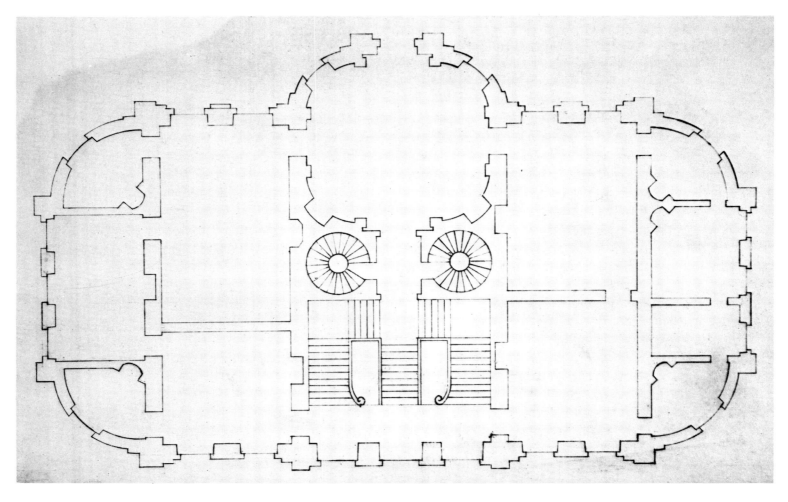

not thought to have practised architecture after 1715, with the single exception of the house in Cavendish Square for his friend Lord Bingley around 1720.

The site which young Squire Chafin chose for his new house was just south of the village church in a sheltered combe, through which a stream runs south-eastwards to join the river Allen in Crichel mere. The plan (Fig. 332) is compact and ingenious. The centrepiece of the west front (Fig. 328) bulges out in a flattened ellipse to present the front door; the centrepiece of the east front (Fig. 331), on the other hand, is straight. The four angles of the house are rounded so as to contain a window-bay in each segment. What make all the elevations most unusual are the giant pilaster strips which, embracing semi-basement, *piano nobile* and first floor, flaunt odd, frilly or tent-like capitals. These carry an entablature (Fig. 329) on the frieze of which curved cantilever brackets are much in evidence. Over the entablature runs a balustrade. The three-bay centrepieces of both west and east fronts are raised into an attic storey. Originally there was some sort of a superstructure with cupola on the roof, but it disappeared long ago. Here, as at Marlow, the material used is a beautiful plum brick, with scarlet gauged brick for window-surrounds. All the dressings are of stone.

The more one looks at Chettle the more extraordinary it appears. One by one unexpected eccentricities, which could only be Archer's, reveal themselves. The squared aprons under the windows are the same as those he used

329 *(above left) The east, garden front.*

330 *(left) Archer's original plan for Chettle.*

331 *(right) The centre of the garden front.*

332 *(below) Plan of the ground floor as it was in 1928.*

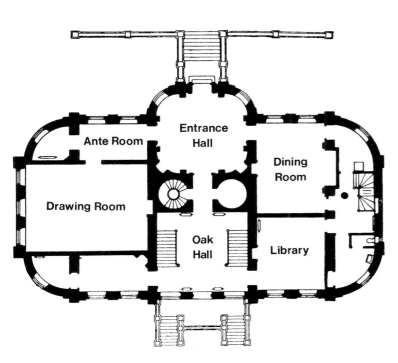

at Roehampton House (1710–12). The front door (Fig. 328) with canted jambs, has counterparts in the Wrest Park pavilion (*c.* 1709) and St Philip's Birmingham (1709–15). The segmental angles of the fronts remind us of Archer's great bow on the north front of Chatsworth (1705). The semi-circular-headed windows on the centrepiece (Fig. 331) of the east front are a small-scale reflection of those on the north-east front of Wentworth Castle (*c.* 1710). The pilasters and frilly capitals are, however, found nowhere else except at Marlow Place.

Before turning to that house we must take a quick glance at the interior of Chettle. It was considerably altered after the Chafins sold the estate to Edward Castleman in 1826. The decorator employed in 1846–50 upon the large Drawing Room then formed out of the south end was a Blandford man and father of Alfred Stevens, the Victorian artist and sculptor. It is thought that the young Alfred may even

333 *The west side of the Entrance Hall.*

334 *The staircase hall with the double flights and two galleries above.*

335 *The entrance front of Marlow Place.*

have modelled the plaster reliefs over the doorways in the
staircase or east hall. The Entrance Hall behind the bowed
centre of the west front remains as originally constructed,
in form a near oval (Fig. 333). It has heavy Doric door
surrounds and fireplaces within the inner curved angles.
A corridor, passing on the right a snail stair from basement
to roof, leads to the east hall (Fig. 334). Here the main
staircase rises in two flights, merges and disappears into
the tunnelled thickness of an inner wall. It then divides
again and emerges upon two galleries apparently added by
the Castlemans so as to link with the original gallery, which
runs along the east wall.

Marlow Place may be less Baroque in plan than Chettle,
for the conspicuous curves of the last house are missing,
yet it is scarcely less Baroque in its distinctive Archerian
detail. Since John Wallop engaged Archer to rebuild his
principal seat, Hurstbourne Priors, in 1712 he probably
turned his attention to Marlow a few years later. He
married in 1716, became a Commissioner of the Treasury
in the following year and was in constant attendance upon
the Hanoverian court. In 1720 he was created Viscount
Lymington.[1] These dates may serve to indicate why John
Wallop thought fit between 1712 and 1720 to build on his
mother's property a smallish house fairly close to Windsor
and midway between London and Hurstbourne.

[1] And in 1743 1st Earl of Portsmouth.

As at Chettle House all four fronts of Marlow Place (Figs. 335 and 336) were meant to be equally admired. The building is of rectangular plan with no unsightly attachments. Tradesmen plunged straight into the basement and the *piano nobile* is approached by steps on the long sides facing road and garden. The projecting centres and four corners are, as at Chettle, articulated by giant pilasters, their plinths demarcating the basement storey. The same stone cantilever brackets support the cornice of each centrepiece, here crowned with a pediment. The angle pilasters have the same tent-like capitals, which instead of being fluted like those at Chettle, are gadrooned. The capitals of the central pilasters are, however, different; they are remarkable for their inturned volutes. Although these eccentric capitals are not found at Chettle they were commonly reproduced in that neighbourhood by the Dorset group of builders, Cartwright, Ireson and the Bastard brothers in the 1730s, 1740s and 1750s. There is little doubt that Archer was the first to introduce to England the inturned volute, which he adapted straight from Borromini's Roman architecture.[1] The fact that this particular conceit came to be so popular in the Blandford area can easily be explained. As Professor Webb suggested, Archer probably supplied Squire Chafin with a design for Chettle, which a local builder—it may have been John or William Bastard—then carried out. Indeed it is more than likely that the same builder was brought by Archer (who had in 1715 purchased for himself a property at Hale Park less than 20 miles from Chettle) to execute the Marlow villa for Chafin's friend, Wallop. The high quality of the workmanship of Chettle must have been a sure recommendation of whosoever was responsible for it. At Marlow the brickwork is if anything superior. The chromatic subtleties in the red stock bricks for facings juxtaposed with scarlet gauged and rubbed bricks for pilasters and window-surrounds are extremely effective.

The Hall (Fig. 337) at Marlow Place, which is entered straight from the front door, is carried into the upper storey. It has two striking features which are shared with Chettle. They are the massive Doric order of pilasters and triglyph frieze, used as frames to fireplace and doorways (as in the western hall of Chettle), and the groined cove of the ceiling which rests on wide pendants (as in the staircase hall at Chettle). The chimney-piece dates from the mid eighteenth century.

Marlow Place has passed through many vicissitudes, and only just weathered them. After serving as a military academy at the turn of this century it became the home of the architect, W. Niven, who illustrated it with photographs and measured drawings in the *Architectural Review* of 1910.

[1] Or, as Mr Whiffen points out, from Domenico de Rossi's three volumes of *Studio d'Archittetura Civile* (published 1702–21) in which this and other Roman High Baroque eccentricities are illustrated.

336 *(above) One of the side elevations.*

337 *(left) The Hall.*

338 *The entrance front framed by the gates to the forecourt.*

BIDDESDEN HOUSE, WILTSHIRE

**In 1711 General John Richmond Webb built Biddes-
den House on land he had purchased in 1692. It is of
ripe plum brick with blue headers. The architect is
not known. (The home of Lord and Lady Moyne.)**

Early eighteenth-century generals, whether Whig or Tory,
had a surprising aptitude for building themselves the sort
of houses which we covet today. There was General Tyrrell
of Shotover, General Hawley of West Green, not to
mention General Wade of Great Burlington Street, London,
whose Palladian box, now demolished, has become the
archetype of the exquisite classical town house in miniature.
General Webb of Biddesden is another. The country house
he built for himself near Ludgershall, just within the
Wiltshire border but geologically within the Berkshire
regional orbit, is like its creator, robust, no-nonsensical and
infinitely pleasing.

John Richmond Webb was a good-looking young officer
when in 1692 he bought a moiety of the Ludgershall
property which had belonged to the Brydges family since

Edward I's reign. On this moiety lay Biddesden, and with
it went the Ludgershall pocket borough which returned
two Members to Parliament. Richmond had by some means
become one of these Members in 1690 at the age of
twenty-three. In 1701 he was joined in the partnership by
his father, Edward Webb, whose family had long resided
at Rodbourne Cheney in Wiltshire. The two Webbs thus
formed a nice little Tory entrenchment in this corner of
the county.

Young Webb was called by a poetaster of the time,
'As Paris handsome and as Hector brave'; years later he
was taken by Thackeray as the model for Henry Esmond.
He was evidently in no hurry to make a home for himself
and he took plenty of time in choosing one of a number of
shallow, wooded combes just protected on the west from
Salisbury Plain for a site on which to build. As it was
his military duties kept him fully occupied for several
years in Flanders. He fought under Marlborough at
Blenheim, Ramillies and Oudenarde, at all of which battles
he distinguished himself. The engagement at which he won

339 *(right) The terraced garden lying to the west.*

340 *(below) The south and west fronts.*

341 *(opposite) The three-bay centrepiece of the south front.*

342 *(above) The round tower attached to the east front. The 'inanimate companions' in the dummy windows were painted by Roland Pym in the 1930s.*

343 *(above right) The Hall. The equestrian portrait, by Wootton, is of General Webb, the builder.*

344 *(opposite) The window wall of the Hall.*

most renown was Wynendael when, in September 1708, he successfully routed a superior French force which attempted to intercept an important British convoy on its way to supply Marlborough's army at Lille. But the credit for this valiant action was unfairly given by the Whig government to Webb's junior officer Cadogan. The consequence was a scream from the outraged Tories which substantially helped to bring down the Government in 1710. Webb was seriously wounded at Malplaquet that same year; and thenceforth unfit for active service. In 1711 he was free to turn his attentions to Biddesden. He straightway began building, and finished in the following year just before being made Commander-in-Chief of the Home Forces. At the Hanoverian succession he was deprived of his command and retired to Biddesden, only making occasional sallies from Wiltshire into the House of Commons.

The General's house faces southwards across a forecourt towards a handsome pair of iron gates with overthrow (Fig. 338), and westwards to receding terraces now grassed

over and practically encircled by fully-grown trees (Fig. 339). It is a square block of seven bays (Fig. 340), two floors and an attic storey over a projecting cornice. A hipped roof rises above the parapet and a lower two-storey extension retreats to the rear. The red-brick walls have, in the words of Christopher Hussey,[1] 'the colour and bloom of a slightly unripe plum', and are interspersed with blue headers. The arched windows are of vermilion gauged brickwork. These windows are the most characteristic feature of Biddesden, for the semi-circular heads are blind and filled with white plaster. Two exceptions are those of the windows flanking the front door which are glazed, the thick sashbars being fanned. As emphatic keynotes to the circle theme three central eye-windows light the upper part of the Entrance Hall; the attic windows and the prominent pediment on this front are segmental.

The centre of the south front (Fig. 341) is brought forward several feet. To add to the rich effect military trophies and the General's arms adorn the pediment, of which the cornice is carved with acanthus. All these dressings are of stone.

The circle theme is repeated along the west and east fronts in what Dr Pevsner has called an 'aqueduct rhythm'. At the northern end of the east front (Fig. 342) an abrupt apostrophe is introduced in the shape of a round tower built to take a bell which the General looted from Lille. It has a round-headed door and windows, and one round eye-opening under a crenellated parapet. The nearest thing

[1] *Country Life,* 2 and 9 April, 1938.

to it is the pair of round towers, also in brick, of Vanbrugh
Castle, Greenwich, built in 1717–18. The three dummy
windows painted in the 1930s by Mr Roland Pym with
figures from Jane Austen, add zest to the considerable
'movement' already imparted to this front by the designer.
In 1932 Dora Carrington had initiated this delightful form
of conceit on the west front with the picture of a kitchen
maid peeling an apple while a tabby cat blandly looks up
at her (Fig. 345).

None of the rooms at Biddesden is elaborately decorated
and several have been thrown into single large living rooms.
But nearly all are wainscoted in long, wide bolection-
moulded panels. The upper part of the two-storeyed Hall
(Fig. 344) is lit by the three round windows which here
break through the box cornice. Confronting the entrance
a huge equestrian canvas by Wootton (Fig. 343) depicts
the General during his finest hour at Wynendael, a plan
of the battle appearing at the foot of the picture. The
canvas was at one time removed, and tradition relates that
the General's shade made such a shindy at night, riding up
and down the staircase on his charger, that it was immediately rehung. The staircase (Fig. 346), occupying a narrow
well, has alternately twisting balusters, and a handrail with
acanthus mould carved on the sides.

Dr Pevsner, in praising Biddesden as 'a very remarkable
house, even from the point of view of English, not of
Wiltshire architecture', classes it in the 'Vanbrugh-
Hawksmoor-Archer group'. And Kerry Downes sees in
the treatment of the windows a link with the Stable Yard
colonnade and old kitchen of St James's Palace by either
Vanbrugh or Archer. But these service additions to the
palace were made after Biddesden was built; and it is
unlikely that so crusted a Tory as General Webb would
have engaged Vanbrugh—whom the Tory Government
had deprived of the Comptrollership in 1710—or for that
matter his close associate Hawksmoor. As for Archer,
there is nothing at Biddesden to correspond to his unmistakable use or abuse of the orders, and his fondness
for sharply broken surfaces. John James is hardly a more
probable claimant. Perhaps the General engaged one of
the anonymous master-builders of those substantial Queen
Anne houses on the outskirts of Newbury, whose richly
chequered brickwork, round-headed windows and angle
pilasters have their counterparts at Biddesden. Whoever
the architect may have been he managed to impart—or his
client saw to it that he imparted—a definite military
element to the design.

General Webb's son succeeded him in 1724. He later
sold Biddesden to the Everett family who owned it for
more than a century. Just before the First World War it
was bought by Colonel the Hon. Guy Baring. He was
killed in action soon afterwards. Lord Moyne acquired it
in 1930. While preserving the house intact he has introduced some charming garden features, including a gazebo,
swimming-pool and statuary, all by distinguished pre-war
architects and artists.

345 (above) The blind window on the west front, painted by
Dora Carrington in 1932.

346 (right) The staircase.

IVER GROVE, BUCKINGHAMSHIRE

Built between 1722 and 1724 for Lady Mohun, this early Georgian villa may have been designed by John James. (The home of Mr and Mrs James Howie Mitchell.)

What in England we term the villa—in Italy the word denotes the whole domain surrounding a 'casino'—is associated with the Palladian style of architecture. Colen Campbell's house for Lord Herbert at Whitehall may have been the first adaptation in this country of the villa 'casino'. That Thames-side offspring of the Veneto was begun soon after 1717. Iver Grove in Buckinghamshire likewise comes into the villa category of small country house. But according to our notions it is far more Baroque than Palladian; and it was built, if we may trust the *Topographer* for 1789–91, in 1722, and finished in 1724. Ackermann's *Repository of Arts* (1824) goes so far as to state categorically that the Grove's architect was Vanbrugh. This is a more controversial matter.

The name Grove at once suggests a small, trim, pretentious, surburban retreat. And this is just what Iver Grove superbly is. Even in George I's reign Iver belonged to the suburbs, and it was within a few hours' trot of London and royal Windsor. Not that its builder can have been particularly well received, if received at all, at St James's Palace and Windsor Castle, for there was something just slightly *déclassée* about Lady Mohun.

In the first place by 1722 she no longer had any right to this title, which legally speaking she had enjoyed for at most six months. Her friends implied that she should have enjoyed it somewhat sooner. Elizabeth Griffin ('Duck' as she was rather equivocally called) was the daughter of Dr Thomas Laurence, physician to Queen Anne. Her first husband, Edward Griffin, had been Clerk of the Board of Green Cloth. Her second, Charles, 5th Lord Mohun, was in the correct words of *Burke's Extinct Peerage* a 'nobleman . . . of a vehement and passionate temper, which led him into many excesses in his youth, and subjected him to be twice arraigned for murder . . .' Acquitted of these charges he challenged the Duke of Hamilton to a duel in Hyde Park; both combatants were killed on 12 November 1712. In 1717 'Duck', by now a rich and still beautiful widow, married for the third and last time Colonel Charles Mordaunt, a nephew of the Earl of Peterborough. After his wife's death in 1725 the Colonel lived on at Iver Grove for another forty years.

347 *The west, entrance front.*

348 *The south front*

349 *The staircase.*

We do not know what brought the newly married Mordaunts to Iver, unless it was the presence of at least two other houses in the village—Hill House owned by the Pagets, and Richings by Lord Bathurst. There is evidence that Lady Mohun was an ornament in Lord Bathurst's circle. But—and this is a question of more moment—whom did she get to design her new villa?

Lord Mohun had been a Whig and a member of the Kit Cat Club with Vanbrugh. Therefore, Mr Laurence Whistler has argued, his widow may have consulted him; but he suggests that Hawksmoor on his behalf supplied a design. Quite understandably Mr Whistler does not detect the hand of Sir John in either the Grove's plan or elevations. Indeed Vanbrugh never showed interest in a dwelling quite so small. Mr John Cornforth and Mr Kerry Downes, on the other hand, advance the claim of John James who was closely attached to the Board of Works, of which Vanbrugh was still nominally Comptroller. Moreover, there are in various known works of James elements that can be compared with those at Iver Grove.

Of them the most outstanding is the colossal temple portico imposed upon the west front (Fig. 347). It may be thought that this somewhat portentous Doric affair has its counterpart in Hawksmoor's Clarendon Building at Oxford, even down to the lunette in the pediment. But would Hawksmoor have translated this monumental stone feature into a brick frontispiece upon so tiny a domestic edifice? Somehow it seems unlikely. His impeccable sense of propriety, not to say limited sense of humour, would never have permitted the squeezing of windows between the pairs of pilasters and doorway within the central space. John James, on the other hand, was not so scrupulous nor so serious. Besides he specialized in small buildings and houses. He had already reduced the Clarendon Building stone columns to brick pilasters upon the side of St Mary's

church, Twickenham, and upon the front of Hursley Park in Hampshire (Fig. 444). Here at Iver the monumental effect in miniature is certainly striking. It is redeemed from absurdity by the splendid texture of the ochre brick of the walls, and the gauged and rubbed vermilion brick used for pilasters, window-heads and quoins.

The south front (Fig. 348) of only three bays is distinguished by a tall and narrow arch motif formed between a pair of panelled chimney-breasts. The two chimneys are linked by a dormer under a segmental head, and the arch rhythm is perpetuated in the rounded heads of all three central windows. A similar but not identical chimney treatment appears on James's own Warbrook House, and may also have appeared on the sides of the house he built for Secretary Johnson at Twickenham. The plan of the latter in *Vitruvius Britannicus*, vol. I, shows that he used corner fireplaces in the end rooms. Their juxtaposition suggests the knitting of flues and chimneys close together.

The plan of Iver Grove, even allowing for many internal changes, is awkward and non-axial, owing to the architect's obligation to space his windows arbitrarily between the pilasters of the west front. No interior fittings, apart from the staircase (Fig. 349) with its slim balusters, have survived. Not even the stair dado is left. We must be grateful to the Ministry of Works that this remarkable little house stands at all. During the last war it fell into terrible disrepair; and later neglect and dry rot so ravaged the structure that it was nearly demolished. Fortunately it was saved in the nick of time by a government grant. The later accretions which disfigured the north and east sides were, to the great advantage of the George I block, removed.

STANFORD HALL, LEICESTERSHIRE

The Caves have owned Stanford since 1430. Sir Roger Cave, 2nd Baronet, commissioned William Smith to build a house on a new site in 1697. In 1730 William's brother Francis Smith began decorating the house for Sir Verney Cave, 4th Baronet, and in 1737 built the stable block for the 5th Baronet. Francis's son William Smith continued decorating in 1743. (The seat of the 7th Lord Braye.)

The claims of Stanford Hall to inclusion in this volume are manifold. The house was begun in the reign of William III; yet it follows the pattern of an earlier period. It was built and decorated by three successive members of the same family of Midland masons over nearly half a century; and yet it presents a beautifully congruous uniformity.

The Smith family is generally associated with country houses of George I's reign, and Mr Hussey has already dealt with several built by the most famous of the family, Francis—commonly styled 'of Warwick'—namely Stone-

leigh, Davenport, Mawley (very probably) and Ditchley (to the designs of Gibbs). These are essentially Rococo by English standards, and Stanford, at which Francis worked, can hardly be so described. It was, however, designed and begun by his brother William who was older than he by eleven years. William's seniority may account for his adherence to a plan and elevations harking back to the Clarendon House (1664–7) prototype of his extreme youth. In fact Stanford might almost have been designed by Sir Roger Pratt. It belongs to Pratt's 'double pile' category, that is to say a modified H-plan, with large central saloon and hall back to back, and doors axially placed in the middle of all four elevations.

William Smith's client was Sir Roger Cave, 2nd Baronet, who in 1670 had succeeded his father, an ardent supporter of Charles I in the Civil War. He was a man well over forty when he decided to pull down the Northamptonshire home which his ancestors had acquired in the fifteenth century, and to build afresh. He rather curiously chose a site on the

350 *The south, entrance front at the end of the avenue.*

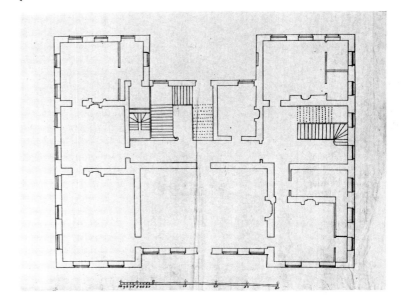

351 *Francis Smith's plan of the ground floor, dated 1730.*

352 *The centre of the south front.*

353 *The Green Drawing Room.*

354 *The main staircase constructed in 1730.*

355 *(right) A view at the head of the main staircase.*

356 *(below) The original staircase of 1700 at the east end of the house.*

357 *(opposite) The east front and stable block.*

358 *(opposite below) The front of the stable block, built in 1737.*

opposite bank of the river Avon, which happens to be in Leicestershire (Stanford village and church are in Northamptonshire).

Sir Roger was probably an old-fashioned sort of baronet with definite views. For the architecture of his new house he engaged a mason from Tettenhall who had not built anything up to date. Did he then dictate the design? It is quite possible. In 1697 William Smith's estimate for the new project, including demolition of the old house, amounted to £2,138. 10s. 3d. Sir Roger undertook to 'find all scaffolding stuff and iron barrs for the casements chimney peices & hearths', also 'carriage of all sand & brick & all old stone'. The old stone may have been re-used and redressed for the south front, which is the only front in this material, the others being of brick, apart from quoins and dressings. Thirty-three windows were to be sashed—quite a high proportion for a provincial house of the period—the rest transomed. The modillion cornice is of wood.

Seen from the end of the straight avenue the south front (Fig. 350), its window-panes and silvery walls glistening in the sun, looks like a compact and vertical French *manoir* embosomed in trees. On getting closer we realize how extremely English the composition really is. Even so there are certain things about this enriched front which are too sophisticated to have sprung direct from a master-builder's earliest endeavour. The bolection-moulded panels under the windows of the wings, the balusters under those of the centre, and the elongated scrolls and mask of the window

359 *The Saloon decorated in 1743 in the Rococo style; the plasterwork by John Wright of Worcester. Ceiling cove painted 1880.*

over the entrance (Fig. 352) suggest that Talman's Thoresby and Dyrham fronts may have presented an idea or two.[1]

Sir Roger Cave died in 1703 having glazed the windows and leaded the roof of his new house. He had also planted the long north and south avenues of oak and elm. His son Sir Thomas, 3rd baronet, had married just before his succession Margaret Verney of Claydon, through whom their great-granddaughter, Sarah Otway, was in 1839 to call out of abeyance the ancient barony of Braye, created three hundred and ten years previously. Sir Thomas does not seem to have done more to the house than decorate 'ye great parlor it is a handsom rome' (now the Green Drawing Room (Fig. 353) in the south-west corner of the house). But his son, Sir Verney Cave, 4th Baronet, put in the main staircase (Fig. 354). This was in 1730, by which time William Smith was dead; his younger and better-known brother, Francis Smith of Warwick, now took over. A plan (Fig. 351) by him of the house shows where the new staircase, with a service stair beside it, was to go. Until 1730 the only staircase had been the one shown on the east front, with dog-leg flights, turned balusters and ball newels (Fig. 356). It is a modest and old-fashioned affair, sturdy and Caroline.

[1] Admittedly these embellishments are not shown in the rather sketchy views of Stanford Hall published in J. Nicholls's *Leicestershire*, Part I, vol. IV, 1807.

A long letter from Francis Smith advised against a main staircase of stone and iron, 'the walls not being sufficient to carry 'em', and proposed instead 'to have it done with some Dutch oak—with handsome rails & barristers & a carv'd braget at ye noseing of the step & ye under side of ye step with wainscot'—all of which was duly carried out, including a handsome ceiling (Fig. 355) 'to be done with stoko'.

Francis then proposed adding a pair of pavilions to accommodate offices and stables, 'to be built on either side ye front Court'. The scheme was interrupted by Sir Verney Cave's death in 1734, so the architect had, after an interval, to start all over again. Instead he designed and, in 1737, built for a second grandson of Sir Roger's, namely Sir Thomas Cave, 5th Baronet, one large stable block of two courtyards to the north-east of the house (Fig. 358). It has a two-storey front with central pediment, clock and cupola. It lies on slightly lower ground than the house which it nicely sets off without impeding views of it from across the river or down the south avenue. Consequently the east front (Fig. 357) of the house was brought into greater prominence. So a central door was provided; the windows of the main floor were given pediments, those of the upper floor architraves and all of them brackets under the sills to match the windows of the stable block. There can be little doubt that Francis Smith was responsible for these improvements. The double-flight perron was added by the 5th Lord Braye in 1880 when the east front was made into the entrance. He also joined house to stables by a building which fortunately was removed in 1924.

Francis Smith died in his turn, and in 1743 we find his son William sending to Sir Thomas Cave a sketch with proposals for heightening the Saloon (Fig. 359) on the south front. This involved 'removing entirely the upper row of windows and sinking the ceiling by a cove'. And now the first introduction to Stanford of Rococo decoration appears in the shell and scroll motif of the cove corners. They were entrusted to one John Wright of Worcester, plasterer, who likewise moulded the cornice, the 'tabernacle frames' on either side of the door-case and the chimney-piece with its 'satyr termes', for all of which he received £270. 12s. 1d. In 1880 the ceiling was painted by a Frenchman, Félix Joubert, and certain minor enrichments including a generous splash of gold leaf were added. In this splendid state room there hangs a collection of portraits of the later Stuarts. They and a number of relics about the house had belonged to Henry Stuart, Cardinal of York, and were bought in Rome by Baroness Braye in 1842.

Stanford Hall is a fascinating repository of portraits, furniture, books, manuscripts and belongings of an ancient county family. When the 7th Baronet died in 1792 the Cave baronetcy passed to an uncle. Stanford was inherited by a sister, Sarah (3rd Baroness Braye), married to Henry Otway. On her death in 1862, aged ninety-four, the barony of Braye for a second time fell into abeyance. It was revived in 1879 in the person of her fourth and last surviving daughter, Henrietta, 4th Baroness Braye, married to Edgell Wyatt-Edgell. The present and 7th Baron is their great-grandson.

360 *The south-west, entrance front.*

CHICHELEY HALL, BUCKINGHAMSHIRE

Chicheley, once monastic property, was bought from the Crown by Anthony Cave in 1545. His daughter married a Chester. In 1713 Sir John Chester, 4th Baronet, commissioned James Oldfield, master-mason, to rebuild. In 1719 Francis Smith took over and in 1722 Henry Flitcroft designed and Isaac Mansfield, plasterer, decorated the two-storey hall. In 1952 the Chesters sold Chicheley. (The home of Earl and Countess Beatty.)

There were two unusual things about Sir John Chester of Chicheley. The first was that he began rebuilding his ancestral seat at the advanced age of fifty-four, and the second that he defied the disapproval of his fashionable protégé, William Kent, at least in so far as the outside of his new house was concerned.

It is true he was not all that young—he was thirty-two—when he succeeded his father as 4th Baronet in 1698. In 1704 his wife Anne Wollaston died and in her memory he got James Oldfield, a local mason, to add a chancel to

Chicheley church, and Francis Baxter, joiner, to make the reredos and three-arched screen. In May 1713 his intimate friend Burrell Massingberd of Ormesby Hall, Lincolnshire, wrote to William Kent in Rome that Sir John was beginning to rebuild the hall. If he thereby meant the present house he may have been referring to the long office block to the north (Fig. 363), which was balanced by the stable block on the south in 1723–4. There is a provincial air about these identical pendant blocks with their steeply pitched roofs, odd aprons under the parapet and pair of niches flanking a central window. They may well have been to James Oldfield's design.

Massingberd had met Kent in Rome in 1711–12 and become his patron and admirer. He likewise persuaded his old crony Chester to help finance the struggling artist. Soon Kent was buying for Sir John *bustos* and pictures which he despatched from Leghorn, and even copying old masters for him.

Had Kent returned to England before Christmas 1719 the outside of Chicheley might now look very different.

361 *(above left) The upper part of the centrepiece of the entrance front.*

362 *(left) The garden front with the stable block beyond.*

363 *(above) The back of the house with the office block on the right.*

364 *(right) The eastern projecting wing at the back of the house.*

As it happened, Sir John that October commissioned the architect Francis Smith to pull down the old house and 'dig ye foundations for a new one'.[1] It was to be 'agreeable to ye model as by ye agreement doth appear for £638'. Early in the New Year of 1720 building began. Sir John's account books mention that Oldfield and Baxter were again employed. Other craftsmen were Thomas Eborall (alias Broval?) of Warwick, joiner, Edward Poynton of Nottingham, stone carver, and John Wilks of Birmingham, locksmith, all of whom were to work for Smith at Sutton Scarsdale in Derbyshire. Within a matter of months Kent visited Chicheley, and he reported to Massingberd that he was not very impressed by what he saw, and that it was now too late to alter the design. The same year Massingberd paid a visit and found the same faults as Kent. In a letter to his wife he said: 'I was so fretted to see such havoc made

[1] Joan D. Tanner—'The Rebuilding of Chicheley Hall', *Records of Bucks.*, vol. XVII, Part I, 1961.

365 *The screen of marble columns dividing the Entrance Hall from the staircase.*

366 *Part of the east wall of Flitcroft's Entrance Hall.*

in the architecture especially in the garden front, which was at first all laid out by my direction, that if Sir John had been at home when I first saw it I should not have foreborne the rudeness of exposing all the faults to the utmost. . . .' But he conceded that the house was good within and the workmanship excellent. 'The Knight, & his builder Smith', he went on, '(who I believe is an honest man and a very good bricklayer) must needs turn all our antique into modern London proportions, etc.'

Kent and Massingberd's disapproval of the exterior is interesting, but hardly surprising. Since the fronts of Chicheley are about the most Baroque of any English country house, the two Palladians must have been shocked indeed. How far and why Sir John Chester was responsible for the design we may never know, because from the sixty surviving letters between Chester and Massingberd it appears that their tastes in architecture coincided. Only in December 1716 the Baronet had written to the squire: 'I shall be extream glad to enjoy your good company at Chichley & to receive instructions in relation to my building, there being no person whose judgment I value more in that as well as all other affaires.'

Francis Smith's hand in the design is apparent. Building was so rapid that there can have been little if no deviation from his model, agreed upon in October 1719. He was a prolific designer in, as it transpires, a variety of styles. Chicheley's style does not conform to that of Stoneleigh (1714) or even Sutton Scarsdale (1724), two early Smith houses; but it does have much in common with that of

367 *Detail of the third flight of the staircase.*

368 *The staircase, the work of Francis Baxter.*

Heythrop (1705–10) which as a young man he had built to the designs of Archer. This was clearly the house from which Smith was deriving a good deal of inspiration with, we must suppose, at least the connivance of his middle-aged client.

Chicheley lies in that lush, Ouse-watered part of Buckinghamshire which we associate with the poet Cowper and which, until threatened with an overspill town at Crawley a mile or two away, we believed to be infinitely remote from the urban sprawl. Originally monastic property, it was purchased from the Crown in 1545 by a rich merchant, Anthony Cave. Through his daughter it passed in Elizabeth's reign to the Chester family. The Cave house, which Sir John Chester demolished, stood on a site between the south-east front of the present hall and the canal. This ornamental piece of water in three arms was formed by George London in 1700, about which time Sir John planted several avenues and embarked upon extensive garden operations.

Arthur Oswald[1] has remarked how the four sides of the house show, if one takes them clock-wise beginning with the north-west, 'a well graduated crescendo of effect' in brickwork and design. Seen across a cobbled yard the north-west side, linked by a quadrant corridor to the office block, is of variegated bricks with windows in no sort of order. Next, the back of the house (Fig. 363) has the same rude brickwork, but the cornice is of stone. Here symmetry and the Tuscan order are introduced. In the projecting

¹ *Country Life*, 9, 16, 23 May 1936.

369 *(above) Carved decoration in the Drawing Room.*

370 *(left) One of the four gilt mirrors in the Drawing Room.*

371 *(right) The Billiard Room (as it was in 1936).*

wings (Fig. 364) giant pilasters embrace the ground and
first floors, and above the cornice lesser pilasters embrace
the attic. The windows are given stone surrounds, and a
special feature is made of shell-headed niches, surely the
work of James Oldfield, since they resemble his Queen
Anne niches on the chancel of the church.

The south-east or garden front is more ambitious. The
brickwork is of fine quality and uniform colour, and the
joints are narrower. The pilasters—the order is Doric—
are now in stone. The windows are given aprons and the
door-case has an oddly curved pediment, both Archerian
touches (Fig. 362). Remarkably fine are the lead rainwater
pipes with Sir John's and the second Lady Chester's monogram on the heads. 'And so', in Mr Oswald's words, 'we
work up to the architectural climax of the main elevation,
with its enriched modillion cornice, fluted Corinthian

pilasters, and (in the central portion) a beautifully carved frieze of masks, foliage and cornucopias', which frieze (Fig. 361) may be the work of Edward Poynton. Not the least eccentricity is the pair of rams (the Chester crest) advancing from the angles of the cornice.

It is, of course, the dramatic manner in which the cornice and parapet have been swept up in the centre which makes the main elevation of Chicheley an essentially Baroque composition (Fig. 360). The architect's intention was to convey by this false perspective an appearance of greater central projection than actually is the case. How far he was successful may be gauged by an inaccurate lithograph in Burke's *Visitation of Seats*, vol. I, 1852, where the artist, presumably drawing from memory, positively canted the centrepiece forward. Other Baroque details are the front door and windows of the centre, directly borrowed from Archer's Heythrop and indirectly from the Rome of Bernini and Borromini. The bat's-wing door pediment on tapering pilasters has been crowned with a curved hood. The rather jejune result is scarcely an improvement upon Bernini's doorway in the Chapel of the Holy Crucifix in St Peter's. The shaped window architraves with double

mouldings taken from the north-west front of Heythrop are distant reflections of those on Borromini's Oratorio dei Filippini.

Massingberd and Kent were, fortunately, too late to prevent the baronet's 'havoc' of the architecture, but they were able to restrain his Baroque tendencies inside the house. All the rooms are impeccably Palladian.

Sir John Chester's accounts reveal that Henry Flitcroft was paid in 1722 for designing the two-storeyed hall (Fig. 366) with its marble pillars. Two years previously Flitcroft had become Lord Burlington's draughtsman and was presumably introduced to Chester by Kent, then lodging in Burlington House. The ceiling painting on two cloths was copied very tolerably by Kent from Domenichino's *Diana and her Nymphs* in the Palazzo Borghese. The niche within a tabernacle in the west wall formerly contained a grisaille figure of Mercury for which Kent received twelve guineas in May 1725. Two steps in the same grey-veined marble as Flitcroft's arched screen lead to the Staircase (Fig. 365). This is a splendid piece of joinery for which Francis Baxter was responsible. The handrail and treads are of oak inlaid with bands of golden walnut; the half-

landings are parquetried, the tread ends panelled with burr walnut. Each of the three balusters to every tread is different, and the moulded soffits and carved brackets (Fig. 367) are exceptionally refined. The simple ceiling compartments and rich cornices of stairwell and hall were finished in 1722 by Isaac Mansfield, the important London plasterer who worked at Castle Howard, Burlington House and Blenheim. The walls of both apartments are now painted a greeny French grey.

The garden front is taken up with a suite of three rooms, similarly panelled in the Palladian style of George I's reign. The raised and fielded wainscot here, as throughout the house, is of the highest quality, and does enormous credit to Baxter and his joiners. The marble fireplaces (Fig. 371) of all three rooms are distinguished by a tabernacular arrangement of fluted Corinthian pilasters and rich entablature pertaining to that order. The wood used is mostly elm, sometimes grained to resemble walnut. Door-heads and spandrels of panelling have applied carvings of birds, cherubs, musical instruments and trophies in limewood. In the Drawing Room, the most opulently treated of the three rooms, hang four gilt mirrors, each with a swan-neck pediment and plumed mask (Fig. 370) which were made for Sir John Chester. The Drawing Room photograph (Fig. 369) shows a contemporary settee and chair in walnut parcel gilt, the seats and backs worked with scriptural and allegorical subjects in *gros* and *petit point*. They are part of a set which is now on loan to Montacute House in Somerset.

On the top floor of the house Sir John Chester fitted up for himself an ingenious library (Figs. 372 and 373). The panels of feathered oak, the fluted pilasters, even the plinths and dados were made to swing or pull open, so as to conceal the baronet's precious books. The room must be unique in the annals of joinery. Hardly less ingenious is the steep staircase (Fig. 374) of divided steps that gives access to the roof. Did it also spring from the inventive brain of the incomparable Francis Baxter?

Sir John Chester died in 1726. On the death of his grandson Sir Charles, 7th Baronet, in 1755 the title (it became extinct in 1769) passed to an uncle. The property, however, went to Sir Charles's mother's nephew, Charles Bagot, who adopted the Chester name. His descendants owned Chicheley Hall until 1952 when it was sold with several of the family portraits and some of the furniture to the present Earl Beatty.

372 (*above left*) *Sir John Chester's Library with the shelving concealed.*

373 (*left*) *The Library with the shelving revealed.*

374 (*above*) *The divided staircase to the roof.*

WENTWORTH CASTLE, YORKSHIRE

In 1708 Thomas Wentworth, 3rd Lord Raby (created Earl of Strafford 1711), bought Stainborough Park from the Cutler family. In 1709 the east front was begun to a design by Jean Bodt. Before 1713 Archer was called in and before 1724 James Gibbs. (The property of Barnsley Corporation.)

Christopher Hussey has recounted[1] the amusing story of the bitter rivalry between the owners of Wentworth Woodhouse and Wentworth Castle, which led to a house-race of fantastic extravagance lasting for at least sixty years. First one and then the other house advanced from a modest manor to a palace of vast proportions. From the start Wentworth Castle led, then Woodhouse after a neck-to-neck spurt finally outstripped the former in becoming the largest country house in England. It all happened in this way.

On the death without issue in 1695 of William Wentworth, 2nd Earl of Strafford (son of Charles I's ill-fated statesman Thomas Wentworth), the family property of Wentworth Woodhouse passed to his sister, Lady Rockingham's younger son, the Hon. Thomas Watson. The Strafford earldom became extinct, but the barony of Raby devolved by special remainder upon the grandson of the 1st Earl's brother, another Thomas Wentworth. This individual, the 3rd Lord Raby, began life as a soldier serving with distinction in Flanders under William III and later under Marlborough. But he was extremely ambitious, consumed with resentment of his Watson cousins, and determined to get revived in his favour, and not in the

[1] *Country Life*, 8 Sept. 1934.

Watsons', the Strafford title, an objective in which he was successful. In 1711 after blatant manœuvring he was made Earl of Strafford of the second creation. He was an unbending Tory, an arch-snob (he prevented Matthew Prior becoming Ambassador at Versailles because of his mean birth) and remarkable for 'excess of bloated pride' in his own descent.

Lord Raby in 1708 bought the Caroline brick house of the Cutler family, called Stainborough, a mere six miles from the ancestral Wentworth Woodhouse. Disregarding the Duke of Marlborough's injunction that the size of his house should be commensurate with his rank Raby, still a mere Baron, at once planned to add to the east end of the existing manor house (Fig. 380) a long range like the stroke of the letter T (Fig. 379). Mr John Harris[1] believes that Raby first commissioned Talman to work out a scheme, but like many other clients fell foul of this impossibly difficult architect. He then handed over Talman's scheme to the architect of the Prussian court to which he, Raby, had been accredited in 1701. The man's name was Jean Bodt, a Huguenot who fled to Holland in 1685 where he entered the service of William of Orange. In 1698 he crossed to England and played an active part in erecting buildings in Whitehall after the palace fire in that year. He even made designs, unexecuted, for Greenwich Hospital before seeking further fortune in Berlin. Bodt's design (Fig. 377) for the Stainborough front is preserved in the Victoria and Albert Museum library.

While abroad Raby kept up a correspondence with his younger brother Peter Wentworth. In 1709 Peter wrote to

[1] 'Bodt and Stainborough', *Architectural Review*, vol. CXXX, July 1961.

375 *The east elevation of Stainborough, as Wentworth Castle was called in 1715, as published in* Vitruvius Britannicus.

The Elevation of Stainborough in Yorkshire the Seat of the R.t Hon.ble The Earl of Strafford &c. Knight of the most Noble Order of the Garter to whom this Plate is most humbly Inscribed

Elevation du Chateau de Stainborough dans la Comté de York

Co. Campbell Delin.

376 *The east front as it is today.*

377 *(below) Bodt's design for the east elevation.*

him that he and their mother feared lest the new front should cost £10,000, but consoled themselves that it would 'make his Great Honour [the owner of Wentworth Woodhouse] burst with envy and his Little Honour [the son, subsequently 1st Marquess of Rockingham] pine and die'. In May 1711 Peter forwarded to him the express advice of Mr Robert Benson of Bramham who since 1709 had been 'looking after' the building, that there should be a competent surveyor on the spot. This counsel seems to have been taken for in August 1713 one Edward Reeves, surveyor, writes to Raby, now *en poste* at the Hague, that the wing is ready for cornice and roof. Then in April of 1714 Raby is writing to Thomas Archer asking him to procure the plan of his gallery from the widow of George London, the gardener at Brompton. Archer acceded to this request. Shortly after the Hanoverian succession in August of this year Strafford was recalled from the Hague and deprived of all his duties. Like other prominent Tories he was driven from public life, never to return. December saw him installed at Stainborough.

In vol. I of *Vitruvius Britannicus* (1715) a plate (Fig. 375) is given of the east front of Stainborough virtually as carried out although Bodt's design had, in fact, been altered in several minor particulars. His single end bays became paired; his attic windows were squared and given lugged corners; his first-floor windows were pedimented. Bodt's ground-floor windows were originally supported by curious overlaid balusters of paper-thin relief, enclosing basement openings (Fig. 375). Unfortunately all but the two central windows were subsequently lowered so that the sills now rest right on top of the openings. The bulbous balusters and the ears of the first-floor windows—which are shadows, so to speak, of the corbels supporting the

378 *(above) The view north along the terrace in front of the east façade.*

379 *(below) Plan of the ground floor (from* Vitruvius Britannicus*).*

380 *(above right) The angle between the two ranges; a view showing the Caroline house that lies behind the centre of Bodt's building.*

381 *(right) The centrepiece of the east front.*

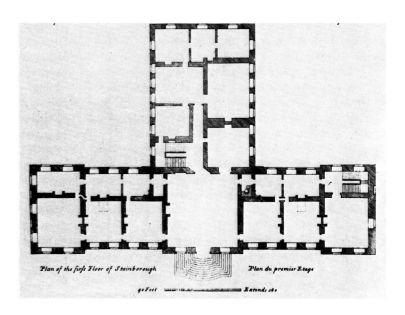

heads—at once suggest the hand of Archer. We may assume then that Archer was engaged by Lord Strafford to modify Bodt's elevation well before 1713, at which date everything but the roof was wanting to the east wing.

A handsome wrought-iron gate (probably by one Richard Booth) leads to the terrace in front of the east wing. The great fifteen-bay elevation (Fig. 378) is of smooth ashlar throughout. Strafford evidently abandoned his intention expressed in a letter of 2 February 1710, that the wing was to be of brick and stone 'as Hampton Court is and which I am assured will look better than all stone'. Doubtless what he then wanted was the wings to be of brick, and only the three-bay centrepiece (Fig. 381) to be in stone, like Wren's garden front at Hampton Court. The round-headed windows between Corinthian pilasters derive, on the other hand, from Wren's Trinity College Library. Can we trace in the Stainborough centrepiece an indirect link with Wren through Talman, of whose design we have no record? The carving here is even richer than anything of the sort at Hampton Court, and far richer than what is indicated in the *Vitruvius Britannicus* plate. Over the masked keystones of the outer bays, fruit, leaves and flowers tumble in festoons; over that of the central bay a gigantic armorial display reaches into the frieze, while military trumpets and trophies rest upon the spandrels. This splendid carving was possibly the work of the French mason, Daniel Harvey, with whom an agreement to make '4 capitals after ye Corinthian order' for the Gallery was reached in 1720.

None of Bodt's suggestions for the interior of Stainborough seems to have been carried out. Work of decoration proceeded slowly during the 1720s. To reach the Gallery it is necessary to pass through the square Hall

(Fig. 382) on the ground floor behind the centrepiece. The ceiling, divided into compartments, is supported by fluted Ionic columns and pilasters. The central compartment was painted with *Aurora and Tithonus* by Giacomo Amiconi in 1735; the others by Clermont in arabesques after Berain. Further opulence is introduced by the doorway surrounds in grey Derbyshire marble. The hall chairs shown in the photograph were painted with 'my Lds arms' by a Wakefield decorator, William Addinall.

Now that Wentworth Castle (its assumption of this grandiose title in 1731 indicated yet another lead in the Wentworth house-race) is a girls' school, the rooms bear little relation to their condition when the house was privately occupied. Detailed description would therefore be misleading. On the other hand Mr Geoffrey Beard[1] has discovered many fresh particulars of how the house was decorated in a series of letters (1714–20) addressed to Lord Strafford at the Hague by the York carpenter-builder, William Thornton. They relate to such items as

[1] *Georgian Craftsmen*, 1966.

glazing bars, stone steps for the stairs (Fig. 385) to the Gallery, marble pedestals and matters of joinery. Resemblances in the cornices and door-heads of the Queen Anne Sitting Room (Fig. 386) and Ante Room to the carved joinery at Beningbrough confirm that Thornton worked extensively at Wentworth Castle. After his death in 1721 his assistant John Goodyear agreed to 'lay ye Gallery floor for sixpence p. yard', although 'Mr Thornton . . . had twelve pence p. yard for laying yr Lordship's other floors.' Ten years later Goodyear died of drink.

The long Gallery (Fig. 383) extends the whole 180-foot length of the first floor. It is lit by fifteen windows on the east wall and a Venetian window at either end, which made it look to hostile contemporaries like a greenhouse. It was, according to Walpole, modelled on the gallery of the Palazzo Colonna in Rome, and filled with pictures and sculpture, which the Earl purchased in Italy. Each end is separated by a screen of two marble Corinthian columns (ordered specially from Leghorn), for which Daniel Harvey was made to supply capitals in 1720. Five years later

382 *(opposite) The Hall in the centre of Bodt's building, as it was in 1924.*

383 *(left) The Gallery running the length of the east front.*

Strafford's cousin Lord Bathurst found the Gallery to be 'a very magnificent room now that the pillars are up'. The high coved ceiling is plastered very simply. There is a pair of splendid chimney-pieces (Fig. 384), each with a pediment on which three eagles perch and—until lately—held garlands in their beaks.

The Gallery is Georgian rather than Queen Anne, and quite unlike any decoration that Bodt and Archer would have designed. In fact the name of another illustrious architect has recently been introduced to Wentworth Castle by Mr Beard. An agreement of 1724 with a London joiner, Charles Griffiths, contains the contract 'to wainscoat ye Gallery att Staineborough as desined by Mr Gibbs in manner following for £225 inc. carriage'. James Gibbs had built for Secretary James Johnston the Octagon Room at Twickenham where Lord Strafford also had a house, and it seems from further passages in the contract that Griffiths worked there too. Mr Beard concludes from this Twickenham connection that the stucco roundels with relief figures and heads, the delicate swags and drops of the staircase in

the north-west angle of Wentworth Castle may be by Artari and Bagutti, the well-known Italian *stuccatori* who were employed by Gibbs in the Octagon.

The first Earl, dying in 1739, was succeeded by his son, aged seventeen, who was a lifelong friend of Horace Walpole. In answer to his 'Little Honour's' addition of the garden front to Wentworth Woodhouse, he built in 1759 the Palladian south front of Wentworth Castle. Walpole wrote, 'Nothing ever came up to the beauty of it.' Then in 1768–72 his 'Little Honour's' son, the 2nd Marquess of Rockingham, finally carried off the house-stakes by engaging Flitcroft to add the 600-foot range of Wentworth Woodhouse.

The 2nd Earl of Strafford lived until 1791, but had no children and Wentworth Castle passed to the grandson of his sister, Lady Henrietta Vernon. In 1804 Frederick Vernon added the Wentworth name to his own. His grandson, Captain Bruce Canning Vernon-Wentworth, who died in 1951 aged eighty-nine, was the last of the family to live in the house.

384 (above) One of the two chimney-pieces in the Gallery.

385 (right) The staircase in the north-west angle of the great front. The stucco roundels and relief work may be by Artari and Bagutti, c. 1724.

386 (below) Queen Anne's Sitting Room, with a view down the enfilade along the east range on the ground floor.

387 (below right) The chimney-piece and overmantel in the East Tapestry Room.

388 *The entrance front and its flanking pavilions from the north.*

BENINGBROUGH HALL, YORKSHIRE

Granted by the Crown in 1544 to John Banister, whose sister Mary Bourchier was his heir. In 1716 John Bourchier built the present house. Archer may have supplied a design. William Thornton was the builder-carpenter and carver of the outstanding wainscot. (A property of the National Trust.)

The Vale of York, flat as a pancake and remarkably sparing of scenery, has nevertheless a charm of its own. It is still a sort of no-man's-land. The little river Ouse flowing from north-west to south-east is not even crossed by a bridge between Great Ouseburn and York, a distance of at least twelve miles. But long before York is reached the Ouse makes a sudden loop round Beningbrough. Through being impassable the river forms a clearly defined boundary to the west and south of the park without, so level is the terrain, contributing notably to the landscape.

Since the reign of King John, Beningbrough had belonged to the Church. In 1539 the Master of the Hospital of St Leonard in York 'surrendered' it to King Henry VIII. Five years later the King granted the reversion of the estate to one John Banister. From 1544 to 1917 Beningbrough passed by inheritance.

John Banister's sister Mary was his heir. While their father Sir Humphrey Banister was serving in Calais she had met and married James, the bastard son of the Deputy Governor, Sir John Bourchier, 2nd Lord Berners, distin-

guished for his ancient lineage and his translation of Froissart's *Chronicles*. Since James Bourchier had no portion to inherit, the Beningbrough property was a windfall for the new family he was founding.

A direct descendant of this union was John Bourchier, builder of Beningbrough Hall. We know this from the cipher JMB (the M standing for John Bourchier's wife Mary, daughter of Roger Bellwood, Serjeant-at-law) in stone over the front door, and their initials, arms and date 1716 in parquetry upon the main staircase (Fig. 397). Apart from having been pricked for High Sheriff of the county in 1719 nothing whatever is known about this Yorkshire squire, nor until lately was there any clue as to the architect of Beningbrough. In 1852 Burke's *Seats* had no hesitation in declaring categorically 'The present mansion was built . . . by Sir Jan Vanburgh [*sic*]', and 'The architecture is Italian.' The last statement is only a little nearer the truth than the first.

Mr Marcus Whiffen[1] was, I believe, the first contemporary scholar to suggest the hand of Thomas Archer. Archer was in correspondence with the owner of Stainborough (Wentworth Castle) in 1714 and may even have supervised its building in the years immediately following. He was certainly a friend of Lord Bingley of Bramham Park, and there is no reason why he should not have known Bourchier and even given him ideas, if not a general

[1] *Thomas Archer*, 1950.

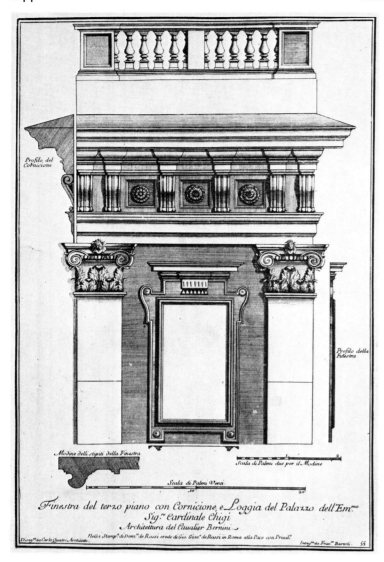

389 (above)
Engraving of a window
from Bernini's Palazzo
Chigi, published in
Rossi's Studio
d'Archittetura Civile.

390 (above right)
The centrepiece of the
north front. The surround
to the first-floor
window derives from
the engraving in Fig. 390.

391 (right) A painting,
dated 1731, showing the
north forecourt flanked
by two blocks which
have disappeared.

392 (opposite) The
south front.

sketch for his new house. As it happens, Dr Eileen Harris recently discovered in a *Builder's Dictionary* of 1730 a marginal note that Beningbrough was designed by Thornton. William Thornton was a York joiner who had made wainscoting at Castle Howard and was to restore the north transept of Beverley Minster in 1716–20. Mr Geoffrey Beard[1] has, more recently still, established that Thornton also worked as a carpenter at Stainborough. In a letter to his employer, Lord Strafford, of 22 March 1714 about glazing bars, amongst other matters, Thornton reminds him that their thickness 'is ye same thickness I have done for Mr Bourchier[2] and others wch hath proved to turn well better than those of thinner stuff'. This extract certainly suggests that he at least made the superlative joinery at Beningbrough, even if he was not solely responsible for the overall design of the house.

A short, straight approach brings us to the north front (Fig. 388). At a glance the eye takes in the periphery of the house, a compact rectangle, connected on this front to a pair of square pavilions by right-angled screen walls built of brick in recesses and projections, and set with niches. The niches and the arches of the pavilions provide the only movement in what is otherwise a curiously static composition, as far from Vanbrugh's lively style as could be imagined. There is no doubt that something seems lacking in this stiff, prim front. If however the painting

[1] *Georgian Craftsmen*, 1966.
[2] Thornton's sashbars were replaced in late Georgian times by ones 'of thinner stuff'.

(Fig. 391), dated 1731, of Beningbrough is a faithful record of what originally existed, then the central raised parapet carrying four jolly figures, and the additional service blocks facing each other across the forecourt, must have considerably relieved the tension which now exists without them. The scarcely perceptible forward break of the wings and the rather more pronounced projection of the centrepiece are emphasized by strips of dressed stones, alternately raised and recessed. The south garden front (Fig. 392), by contrast, has single-bay projections at either end only. The walls are of hard, claret, crusted bricks, finely pointed.

For all its apparent simplicity the exterior of Beningbrough has some very unconventional details. The cornice is supported by pairs of massive console brackets made of wood. They are scaled and scalloped and terminate in dentils of the Doric order. These features appear singly on the front of Archer's Heythrop Hall and in the nave of his St Paul's church at Deptford. In the wide spaces between the pairs of consoles here attic windows are cut into the frieze, as on the north-east front of Heythrop. A sketch (Fig. 393), c. 1720, of part of the south front shows all these features exactly as they are today.

The front door (Fig. 390) is entered from splayed steps with Tijou-like balustrades of wrought iron. The porch is of the Doric order and bears on its cornice a pair of emergent horses and drapery carved in stone. The curiously Prussian device flanks the Bourchier cipher and knot (to which this bastard branch of the family had, strictly

393 (above) A drawing by Samuel Buck, c. 1720, of the east end of the south front and part of the gardens.

394 (above right) The Great Staircase Hall to the west of the Great Hall, as it was in 1927.

speaking, no heraldic right) on a cartouche. The high quality of the carving on this portal is matched by that of the south. The way the escutcheon has been allowed to overlap the keystone of the south portal corresponds with the treatment of the principal window-heads at Wentworth Castle. Over the north door is another very unconventional feature in the form of a central window with ears and scalloped keystones. Mr Whiffen has observed that this window was filched straight from Bernini's Palazzo Chigi (now Odeschalchi) in Rome, illustrated in Rossi's *Studio d'Architettura Civile*, vol. I, published in 1702 (Fig. 389). The same window had been adapted by Archer on the north-west front of Heythrop (begun 1705); and earlier still (at latest in 1703) by Talman on a revised front for Welbeck Abbey.

The carving of the stonework without and the woodwork within constitutes the outstanding excellence of Beningbrough. There is evidence of amateurishness in the planning of the house, as though Thornton was carrying out a scheme beyond his architectural capacities, splendid craftsman though he was. If the door from the Hall to the Dining Room is open it can be seen that the axis from

north to south portal is slightly off centre, and the juxtaposition of these two rooms is awkwardly managed. The Hall is in fact the only ground-floor room with any justifiable claim to the prefix 'state', which is also limited on the first floor to the gallery. All the other rooms in this large house are smallish, and generally high in relation to their length and breadth.

The front door opens straight into the Hall (Fig. 396) which occupies two storeys. Corinthian pilasters on high plinths support a very individual form of groined cove, found also at nearby Gilling Castle (Fig. 438) and formerly at Oulton Park, Cheshire. At Beningbrough plaster decoration is used economically, but effectively; the sharp ribs of the vaulting are slightly raised from the plaster ground and trimmed with a ribbon and flower moulding. The round-headed doorways have elaborately carved keystones which do a double duty in supporting large wall panels that look like mural tablets in a church, and the recessed door-heads are given extraordinary box-like superstructures, more Mannerist than Baroque. The portrait over the fireplace is by Jonathan Richardson of Philip, 4th Earl of Chesterfield, resplendent in brown velvet coat and blue Garter sash.

A door at the south-east corner of the Hall leads down one length of the great cross-corridor to the so-called State Bedroom and two attendant State Dressing Rooms, all of which face south. The corner Dressing Room (like its fellow at the opposite corner of the south front) has a

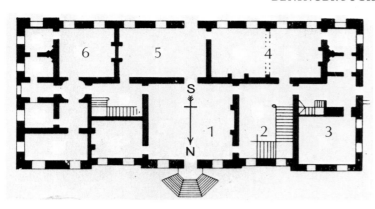

395 *Plan of the ground floor*

1 Great Hall
2 Great Staircase
3 Study
4 Drawing Room
5 Dining Room
6 State Bedroom

396 *The Great Hall.*

397 (above left) The initials and coat-of-arms of John and Mary Bourchier; inlaid parquetry on the main staircase.

398 (above top) The corridor on the first floor. The vista is interrupted by the balcony which overlooks the Great Hall (see Fig. 396).

399 (left) The crimson damask state bed of c. 1710, formerly at Holme Lacy.

400 (above) Detail of the carved cornice in the State Bedroom.

401 & 402 *The corner chimney-pieces in the Green Silk Dressing Room and the State Dressing Room.*

domed ceiling and pine panelling with acanthus frieze. In both dressing rooms the chimney-pieces (Figs. 401 and 402) are set cornerwise in the manner introduced by Wren at Kensington Palace and Hampton Court, and stepped with ledges for the display of blue and white delftware. These chimney-pieces appear in several of the closets at Beningbrough and no one exactly resembles another. Some of the fireplace surrounds are in grey-veined polished marble of bolection mould; others in a white-veined marble with flat surface.

The chimney-piece of the State Bedroom is, however, set in the middle of one wall. The overmantel and raised overframe are carved with truly amazing virtuosity and delicacy, which put Thornton and his men high in the tradition established by Grinling Gibbons. In the surrounds of the doors the cavetto mould (Fig. 35) contains leaves which curl round upon themselves with convincing naturalness. The frames, too, of the overdoor portraits of now-forgotten Bourchiers are carved with sunflowers and other blooms. Above the bolection-moulded wall panels the entablature has a distinctive frieze (Fig. 400) in which, between sprays of acanthus, carved masks are encircled by foliage and drapery. The very handsome William and Mary state bed (Fig. 399), upholstered in crimson and with fringed valances, came from Holme Lacy, having been made for the 2nd Viscount Scudamore, whose coronet is worked on the bedhead.

The Dining Room is by contrast correctly Palladian. It has simple bolection panels and a rich but straightforward

cornice. Not so the next apartment on the south front. What was formerly two apartments is now the Great Drawing Room (Fig. 403). In both sections the carved work reaches a crescendo of excellence. The decoration of each is widely different, and it is a tragedy that the dividing wall was ever taken down. The result may be a decent-sized room for entertainment, but it has meant a clashing of harmonies.

Of the two Drawing Room sections the western has the more extraordinary entablature (Fig. 404). The frieze consists of a series of rising plinths (a device found at Gilling Castle) which support projecting portions of the lower member of the cornice. Interspersed in the frieze are acanthus, palm and shell scrolls, bearing ciphers and vases. The interlaced carving, which forms a canopy with swags in the overmantel, is no less minutely undercut and the overdoor portraits are framed in the same sumptuous style (Fig. 405). We find birds, shells, fruits, flowers, baskets and tasselled valances among the objects represented. The eastern section has for entablature the same theme as the roof entablature outside the house, that is to say pairs of carved consoles which uphold projecting parts of the cornice. These paired consoles are likewise found indoors at Wentworth Castle. The acanthus carving on the scrolls is as meticulous and crisp as elsewhere and the whole effect is immensely rich and pleasing.

Whereas Vanbrugh at Castle Howard and Grimsthorpe provided an identical pair of stairwells, corresponding with the length of the halls they flanked, the builder of

403 *The west end of the*
Drawing Room.

Beningbrough evolved a different arrangement. To the east of his hall a fairly modest staircase occupies a small space without windows, but top-lit; to the west a more ambitious ascent fills a very much larger space (Fig. 394). Instead of stone for steps and iron for handrail, here the material is wholly wood. Like the rest of Thornton's wainscot at Beningbrough the main staircase is of superlative craftsmanship. The steps are nicely poised one upon another, the undersurfaces being panelled in deeply carved moulds. The treads are parquetried and on the landing different veneers indicate John and Mary Bourchier's arms, initials, knots and date, to which I have already referred. Most remarkable of all, the balustrade simulates metal in the slim uprights and perforated panels, which in the photograph might easily be mistaken for the wrought ironwork of Tijou.

The long upstairs corridor (Fig. 398) provides from end

to end a dramatic vista, through arches with splayed jambs, and across two iron balconies overlooking the Hall. To get round the Hall on the first floor it is necessary to pass through the Gallery, not a highly convenient arrangement. This apartment has five windows facing south and has similar Palladian decoration to that of the Dining Room, with the addition of fluted Corinthian pilasters forming bays.

In 1768 Beningbrough passed to the last of the Bourchiers, Margaret, wife of Giles Earle. She left it in 1827 to a friend of her deceased son, the Rev. and Hon. W. H. Dawnay, who in 1833 became the 6th Viscount Downe. In 1917 it was bought by the widow of the 1st Lord Nunburnholme for her son-in-law and daughter, the 10th Earl and Countess of Chesterfield. On the death of Lady Chesterfield in 1957 the house was transferred by the Treasury to the National Trust.

404 (above) The entablature and part of the picture-frame over the west wall of the Drawing Room.

405 A carved overdoor in the Drawing Room.

SHOTOVER PARK, OXFORDSHIRE

Shotover came to the Tyrrell family in 1519. The present house was built for James Tyrrell in 1713–18. His son General James Tyrrell completed the decoration and laid out the grounds. House and Gothic lodge were probably carried out by William Townesend. (The seat of Major A. A. Miller.)

406 *The obelisk, designed by Kent, placed on the axis of the west front.*

'It is within four miles of Oxford, a magnificent place, an elegant stone house, which stands in the centre of very fine gardens, . . . straight avenues terminated by obelisks, temples, porticoes, etc; it has an air of grandeur.' This is how Mrs Lybbe Powys wrote about Shotover in 1769; the description applies equally well today. The house, rather more 'magnificent' now than then on account of the wings added in 1855 at either side, the formal landscape and all the embellishments observed two hundred years ago survive intact.

We do not know for certain what architect was responsible for the house; we only know who was not. When Avray Tipping was writing in 1928[1] he jumped to the conclusion that it was Vanbrugh on the strength of a visit which Sir John paid to Shotover in 1725. But in the course of his journeys Vanbrugh frequently looked at houses which he was not building. Besides by 1725 Shotover was finished. Also the style evinces nothing of the heroic flamboyance which we associate with that unequivocal hand. The west (Fig. 406) and east elevations—Haseley stone has been used throughout—could hardly look less like those of neighbouring Blenheim, which was rearing its immense bulk contemporaneously. They are staid and static, each consisting of seven bays of two storeys and an attic floor over a well-accented cornice. A hipped roof just peers over the parapet. The east front (Fig. 407) is redeemed from dullness by being constructed upon an open arcade, or loggia, owing to the fall of the ground on this side. The arcades are treated in horizontal rustication, as are the quoins which form pilaster strips at the angles. It is the loggia which has provided the hint as to who the architect may have been.

But first of all the client. James Tyrrell of Oakley in Buckinghamshire inherited Shotover in 1701 when he was forty-eight years old. The property had passed to his Tyrrell forebears through marriage in 1519. James, who was a doctrinaire Whig and a bit of a pedant, had an only son also christened James, a soldier and subsequently a general who fought in Marlborough's campaigns. It appears that the father, a retiring and diffident man, delayed rebuilding his Oxfordshire home until the safe return of his son from the wars. This puts the start of the new Shotover soon after the Treaty of Utrecht in 1713. The date 1718 on a rainwater head marks the finish of the structure. It also records the year in which the father died. Thereupon the General completed the decoration of the house and the layout of the grounds. We learn this from the Latin epitaph on his monument in Oakley church, a translation of part of which runs thus: 'Lest after the hardships of war his leisure should be misspent, this remarkable lover and cultivator of all elegant things pressed on with the completion of his house and gardens at Shotover.' The General had until 1742, time in which to devote his energies to this laudable end. An engraving (Fig. 408) of *c.* 1750 shows what his father and he had achieved.

[1] *English Homes*, Period IV, vol. II, *Sir John Vanbrugh and His School.*

Although gardens are not the concern of this volume it is virtually impossible, and unprofitable, to divorce the house at Shotover from its surroundings. Without the layout the house loses its *raison-d'être*. Frankly, it is not important enough on its own to merit more than a passing reference, but taken together the two make an historic and stylistic whole.

For all we know James Tyrrell may have begun work on the gardens before the house. There are no records of whom he consulted, if indeed he did call upon a professional adviser at all. It is much more likely that father and son went their own sweet way. At all events two focal orna-ments were added by the son. In the middle of the west arm of the long, straight axis the Obelisk (Fig. 406) was, according to Isaac Ware,[1] designed by William Kent. So, too, was the domed octagonal temple (Fig. 412) set on a mound to the south of the Wilderness Garden, so as to command radiating vistas. Both probably date from 1738–40 when Kent was establishing the garden of another retired Oxfordshire soldier, General James Dormer of Rousham. At the extreme east end of the axis the

[1] *Designs of Inigo Jones and Others*, 1743.

407 *The east front with the canal in the foreground.*

408 (above) A bird's-eye view from the east showing the Gothic Lodge, the canal and the house; an engraving of c. 1750.

409 (above right) The view from the house to the Gothic Lodge.

410 (right) The facade of the Gothic Lodge.

411 (above) The vaulting inside the Gothic Lodge.

412 The octagonal temple, designed by Kent 1738–40.

Gothic Lodge (Fig. 410) was doubtless designed by the architect of the house, and so will be of earlier date. This is suggested by the similarity of its vaulting (Fig. 411) to that of the east loggia.

James Tyrrell senior had matriculated from Queen's College, Oxford which between 1693 and 1720 was being rebuilt in a very big way. Nicholas Hawksmoor was the principal architect, but after 1709 William Townesend was in charge and probably designed the front quadrangle, hall and chapel. He certainly decorated the two last to his own designs. Mr W. G. Hiscock[1] has seen in the flattened vault arches, the wide plaster ribs and in the floral ornaments of the arcaded loggia (Fig. 413) at Shotover an extension of Townesend's style in the Hall and Chapel of Queen's College. Furthermore the horizontal rustication and the block-like imposts make the arcades at Shotover identical with those below the library of that college.

William Townesend had in the later part of Queen Anne's reign risen from the status of master-mason to that of an architect in wide demand. Thomas Hearne, the antiquary, declared in 1720 that he 'hath a hand in all the buildings of Oxford, and gets a vast deal of money that way', and not only buildings in Oxford city but the neighbourhood as well. It is very probable that his services would be enlisted by an old Queen's man living a mere

[1] 'William Townesend', *Architectural Review*, Oct. 1945.

413 *(opposite above)*
Inside the loggia on the east
side of the house.

414 *(opposite below) The*
Doric Entrance Hall.

415 *(left) The*
chimney-piece and carved
overmantel in the Saloon.

four miles from the university. Moreover there are details
in the interior of Shotover which we would expect from a
provincial follower of Hawksmoor, and not from the master
himself. Of such are, in the Doric Entrance Hall (Fig. 414),
the unorthodox introduction of the Tyrrell crest in the
frieze, and the daring but uncouth chimney-piece with
outsize shell in the cleft pediment. The chimney-piece has
its counterpart in Queen's College hall, only without the
robust swags suspended from a helmet, all in plaster, in the
overmantel. Another unorthodox, but not unsuccessful,
touch is the screen of which the columns have their plinths
on the steps. These four steps lead to a Saloon (Fig. 415).
In this room the oak wainscoting and carved gilt cornice
are not unusual; nor are the carved wood swags of the
overmantel in the style of Gibbons.

As for the Gothic Lodge (Fig. 410) Mr Tipping was the
first to observe a likeness in its miniature twin turrets to
that pair of towers which Hawksmoor conceived and

Townesend certainly gave to the north quadrangle of
All Souls College in 1716—a likeness all the more perceptible when its finials, shown in the engravings, were
still in place. It was a picturesque notion to make this little
fantasy face the big house down the two long canals,
flanked by a double row of oaks, elms and Spanish chest-
nuts (Fig. 409). Like the classical house the Gothic Lodge
was surely contrived 'by that ingenious artist of a mason
Mr Townesend of Oxford', as a contemporary described
him.

General Tyrrell never married. He left Shotover to
his cousin Penelope Madan, wife of Augustus Schutz, a
second cousin of George II. Schutz continued to improve
the gardens, 'every year making openings', to quote
Mrs Powys again, 'to an extensive country before altogether excluded'. Shotover remained in the Schutz family
until 1839. In 1870 it was bought by Lieutenant-Colonel
James Miller, the grandfather of the present owner.

NOTES ON THE PRINCIPAL BAROQUE HOUSES

This list comprises country houses of the period **1685–1715**—with only a few of earlier and several of later date—which have not been described in the main text. Some have been mentioned in the Introduction. The abbreviation *C.L.* with date refers to the *Country Life* article or, if there have been more than one, the first of the series of articles on the houses listed below. In the case of those houses which have not been written up in *Country Life* I have given some other available reference, wherever possible.

The list makes no claim to be exhaustive.

Acton Round Hall, Shropshire

In a remote, secluded corner of the county. Built *c.* 1695 as a dower house for the Actons of Aldenham Park. Pevsner calls it 'a very fine, noble and restrained design'. Indeed it is almost the perfect specimen of a William and Mary manor house. Of red brick, with perpendicular stone strips. Elliptical doorway of stone. Eaves, cornice and carved brackets of wood. Hipped slate roof; dormers and four symmetrically set chimney-stacks. A vertical window in the pediment.

Plan simple and straightforward. Two large rooms addorsed with central doors on the axis. A transverse passage and staircase of two long flights in the middle of the south end. Panelled rooms and oak floors, except those of the attic floor which are of gypsum. Two bedroom fireplaces have wooden surrounds lacquered in Chinese vignettes.

N. Pevsner—*Buildings of England, Shropshire*, 1958.

Addiscombe House, Surrey

(demolished *c.* 1861)

Built 1702–3 for William Draper, son-in-law to John Evelyn whom he succeeded as Treasurer of the Commission for Greenwich Hospital. The mason, and in Kerry Downes's opinion the designer, was Edward Strong, who worked on Hawksmoor's King William block at Greenwich Hospital. Untutored resemblances to the east side of the block are apparent in the attenuated Ionic pilasters and portico columns, embracing three storeys. The Greenwich treatment has become eccentric in a country house. Comparison with Cound Hall, Shropshire, is called for.

John Evelyn on 11 July 1703 praised Addiscombe in his *Diary*: 'The outsides to the covering being so excellent brickwork, based with Portland stone . . . that I pronounce it, in all the points of good and solid architecture, to be one of the very best gent: houses in Surry, when finished.'

Saloon and staircase had Bacchic decorations by Thornhill.

Kerry Downes—*English Baroque Architecture*, 1966.

Aldby Park, North Riding, Yorkshire

Although dated 1726 the house shows traces of Vanbrugh influence. Built for the Darley family, possibly by William Etty of York. Compact, rectangular; of brick, with three-bay stone frontispiece on each long front. The round arched windows and naturalistic carving of pediment and frieze—pheasant and foxes—are reminiscent of Wentworth Castle and Wentworth Woodhouse.

Entrance Hall chimney-piece and Breakfast Room Doric frieze both Vanbrughian. The Staircase was inserted in 1840 when two wings (demolished 1951) were added. *C.L.*, 9 Nov. 1935.

Alveston House, Warwickshire

Built 1689 for Thomas Peers, whose descendants owned it until 1803. The ideal of the smaller William and Mary house. Set on the river Avon. Red brick diapered with flared headers; stone quoins and keystones. Hipped roof with dormers, and modillioned eaves like a wide-awake hat brim.

Rusticated brick frame to central window of south front. Fluted Doric porch of west front *c.* 1750. *C.L.*, 25 May 1945.

Ampthill Park, Bedfordshire

On the advice of Lord Nottingham of Burley-on-the-Hill his friend, Lord Ashburnham engaged John Lumley of Northampton to design Ampthill Park. Built 1704–7 in red brick and blue glazed headers. A two-storey, eleven-bay front. Basement and dormered attic. A perron with wrought-iron balustrade, possibly by Tijou, leads to a Tuscan doorway with swan-neck pediment. The three-bay centre is dominated by a pediment displaying the arms of the Earl of Upper Ossory (mid eighteenth century).

Three-bay corridors connect the centre block—which bears little resemblance to Burley-on-the-Hill—with pavilions projecting at right angles. William Winde was consulted 1706–7. Edward Chapman provided five marble chimney-pieces in 1699.

William Chambers made alterations 1769–71. J. P. Neale—*Seats*, vol. VI, 1st series, 1823. Victoria County History, *Bedfordshire*, vol. III, 1912.

Antony House, Cornwall

On the northernmost tip of a wooded peninsula in Plymouth Sound. Inherited by the Carews through marriage with a Courtenay heiress in the fifteenth century, and the property of Cornwall's well known chronicler, Richard Carew (d. 1620). Still the home of his descendant, Sir John Carew Pole, 12th Baronet.

The present house was built between 1710 and 1721 for Sir William Carew, 5th Baronet. The names of James Gibbs and Thomas Edwards have been suggested as architect. John Moyle was master-mason throughout.

For its date the house is old-fashioned, neither Palladian without nor Baroque within, but pertaining to the Wren tradition of two generations back. It consists of an austere two-storey block (double pile) of silvery Pentewen stone (*porte-cochère* nineteenth century), hipped slate roof and dormers. Narrow windows without entablatures; minimum adornment.

Long arcaded corridors are at right angles to front of house with seven-bay pavilions raised upon them, all in

416 *(left) Aldby Park, Yorkshire, 1726.*

417 *(below) Ampthill Park, Bedfordshire, by John Lumley, 1704–7. Neale's View.*

418 *(bottom) Antony House, Cornwall, 1710–21. The south front.*

glowing red brick. At the corners of the forecourt little lead cupolas. Below the north front are long brick terraces, and on the west side massive clipped yew hedges.

Nearly every room panelled in oak, and containing much fine contemporary furniture and many family portraits. Staircase in two long flights.

C.L., 19 Aug. 1933.

Appuldurcombe House, Isle of Wight

Brought to the Worsleys after the Dissolution by marriage with a daughter of the Leigh family. The present house, now carefully preserved as a ruin, was built for Sir Robert Worsley, 4th Baronet.

L. O. J. Boynton (Ministry of Works guidebook, 1967) has revealed that Appuldurcombe was begun in 1701, and the architect was John James, with William Reynolds, Joseph and James Clarke and John Davis as masons.

Exterior noted for the green and silvery texture of the stone, and crispness of the carving. The main east front is much the same as when *Vitruvius Britannicus* published a plate, 1725. Pediment over front door has been replaced by a straight entablature; urns and statues on skyline have given way to a balustrade.

Corinthian giant order imposed upon French horizontal rustication, of centre block and deeply advanced wings alike. The wings have pediments like the Charles II block at Greenwich, and on the return sides are given niches for windows. The pairs of chimney-stacks coupled by arches are typical of James. The attic storey over main entablature and wide central bay point to the influence of Thoresby House. Were the wings later additions by James?

Sir Richard Worsley, 7th Baronet, completed the house after 1772, probably calling in James Wyatt, but none of his rooms has survived. On Sir Richard's death in 1805 the house passed to the Earls of Yarborough until 1855. From 1909 it was unoccupied, slowly deteriorating until acquired by the Ministry of Works in 1952.

C.L., 19 Nov. 1932.

Aspley Guise House, Bedfordshire

Circa 1695. Of seven bays and two storeys, with hipped roof and dormers. Red brick and modillion cornice of wood. The three-bay centre projects and has an eye-window within the pediment. Front door with broken pediment.

Curiously muddled garden front, the centrepiece being a chimney-breast containing two Venetian windows. The cornice is raked sharply up to the chimney in an acute angle. Staircase with twisted balusters.

A. E. Richardson—*Smaller Houses of the Renaissance*, 1925.

Audley End, Essex

In 1721–2 the 7th Earl of Suffolk began demolishing two-thirds of what was the greatest and grandest Jacobean palace in England. Vanbrugh was certainly associated with this sorry business. No less unsavoury had been his intrigue with the 6th Earl, acting Earl Marshal, to get the office of Garter King of Arms.

Vanbrugh's constructive work at Audley End amounted

419 *Audley End, Essex. Vanbrugh's staircase and screen, c. 1718.*

to the staircase and stone screen in two tiers of arcades at the south end of the Great Hall. Stone steps with wrought-iron balusters (ciphers and coronets) rise through Doric arches in two straight flights to a landing. There are echoes here of Blenheim and Grimsthorpe staircases. Date of this work *c.* 1718.

C.L., 19 June 1926.

Aylsham Old Hall, Norfolk

Dated on a chimney 1689 and unaltered. Red brick of seven bays. Projecting wings. Quoins of rubbed red brick. The roof is pantiled over a wooden block cornice. Sash windows except for casements on the north side.

Doorway with Ionic pilasters and broad segmental pediment leads into a transverse hall. Behind is the staircase with sturdy twisted balusters.

In the grounds are a small rectangular canal and a barn with curvilinear gable. A straight oak avenue across the road is axial with the front door.

N. Pevsner—*Buildings of England, Norfolk*, 1952.

Aynhoe Park, Northamptonshire

The Cartwright family owned Aynhoe from the early seventeenth century until the 1950s. A drawing of 1683 shows how the south front built by Edward Marshall after 1660 has since been altered by Thomas Archer (1707–11) and again by Sir John Soane (1800–5).

On the south front Archer added to Marshall's block the top storey and pediment and the Tuscan entrance. He also

420 & 421 *Aynhoe Park, Northamptonshire. Archer's east flanking wing and its Borrominesque central feature, 1707–11.*

added the seven-bay library and orangery wings with window arches resting directly on pilasters. The involuted scrolls of the capitals are typical of Archer's Borrominesque touch. Soane put the upper storey on the wings.

Archer's contribution to the gloomy stucco north front is the detached office and stable blocks forming the forecourt. They are conventional enough except for the central door of each, which is distinctly bizarre. The moulding is continuous from surround into arch, with only a small block where the impost should be. The doorway is framed by tapering canted pilasters carrying a concave entablature.

Little of Archer remains indoors. The Entrance Hall screen of Doric columns is his. So, too, is the Staircase, the treads marquetried and the tread ends carved.
C.L., 2 July 1953.

Ayot St Lawrence Place, Hertfordshire
Queen Anne with segmental headed windows, vertical strips and rubbed brick dressings. Three storeys, the middle bay slightly advanced. Pine staircase and bolection-mould panelling. Additions *c.* 1850 and 1933. Stables with cupola and verandah of thin, polygonal timber posts.
N. Pevsner—*Buildings of England, Hertfordshire*, 1953.

Barham Court, Kent
Like Bourne Park and Goodnestone Park, Barham Court is distinguished by a long front with five-bay projecting centre under a wide pediment. In this case the pediment contains one vertical and two circular windows. Hipped

roof and dormers. Built presumably in Queen Anne's reign by the Fotherbyes, from whom it passed in George I's reign to the Derings. Fine contemporary staircase.

North entrance and north-east wing added by Sir Edwin Lutyens *c.* 1913.
C.L., 8 Feb. 1919.

Baylis House, Slough, Buckinghamshire
For Dean Hascard of Windsor *c.* 1695. Red brick and orange brick pilaster strips. Simple entrance and garden fronts, with slight central projection of three bays under a pediment. Recessed blind lunettes over ground-floor windows, and blind parapet panels.

Alterations in 1725–6 for Dr Godolphin, Provost of Eton, by Thomas Rowland, and 1733–5 for the Provost's son by John James. The stables with lantern and clock dated 1735 are by James; also the quadrant wall linking them to the house. The forecourt pavilions with pyramidal roofs are perhaps late Georgian. Wrought-iron gates incorporate Godolphin dolphin.
Victoria County History—*Buckinghamshire*, vol. III, 1925.
N. Pevsner—*Buildings of England, Buckinghamshire*, 1960.

Beechwood Park, Hertfordshire
Inherited 1693 by Sir Edward Sebright, 3rd Baronet, who added extensively to an older house. The principal range is rectangular of vitrified purple and mellow red brick; two storeys and central pediment contain a cartouche of Sir Edward's arms and supporting putti, all in lead.

422 *Beechwood Park, Hertfordshire, c. 1702.*

Dentilled eaves cornice and hipped roof with dormers. Quoins small in scale. The rainwater heads are dated 1702.

Stone paved hall and, reached through three arches, an inner hall and staircase. The oak stairs rise into a long gallery overlooking a courtyard enclosed in 1859. Oak dado and cornice of acanthus foliage. 1740 decoration in hall and drawing room. Library wing added by Roger Morris.

The house last inhabited by Sir Giles Sebright, 13th Baronet, who died in 1954.

C.L., 12 Nov. 1938.

Belgrave Hall, Leicester

A small red and dark blue brick house, once the home of the Hastings family, now a well-arranged museum. Entrance front with flat roof-line and deeply recessed centre. Garden front with three pointed gables. Stalwart lead hopper heads dated 1709 and 1711. Iron railings and gates to the front. Narrow pedimented doorways.

From a spacious hall, the length of the house, a staircase rises to a wide first-floor landing; and thence from the opposite wall to the second floor.

N. Pevsner—*Buildings of England, Leicestershire*, 1960.

Biddick Hall, Durham

Probably built in 1721–3 for Freville Lambton the younger. Now the home of Viscount Lambton, M.P. A box-like structure of red brick with, on the south front, five closely packed bays. The central bay is contained within a narrowly vertical feature of fluted Ionic pilasters carrying a pediment. Like the window-surrounds and quoins it is of white painted stone. Urns adorn the blind parapet. Staircase with iron balusters of anthemion pattern. Ceiling of the stairwell in Baroque volutes may be by the Italian plasterer who worked at Lumley Castle. At the rear, extensions of 1954–5.

C.L., 28 April 1966.

Bishopsworth Manor House, Somerset

Circa 1730. A local craftsman's reaction to Kings Weston in that he has crowned the small mansard roof with twelve arcaded chimneys, four on each side. The front door and window above have segmental heads. Contrast of white stone with yellow stone dressings.

Kerry Downes—*English Baroque Architecture* 1966.

Bourne Park, Kent

In the valley of the Little Stour the luxuriant park landscape was laid out by W. A. Nesfield in 1848. The house was built in 1701 by Dame Elizabeth Aucher during the minority of her son, Sir Hewitt Aucher. In 1841 it was bought by Matthew Bell and in 1927 by Sir John Prestige.

Two long fronts of thirteen bays are only slightly broken forward in five central bays under an unusually wide pediment. The pediment contains three windows arranged in Venetian fashion. Hipped roof and dormers.

The front door opens into one end of the hall which has a fireplace in Bethesden marble.

In 1848 the interior was much altered by John Shaw. Staircase with balustrade of fluted columns, and ceiling of heavy stucco compartments are contemporary. So too is the Morning Room ceiling.

Horace Walpole's friend Sir Horace Mann rented Bourne at the end of the eighteenth century.

C.L., 6 May 1922.

Bourton House, Bourton-on-the-Hill, Gloucestershire

Bought by Alexander Popham in 1680. Built probably in Queen Anne's reign on the base of a late sixteenth-century house (the splendid barn is dated 1570). Of Cotswold stone.

A rectangular plan made unusual by deep projections at all four angles. The tower-like wings are of one bay each. Entrance and garden fronts have three-bay centres within giant Ionic pilasters supporting a pediment. The blank parapet is broken forward over the wings. Dormers lie half hidden behind the parapet. Two pairs of panelled chimney-stacks over each side elevation.

Hall and staircase—two fluted balusters to the tread—and several panelled rooms.

Purchased 1851 by Sir James Buller East.

C.L., 23 March 1940.

Bradbourne, Kent

Many people's ideal of a Queen Anne country house. Bradbourne was completely remodelled in 1713–15 by Sir Thomas Twisden, 3rd Baronet, grandson of Sir Thomas Twisden, Kt, who bought the property *c.* 1656. Architect unknown, but probably from Maidstone. He certainly was a master of brickwork.

West and south fronts are the showpieces. The walls are of stock brick, but of varying shades, red, mauve, buff, pink and even green. The dressings of windows and pilaster strips are of scarlet rubbed brick. *Oeil-de-bœuf* windows appear in the west pediment and in pairs on the wings of the south front. The south central bow added in 1774. A ceiling and some chimney-pieces are of this date. But the Queen Anne staircase, the upper flight 'flying' and the undertreads richly carved, is of superb joinery.

On the death of the 12th and last Baronet, Sir Thomas R. Twisden, in 1937 Bradbourne was sold to the East Malling Research Station.

C.L., 6 April 1967.

423 *(above left) Belgrave Hall, Leicester, 1709–11.*

424 *(above) Bradbourne, Kent. The carved and moulded soffit of the oak staircase.*

425 *(left) Bradbourne, 1713–15.*

426 *Britwell Court, Oxfordshire, c. 1728. The Doric Hall as it was in 1927.*

Britwell Court, Oxfordshire

Avray Tipping associated Vanbrugh with this house built *c.* 1728. But a more likely architect is William Townesend of Oxford, who probably designed Shotover, Woodperry and Haseley, all nearby Oxfordshire houses.

The Doric hall has a robust chimney-piece with scrolled pediment, containing a socle which bears a vase of flowers. The fanciful design and the vigorous carving call to mind the chimney-piece at Shotover.

In the grounds are an Ionic shaft bearing an urn, and a hexagonal obelisk bearing a pine-cone.

Bruern Abbey, Oxfordshire

Built on the site, if not out of the ruins, of a Cistercian abbey, for the Cope family *c.* 1710–20. Of this date only the high and narrow south front survives. It is of two tall storeys under a balustrade. A massive pediment containing an eye-window spreads across the three-bay centre. The heavily banded angle strips, keys of the windows rising into oblong panels, and central doorway of the Doric order have a distinctly Vanbrughian character. Was William Townesend the designer? Inside, nothing of the period survived a serious fire of 1780.

Buckingham House, St James's, London

(destroyed 1825)

An extremely important Baroque prototype, ascribed to William Winde, but possibly designed by Talman. Built 1703–5 for John Sheffield, 1st Duke of Buckingham and Normanby, with whom, amongst other clients, Talman, according to Vanbrugh, quarrelled.

A nine-bay front of two storeys, basement and attic in brick with stone dressings. The centrepiece was contained within a giant tetrastyle order. Attic windows were contained between the entablature and a parapet with figures. The skyline was flat. Quadrant arcades linked the centre block to a pair of pavilions facing each other and forming a large forecourt. The entrance was approached by stone steps. Central hall separated from stairwell on the left by a screen of columns (cf. Thoresby and Fetcham by Talman, and Hanbury Hall). Laguerre decorated hall and staircase in 1706.

The Buckingham House formula was repeated at Wotton House near Aylesbury, Waldershare Park, Cottesbrooke Hall and elsewhere.

C.L., 12 July 1962.

Buntingsdale, Shropshire

Acquired by the Mackworth family in 1501. Built in 1721 for Bulkeley Mackworth by Francis Smith, who stipulated to be allowed 'a pad nag to ride hither from Warwick'. The Mackworths sold house and property to their cousins, the Tayleurs, in 1733.

Material brick and pink and yellow sandstone, crisper than that used for Mawley Hall. West and east fronts almost identical, but east has two additional unfluted Composite pilasters. The four giant fluted pilasters carrying a continuous entablature, only broken below the three-bay pediment, are the distinguishing feature of each front. Principal windows have segmental heads. The attic storey above the cornice has on the east front single-bay pediments at the angles. The south end has a central bow throughout all floors. Balustrades crown the skyline. North wing added 1857 by — Smith of Shrewsbury.

Front door leads straight into the two-storeyed hall. It has a balustraded gallery (cf. Ombersley Court by Smith). Since the house was sold by the Tayleurs in 1923 many alterations have taken place.

C.L., 3 Nov. 1917.

427 *Buntingsdale, Shropshire. By Francis Smith, 1721.*

Buscot Old Parsonage, Berkshire

Of its date, *c.* 1700, one of the most desirable small houses about which little more can be said. It is rectangular, five by three bays, compact and high; of limestone and its hipped roof stone tiled. The windows have thick sashbars. The stairs and small panelled rooms are of contemporary wainscot. There is an enclosed wall garden with gazebos.

Calke Abbey, Derbyshire

In 1621 the Augustinian Calke Abbey was bought by Henry Harpur. It was rebuilt round an irregular court for Sir Henry Harpur, Bart, in 1703 (embossed on rainwater heads), a very early date for the type of house. South front of three storeys; a seven-bay centre and projecting wings of three bays. Giant order of (originally) fluted Corinthian pilasters at the angles and the flanks of the three centre bays. In late Georgian times the exterior was somewhat altered, and a portico took the place of stairs by Gibbs.

Kerry Downes believes Calke to be Francis Smith's first house. Talman's influence is fairly clear.

The Entrance Hall on the *piano nobile* takes up two storeys. The Saloon has Corinthian pilasters.

Calke passed to the daughter of Sir Vauncey Harpur Crewe, 10th and last Baronet, who was the mother of the present owner.

Cannons Park, Middlesex

(demolished 1747)

This short-lived palace was the acme of refined taste and splendour. Innumerable artists were enlisted. In 1713 James Brydges, afterwards Duke of Chandos, appointed William Talman architect. Within a year Talman proved intractable and was replaced by John James. In 1716 James was replaced by James Gibbs, who may have been responsible for the final look of the south and east fronts. On the other hand the credit may belong to John Price. His engravings of 1720 show the fronts rusticated, the centres brought forward in engaged hexastyle porticoes (Ionic), with an attic floor above the cornice.

Work inside and in the grounds proceeded until 1725. In 1744 the Duke died, and in 1747 the whole place was sold and demolished.

Among decorative painters Bellucci, Thornhill, Laguerre, Sleter, Grisoni and Kent were employed. Panels by the first are now in Great Witley church, Worcestershire. Among leading *stuccatori* employed was Bagutti; among master-masons Edward Strong, junior; and landscape gardeners George London. Pepusch and Handel were the Duke's private organists.

C. H. Collins and M. I. Baker—*James Brydges, Duke of Chandos,* 1949.

428 *(below) Calke Abbey, Derbyshire, 1703. An early 18th-century painting of the house before alteration.*

429 *(left) Cannons Park, Middlesex, 1713–20.*

430 *Cliveden House, Buckinghamshire (rebuilt).*

Cefn Mably, Glamorganshire

Home of the Kemeys family since the fifteenth century until it passed to the Kemeys-Tyntes in 1735. The present house dates from *c.* 1713. It is long, low and unpretentious, of two storeys and a pitched roof with dormers. Porch set with three lead urns. A wing projects to the south-west; beyond that the small parish church.

Entry into the Hall of which the ceiling beams are sixteenth century and the panelling is Queen Anne. Drawing room panelled in Palladian manner, with pedimented door-cases and dentilled cornice; lately dismantled for hospital use.

C.L., 28 Nov. 1908.

Charborough Park, Dorset

From the Wykes Charborough was inherited in the mid sixteenth century by the Erles. Sir Walter Erle rebuilt the house during the Commonwealth in cubic form with hipped roof and dormers. It is graphically described in Celia Fiennes's *Diary*. Greatly altered and enlarged *c.* 1810.

Sir Walter's grandson, General Thomas Erle, a supporter of William III, was responsible for painted staircase and hall. The oak staircase, the work of a Blandford joiner, has richly carved balusters, newels and handrail ending in a scroll and urn. Thornhill painted the walls of stairs and hall, 1718. The theme is *The Triumph of Love*, illustrated in several compartments. Architectural features, niches and trophy panels are in grisaille.

From the Erles Charborough passed to the Ernles, and in 1729 to the Drax family. Charborough is Hardy's 'Welland House' in *Two on a Tower*.

C.L., 30 March 1935.

Chilston Park, Kent

An early Tudor house round a quadrangle bought *c.* 1650 by Edward Hales.

The north front given a pedimented centre and projecting wings of red brick *c.* 1710–28 for William Hamilton (date stone 1728). Hipped roof and dormer windows. Subsequent alterations 1782 and enlargements 1880. Acquired 1821 by Douglas family and inherited 1875 by Akers family.

C.L., 19 Dec. 1952.

Cliveden House, Buckinghamshire

Begun for George Villiers, 2nd Duke of Buckingham by William Winde *c.* 1665–80 on a splendid site overlooking the Thames. It was never finished. In 1706 the Earl of Orkney purchased it and employed Thomas Archer to link house to pavilions with quadrant arcades, which survive. At the same time Archer probably transformed Winde's house. (Compare plate in *Vitruvius Britannicus*, vol. II with that of Umberslade in vol. III.) The history of Cliveden needs investigating.

Present house, rebuilt after a fire by Charles Barry 1850, still bears a faint resemblance to the Winde-Archer house.

C.L., 11 July 1931.

Compton Beauchamp House, Berkshire

Surrounded on all four sides by a moat. House dates from the early sixteenth, early and late seventeenth and early eighteenth centuries. From the forecourt a bridge leads to the stone entrance front of *c.* 1710, which might be yet another example of Townesend's work.

This front is of three bays and three storeys under a balustrade; on either side two-storey wings are imposed upon the mediaeval house like a screen. The centre block has giant Doric pilasters on a rusticated base. There is an inner rectangular courtyard.

431 *Compton Beauchamp House, Berkshire, c. 1710.*

The wrought-iron gates to the forecourt have a double whorl in the feet of the dog-bars, and an overthrow of two foliated scrolls. There is a pair of facing outbuildings in clunch and brick. Walled and terraced lawns.
C.L., 30 Nov. 1918.

Compton Verney, Warwickshire

Takes its name from the Verneys, Barons Willoughby de Broke. George Verney, 12th Baron and Dean of Windsor, built the south-west front in 1714.

The style is more like Vanbrugh's than that of most undocumented houses ascribed to this architect.

Stone, of two storeys and eleven bays. The five central bays project under a balustrade. The ashlar is of solid blocks. Each end bay of the centrepiece is contained within giant Tuscan pilasters. All the windows are arched with wedge-like keystones rising into the features above them. Doorway of Gibbs surrounds supporting a triglyph frieze. The quoins at each outer angle are in blocks. It is a satisfying front. In 1760 Robert Adam added long wings and a great portico at the rear. His style conforms astonishingly with that of the south-west front.

The stable block is by Gibbs: the Chapel by Capability Brown, who was also responsible for the landscape setting, one of the most beautiful in England.
H. Avray Tipping and C. Hussey—*English Homes*, Period IV, vol. II, *Vanbrugh and His School*, 1928.

Cowick Hall, West Riding, Yorkshire

Of creamy-grey stone. James Paine gives a plan and elevation in *Noblemen's and Gentlemen's Houses* of Cowick Hall as 'new modelled' by him for the 3rd Viscount Downe after 1752. But the centre block as illustrated looks much the same as it does today, and is of *c*. 1695, in which year Henry Dawnay, 2nd Viscount Downe, succeeded his father. The Dawnays had been seated at Cowick since Henry VII's reign. Paine's wings were never added.

Giant pilasters, Ionic and Tuscan, unite three sides of the house. Both long fronts have nine bays of two storeys with central pediment carrying the Dawnay arms. Over deep eaves, upheld by enormous brackets, are a balustrade, hipped roof and dormers. Ground-floor windows alternately pedimented.

Paine doubtless remodelled the interior. His work was swept away after the Dawnays sold Cowick in 1869 to a cotton spinner from Cleckheaton. The Hall has been saved by the Croda chemical group with the aid of the Historic Buildings Council.

Cransley Hall, Northamptonshire

Belonged to the Robinsons 1595 to 1791 when it passed to illegitimate offspring, the Roses, until 1904.

The south and east fronts added *c*. 1708 to a house begun *c*. 1677. Grey and brown stone used for walls, and for hipped roof silvery-grey stone tiles. Sashed windows and dormers. The arms of Robinson appear in the pediment of the east front door. Dining Room ceiling and walls decorated with Baroque stucco work. Stable block square tower with blind roundel and two urns on the parapet.
J. A. Gotch—*Squires' Homes of Northamptonshire*, 1939.

Croan, Cornwall

Circa 1696 for Edward Hoblyn, attorney-at-law. Seven bays, two storeys. Hipped roof and three dormers. Deep block cornice. Central door and porch. Panelled study. On the east wall the Tremayne arms under carved swags.
C.L., 28 July 1960.

Croxteth Hall, Lancashire

Since the reign of Henry VI the seat of the Molyneux family (Earls of Sefton).

A large brick and stone house round a courtyard, incorporating Jacobean parts. The principal south-west front, dated 1702, has eleven bays of two storeys over a terrace. The ground-floor windows, except those of the central bay, are grouped in couples and alternately pedimented. Front door has a broken pediment, and above it, in place of a window, is a large panel of carved trophies in stone.

There are ample additions of 1874 and 1902.
P. Fleetwood-Hesketh—*Murray's Lancashire Guide*, 1955.

Culverthorpe Hall, Lincolnshire

Sir John Newton, Bart, succeeded in 1699 to Culverthorpe which had been begun by his father *c*. 1679. He gave the north front its strangely individual form, amounting to a single-bay projection to contain a new staircase. It is lit by one large tall window, with fruit swags and scrolls at the sides and a panel of fruit and flowers over the lintel. Below it a doorway of Ionic columns. The cornice brackets are scaled and decked with acanthus leaf in a manner suggestive of Thomas Archer, whose first wife was actually a sister of Sir John Newton's son-in-law. The mason-contractors, however, are known to have been William and Edward Stanton.

By 1734 Sir Michael Newton added wings and redecorated the interior. The staircase, however, with thin twisted balusters dates from *c*. 1699. The walls, painted

432 *Culverthorpe Hall, Lincolnshire. The north front, c. 1699.*

1704–5 by Louis Hauduroy (*Story of Psyche*), have lately been destroyed.

C.L., 15 Sept. 1923.

N. Pevsner and J. Harris—*Buildings of England, Lincoln-shire*, 1964.

Dewlish House, Dorset

A long, sleepy Queen Anne house among beeches and cedars in a gentle valley with a stream. Built 1702 for Thomas Skinner, merchant. South front of mellow brick, north front grey Portisham stone, east side Ham stone.

The south front of eleven bays has a central three-bay break and one long arched window. The north front has a curvilinear tympanum and porch with a carved shield. Inside, the staircase is of oak with carved brackets and twisted balusters.

Arthur Oswald—*Country Houses of Dorset*, 1935.

Droxford Old Rectory, Hampshire

Circa 1720, of patterned grey and red brick built on to a Jacobean portion. The main north front has a slightly advanced centre with a parapet. The east front of five bays, hipped roof and dormers. Long, slender sash windows. A Late Georgian Tuscan doorway and simple Late Georgian staircase.

N. Pevsner and D. Lloyd—*Buildings of England, Hamp-shire*, 1967.

Duncombe Park, North Riding, Yorkshire

Sir Charles Duncombe, dying unmarried in 1711, left the estate to his niece Ursula, married to Thomas Browne, a City business colleague of the uncle. Browne assumed the name of Duncombe for himself and heirs.

In 1713 Thomas Duncombe began to build. William Wakefield was architect according to *Vitruvius Britannicus*, vol. III (1725), and Francis Drake's *Eboracum* (1736). After a disastrous fire the house was reconstituted in 1891. The saloon on the east front was scrapped and the portico previously projecting was recessed. The hall in consequence was reduced from a rectangle to a square. The west entrance front was unaltered. The bold use of Doric pilasters (Castle Howard) coupled at the outer angles, the arcaded turrets (Kings Weston), and the raised central clerestory (Seaton Delaval) are distinctive if pale reflections of Vanbrugh.

The treatment of the hall walls, namely with Corinthian columns, arched doorways, niches and fireplaces, is surely a faithful repetition of what previously existed within the five original bays.

H. Avray Tipping and C. Hussey—*English Homes*, Period IV, vol. II, *Vanbrugh and His School*, 1928.

Eagle House, Mitcham, Surrey

Built *c.* 1705 in the manner of Pratt's Coleshill for Sir James Dolliffe, a director of the South Sea Company.

A miniature house of yellow and red brick. Square plan, two storeys and attic. Dormers with segmental heads in a hipped roof with balustrade and cupola. Five bays of which the central three project under a pediment in continuation of the blocked cornice. Front door very modest under a hood.

433 *Dewlish House, Dorset, 1702. The north front.*

The forecourt approached through a wrought-iron gate with overthrow and *clairvoie*.

T. Small and C. Woodbridge—*Houses of Wren and Early Georgian Period*, 1928.

Eastbury Park, Dorset

All that survives of Vanbrugh's great palace for George Bubb Dodington, Lord Melcombe of Melcombe Regis, is the north kitchen wing, with projecting arcade and the prodigious archway with two Scots firs triumphantly growing out of the top. The rest was blown up in 1775.

Vanbrugh's first two designs were prepared for Melcombe's uncle, George Dodington (d. 1720). The second figures in *Vitruvius Britannicus*, vol. II (1717). After 1724 building to a third design (*Vitruvius Britannicus*, vol. III, 1725) began in earnest. Eastbury was still in train at the date of Vanbrugh's death (1726), and only finished in 1738. Two oil paintings show how the actual house differed from the architect's intentions. The towering superstructure to light the twin staircases was not put on. But the vast portico with typical Vanbrughian ringed columns and the square corner towers with Venetian windows were faithfully carried out by Roger Morris, who succeeded Vanbrugh.

On the far east side a formal parterre garden was designed by Bridgeman and Vanbrugh, with prospects into the open country. Eastbury has belonged to the Farquharson family since 1806.

C.L., 3 Sept. 1927 and 31 Dec. 1948.

Egginton Manor, Bedfordshire

Four-square and upright with a flat façade like that of a town house. Floors divided by thin platbands. Urns on the parapet. Built for a Huguenot by the name of Renouille, 1696. The rooms have contemporary wainscot.

A. E. Richardson—*Smaller Houses of the Renaissance*, 1925.

434 (top) Duncombe Park, Yorkshire. By William Wakefield, 1713. The entrance front.

435 (above left) Eastbury Park House. The surviving wing of Vanbrugh's house, 1724–38.

436 (left) Eastbury; the house as it was built. A painting which dates from before 1775, when it was demolished.

Emral Hall, Flintshire

(demolished 1936)

The moated home of the Puleston family since Edward I's reign. An essentially Jacobean house, with Hall of Hercules adorned with a barrel ceiling of deep relief scenes amidst strapwork. Two wings and front rebuilt 1724–7 in brick and stone dressings by Richard Trubshaw and Joseph Evans. Ambitious front door of frostwork under a central window with pronounced acanthus scrolls. Another doorway with bat's-wing pediment, the acme of provincial Baroque.

Fine urned piers and somewhat flimsy wrought-iron overthrow by Davies brothers of Wrexham. Also low entrance gates between pair of sentry boxes with ogival cupolas.

C.L., 19 Feb. 1910.

Eversley Manor (formerly Fir Grove), Hampshire

In a setting of Scotch pines. Built for Mr Wadham Wyndham in 1736, almost certainly by John James. Red brick. Centre block of three bays and three storeys under a pediment. There is an Ionic front door-case. On either side are two canted bays of two storeys and a balustrade.

Elegant staircase with slender balusters.

C.L., 19 March 1943.

Farnborough Hall, Warwickshire

Bought by Ambrose Holbech 1684 and still inhabited by his descendants.

West front, built in tawny yellow Hornton stone 1685–90, has slightly projecting centrepiece of one bay, with raised attic window and scroll surround under a pediment (cf. Moat House, Sutton Coldfield by Sir William Wilson). Contemporary lead rainwater heads embossed with escallops. Behind the front, staircase ceiling with oval wreath of flowers. The dome, however, treated c. 1745–55, when extensive alterations were made outside and in. William Holbech rebuilt all the rest of his father's house, engaging possibly the advice of his neighbour, Sanderson Miller. Rich interior decoration of these years.

C.L., 11 Feb. 1954.

Fenton House, Hampstead, London

Built when Hampstead was still an isolated Middlesex village. The date 1693 is scratched on one of the chimneys and carved on a lead pump-head in the garden. Neither architect nor client known. In 1793 the Clock House, as it was called, was acquired by P. I. Fenton, a Riga merchant.

Plan of the house a perfect square. Material deep brown brick with rubbed brick dressings. Two storeys, basement and attic with dormers. Under widely projecting eaves a wooden modillion cornice is carried into a pediment on the south front. A feature of the house is the small closet which opens off the fireplace of each principal room.

The east front wings are joined by a Regency colonnade and crowned by a white balustrade.

The sturdy wrought-iron gates overlooking Holly Hill are contemporary.

C.L., 24 March 1950.

Fetcham Park, Surrey

Arthur Moore, a commissioner of trade and plantations and a director of the South Sea Company, purchased the property from the Vincent family. In 1705–10 William Talman built him a simple brick house, graphically described by Celia Fiennes. It was re-encased c. 1870 and is now extremely ugly.

Inside, the staircase leading straight into the Hall—both painted by Laguerre—survives. The arrangement is also seen at Hanbury Hall c. 1710. Here the balusters and undersides of the stair treads are most delicately carved.

Ian Nairn and N. Pevsner—*Buildings of England, Surrey*, 1962.

Gilling Castle, North Riding, Yorkshire

The Viscounts Fairfax, who succeeded each other in rapid succession, altered the west front and projecting wings in the early eighteenth century. William Wakefield, according to Francis Drake's *Eboracum* (1736), was architect, 1715–25. The window-surrounds suggest Gibbs's influence.

When the house became a school in 1929 the long gallery (Wakefield) with columned end screens and rich carving was removed. It is now in the Bowes Museum, Barnard Castle. But the hall remains. The groined coving resembles that at Beningbrough. Giuseppe Cortese probably did the stucco cartouches, swags, drapery and coronets which assume Rococo patterns (c. 1740).

The staircase balusters, imitating ironwork, also resemble those by Thornton at Beningbrough, though less refined. Some carved chimney-pieces and friezes about the house have their counterparts at Beningbrough.

Gilling is a castle of fourteenth-century foundation set on a hill. Its most important apartment is the Great Chamber (1575–85).

H. Avray Tipping and C. Hussey—*English Homes*, Period IV, vol. II, *Vanbrugh and His School*, 1928.

Goodnestone Park, Kent

Originally another house of the Canterbury group (cf. Bourne, Barham, Kenfield). Red brick with purple headers (renewed). East and west fronts of two storeys, hipped roof and dormers. Five-bay centre slightly broken forward under a long pediment containing window and two roundels.

Built for Brook Bridges, Auditor of Imprest Accounts, after 1705. Inside only oak staircase with fluted and twisted balusters survives from Queen Anne's reign. Alterations c. 1780 when attic floor turned to upper storey and pediment raised, and again c. 1820–30.

Descended to present owner, Brook Plumptre, 21st Baron FitzWalter.

T. Badeslade engraving, c. 1720.

Great Hundridge Manor, Buckinghamshire

Anciently the manor of the De Broc, or Broke family until c. 1530, then of the Dormers. In 1681 bought by William Hobbs, apothecary of London; and in 1742 by Richard Lowndes.

The builder was probably Hobbs's son, styled a doctor of Covent Garden. His rectangular, U-shaped house is

437 *(above) Emral Hall, Flintshire, 1724–7, Borrominesque decoration over a door (demolished).*

438 *(right) Gilling Castle, Yorkshire. The Hall, 1715–25, with plasterwork added, c. 1740.*

attached to the twelfth-century de Brock chapel. The date 1696 appears on a rainwater head. Brick walls diapered with flared headers, and a brick stringcourse between the floors. Casement windows with elaborate hasps. Brick walls enclose a court, formerly the 'nut orchard'.

A steep pine staircase with spiral balusters. Three west rooms, wainscoted with bolection panelling and box cornices, retain original decoration of considerable interest. The parlour is painted in realistic burr walnut with black and gold lacquer stiles *à la Chinoise*; the pilasters marbled in Sienna. Blue bedroom in yellow Sienna panelling, the stiles grained walnut, the fireplace painted black and gold; the second bedroom in umber, burnt Sienna, ochre and Indian red imitating scagliola. In an overmantel panel a grotesque landscape. House much added to in twentieth century. *C.L.*, 15 Feb. 1941.

Great Treverran, Tywardreath, Cornwall
Circa 1720. Small stone house, two storeys, five bays. Front door with segmental broken pediment. Pronounced window voussoirs. Hipped roof and dormers on sides only.

The remarkable feature consists in four Ionic three-quarter columns with dosserets embracing both storeys, two at the angles, and two enclosing the door and window over it. On the dosserets are plinths, suggesting that the giant order once carried a balustrade.

Greenhill, Upper Westwood, Wiltshire
Circa 1695 of five bays and two storeys with hipped roof. There are giant pilaster strips and pedimented ground-floor windows. All in stone, behind gate-piers and a garden wall.

J. Belcher and M. Macartney—*Later Renaissance Architecture in England*, 1898.

Gregories, Beaconsfield, Buckinghamshire
(demolished 1813)
Vitruvius Britannicus, vol. II, states that the house was 'designed by Thomas Milner, esq., Anno 1712'. The client was John Waller, son of Edmund the poet, who inherited the property in 1616 aged ten.

It was a seven-bay house of two storeys and a basement, the three central bays under a heavily carved pediment. Urns on a blind parapet. Quadrant colonnades linked house with facing pavilions. Edmund Burke, who made alterations, died here 1797.

The house was burnt and demolished 1813.

439 Gunby Hall, Lincolnshire, 1700.

440 Hale Manor, Lancashire, c. 1700.

Gunby Hall, Lincolnshire

The Massingberds were seated at Bratoft by Gunby as squires in Henry V's reign. The present house was built in 1700 for Sir William Massingberd. Rectangular in three vertical planes with straight, severe skyline. Deep plum brick and stone strings and dressings. Doorway with broken, scrolled pediment and shield of arms. In 1873 the north wing was added.

Simple contemporary wainscot of fielded panels. Oak staircase with twisted balusters and moulded handrail.

The Massingberd name went with the property in descent through the female line until Gunby was given to the National Trust in 1944. Gunby is Tennyson's 'haunt of ancient peace'.

C.L., 5 Nov. 1943.

Hackwood Park, Hampshire

Although much disguised by Samuel Wyatt's alterations (1805–10) for 1st Lord Bolton, the bones of the house built 1683–7 (probably by Talman) for Charles Paulet, 1st Duke of Bolton, remain. (Plan in Bodleian, Gough A/34.) A long, low, three-storeyed centre block was attached to single-bay wings on the south side. Awkward segmental corridors connected the block with two-storeyed pavilions at right angles on the north side. They formed a deep forecourt. The material was then brick with stone facings, whereas now it is Roman cement. In the house are several friezes, swags and drops in carved wood by Grinling Gibbons. They were brought to Hackwood by the 5th Duke of Bolton from Abbotstone, another Hampshire seat of the Paulet family.

C.L., 17 May 1913.

Hale Manor, Lancashire

The west front, which makes such a striking impression out of little, was added to an older house by the Vicar of Hale, the Rev. William Langford, *c.* 1700. No date, no documents have been forthcoming. The Vicar's monogram and coat of arms bear the only testimony within the swan-neck pediment over the door. The single-bay centrepiece is broad.

Rose brick and soft sandstone dressings. Doric pilaster strips, with entablatures, at the angles. The oval attic windows (blind) and balustrade are a distant and provincial echo of Hampton Court. The carved military trophies in the pediment are another. The ends of the house were never finished.

Hall passage and main stairs are contemporary. Back stairs have flat, raked, classical balusters.

C.L., 30 June 1960.

Hale Park, Hampshire

Built for himself by Thomas Archer soon after 1715. A centre block and, connected by curved corridors, stable and service pavilions, each of seven bays. Outside greatly altered in 1770 by Henry Holland, who added a large portico and rendered the red brick with Roman cement. But on the garden front the double-flight perron, with wrought-iron balusters, remains. No Archer work within.

C.L., 8 Aug. 1941.

Halswell House, Somerset

John Tynte married Jane, daughter and heiress of the Rev. Hugh Halswell of Halswell. Their son Sir Halswell Tynte, 1st Bart, added in 1689 the present house to the old Halswell block at the rear.

The main front facing north is of lichened, buff stone

441 *Halswell House, Somerset. The centre of the main front.*

442 *Harrowden Hall, Northamptonshire. The garden front.*

and of three tall storeys, three central bays and slightly advanced wings of two bays each. Ground- and first-floor windows have segmental and rounded heads. Strange box-like crests crown the latter. The doorway and window over it are highly complex. The door is set back in a curved niche and has carved trophies in the spandrels. It is framed by rusticated piers and a pair of three-quarter columns. The window is framed within a tabernacle, of which the pediment is crammed with a huge shield and garlands. Pilasters with sunk panels, pilasters carved, and pilasters ending in outer scrolls support the heavy headpiece.

The staircase of stout, turned balusters fills a large square well. Ceiling and cove adorned with stucco wreaths and *amorini*. A fire did much damage to the interior in 1923.

Sir Halswell's son married the heiress of Sir Charles Kemeys of Cefn Mably. Through their daughter the property descended to the 9th Lord Wharton who sold it after the Second World War.

C.L., 21 Nov. 1908.

Hardwick Hall, Shropshire

John Kynaston inherited 1693, and died 1733. The house he built in brick appears at first sight to date from 1700, but was probably not begun much before 1720.

It has a seven-bay front of three storeys and is immensely tall on account of a massive elliptical tympanum, rather than pediment, over the stone three-bay centre. Within the tympanum a shield and garlands. This centre is flanked by Corinthian pilasters carrying entablatures in the manner of Francis Smith's Buntingsdale. The angles of the front have quoin strips of horizontal rustication. Main windows have segmental heads and brick aprons.

Semi-circular walls connect the house to facing pavilions, each of which has a central square stack, hipped roof

and dormers with steep alternating pediments in the style of 1700.

Interior much altered, but the staircase which occupies a square well has a handrail ramped at the angles (no newels) and carved tread ends.

Hardwick passed in 1868 to the Owens who took the name of Kynaston.

C.L., 15 June 1918.

Harrowden Hall, Northamptonshire

John Bridges wrote succinctly *c.* 1720: 'The manor-house new built by Mr Wentworth stands high and hath good gardens.' In 1694 the Hon. Thomas Watson (he added Wentworth on succeeding to his mother's Yorkshire estates the following year), younger son of the 2nd Lord Rockingham, bought the Harrowden estate. Did he start building immediately? The Wentworth arms are not quartered on the Watson shield displayed on the fine wrought-iron gates and *clairvoies*. These gates, stone piers, terraces, steps, statues and walls form an interesting garden layout of William III's reign.

The house is exceedingly plain—five-bay centre, three-storey block with flat skyline—and may date from 1694. The two-storey wings seem afterthoughts; the date 1719 appears on a downpipe. The staircase walls are hung with painted canvases, architecturally treated in the style of Verrio. They are dim with age (1967).

In 1895 the 7th Lord Vaux of Harrowden bought back the property which had been alienated by his Vaux forebears in 1694. It was again sold in 1966 and is being repaired.

C.L., 26 Dec. 1908.

J. A. Gotch—*Old Halls and Manor Houses of Northamptonshire*, 1936.

Haseley Court, Oxfordshire

The core of the main front added 1709 by Edmund Boulter to a fourteenth-century building at the rear. Architect unknown.

The 1709 front was of seven bays, probably with hipped roof and dormers. After Haseley was inherited by Boulter's great-niece, married in 1737 to John Woolfe, two-bay wings were added and the present shape of the front assumed. It is of coursed and dressed rubble, central bays under a pediment, and roof concealed by a plain parapet. Front door given a segmental head, probably by the Woolfes.

The ambitious hall fireplace of two tiers, with richly carved masks and swags in the lower and a broken pediment with fat pine-cone in the upper, suggests the hand of William Townesend, c. 1720. Simple staircase of painted pine with cluster of four turned balusters where newels should be, and dining room of fluted Doric pilasters are of 1709 date.

Later eighteenth-century alterations. This house was saved from utter disintegration by Mrs Lancaster in 1955.
C.L., 11 Feb. 1960.

Henlow Grange, Bedfordshire

Queen Anne house of three storeys and five bays in red brick. Burnt headers and rubbed and gauged brick for dressings. At the four angles pilaster strips support a shallow parapet, and over each strip a chimney-stack. Central wooden porch with pediment. The contemporary staircase, some fireplaces and panelling remain (1953). Later three-bay wings.

The forecourt piers and iron gates and railing are twentieth century.
Victoria County History—*Bedfordshire*, vol. II, 1908.

Herriard Park, Hampshire

(demolished 1965)
The Jervoise family have owned the property without break since the thirteenth century. Rainwater heads were dated 1704. The nine-bay fronts were as gaunt as those of Cound, which Herriard resembled. Unlike Cound, Herriard had been stuccoed over c. 1775. Doric pilasters of the giant order were used, the attic windows being pushed into the entablature. The raised central parapet has suggested tentatively to Mr Kerry Downes the name of William Dickinson as architect. John James's name is even more plausible. The original wooden model exists.
C.L., 1 July 1965.

Hewell Grange, Worcestershire

(dismantled 1890)
In 1542 Andrew Lord Windsor was obliged much against his will to exchange with Henry VIII his ancestral property in Middlesex for the manor of Tardebigge, Worcestershire. In 1712 Other, 2nd Earl of Plymouth, built a two-storey block round a court, close to a lake. In 1887 the foundations began sinking, and the house was dismantled.

A plate in Nash's *Worcestershire* (1799) shows the north and east fronts before the addition to the north in 1816 of a portico by Thomas Cundy. Giant order of Tuscan pilasters supported a heavy entablature with balustrade.

On the east front the cornice was broken over the central bay by a semi-circular tympanum. Remarkably small keystones to windows. Architect may have been Thomas Archer.

In 1884–92 Bodley and Garner built for the 1st Earl of Plymouth (of 1905 creation) on a new site, an inflated version of Montacute House in sombre Tardebigge stone.

Heythrop House, Oxfordshire

Charles Talbot, 12th Earl and 1st and only Duke of Shrewsbury, Lord High Treasurer and Lord Chamberlain, was a staunch supporter of William III and secured the Hanoverian succession. He was much travelled and had an Italian wife.

On the Duke's return from Rome in 1706 Thomas Archer began Heythrop, with Francis Smith as master-mason in charge. Roofed 1709; still unfinished by 1716. Design may possibly have been supplied by Paolo Falconieri, amateur Roman architect who gave Shrewsbury a plan for a royal palace in 1704. Rossi's *Architettura Civile* (1702) was undoubtedly the source of much detail, viz: the curvilinear heads and the ears of windows, the swan-neck and bat's-wing pediments, the tapered pilasters, and the scaled cornice consoles, which derive from Bernini and Borromini. Yet the markedly contrasting treatment of the elevations recalls Talman's fronts at Chatsworth.

Heythrop was gutted by fire in 1831 and left a ruin until c. 1870 when it was entirely remodelled inside for Albert Brassey. It was Archer's most important house to which Vanbrugh and his contemporaries referred admiringly.
C.L., 26 Aug. 1905
Kerry Downes—*English Baroque Architecture*, 1966.

Hill Court, Herefordshire

Centre part begun 1698 for Richard Clarke and finished c. 1708 for his brother Joseph. The Clarkes, of yeoman stock, were granted arms in 1663.

443 *Herriard Park, Hampshire (demolished). The wooden model.*

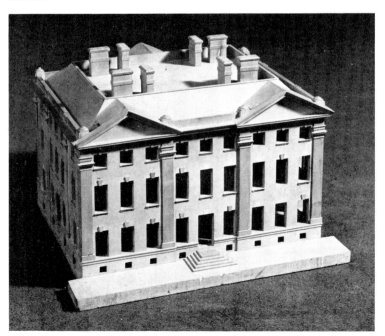

Originally a rectangular block with hipped roof, balustrade and cupola and an unusually large segmental pediment over three bays. A double-pile plan, with hall in front and 'great staires' behind. 'I would persuade you to make them of the new mode . . .', wrote Joseph Clarke to the model-maker. Hall wainscot survives and stairs (1708) of walnut, yew, twisted balusters and inlaid half-landings. Fine plaster ceiling with wreath of fruit and flowers in bold relief.

Of several surviving panelled rooms of this period the most interesting is the Painted Bedroom. It has panels of reds, browns and creams simulating rockwork, the moulds marbled white with grey veins. On rails and stiles are chinoiserie scenes simulating lacquer, and two ruin pieces in grisaille by (?) Isaac Bayly (see Stoke Edith). Bills of all craftsmen's work exist.

In early eighteenth century the upper floor and roof-line were altered and wings added. Bought 1888 by Major Lionel Trafford.
C.L., 27 Jan. 1966.

Hinton Admiral Park, Hampshire
Bought 1708 by Sir Peter Mews. Went by inheritance through his widow's nephew Benjamin Clarke, and his heirs to the Meyrick family. Can claim a place in the group of houses possibly by John James.

Sir Peter Mews, on his marriage with Lydia Jarvis of Islington 1719, began building. Tetrastyle centre block of pink-white ashlar, Composite pilasters and pediment: arched windows. Two-bay ends of brick. Long pavilions at right angles linked by quadrant colonnades, originally open. After a severe fire in 1777 wings added at either end of the garden front and interior reconstituted. Some alterations took place *c.* 1898, when the ballroom was formed and the terraces were laid out by Harold Peto.
C.L., 8 Oct. 1910.

Holt, The Courts, Wiltshire
To a fifteenth or early sixteenth-century hall house the astonishing façade of *c.* 1700 was tacked on at right angles, possibly for a rich mill owner by a Bradford-on-Avon mason.

Façade of two storeys, the windows of both with alternate broken and scrolled heads. In the centrepiece a wide entrance porch with elliptical pediment and window above with scrolled pediment. These are flanked by narrow windows with rounded heads. The cornice rises into a sharp pediment containing a long, thin window. Two dormers in hipped roof. The whole composition very flamboyant and provincial.

A narrow staircase with panelled dado and turned balusters is separated from the hall by a wainscot arch.
C.L., 1 Jan. 1943.

Hursley Park, Hampshire
Sir William Heathcote, 1st Bart, M.P., bought the property in 1712 and in 1718 rebuilt the house, which is illustrated in vol. I of Neale's *Seats* (1818). It there appears as a red-brick building with long first- and second-floor windows and blind panels over them. Steps led to the entrance within a stone tetrastyle centrepiece of Doric pilasters and pediment. Dormers in a hipped roof.

Before considerable alterations and aggrandizements *c.* 1905, Hursley suggested the hand of John James, who is named architect in G. F. Prosser's *Select Illustrations of Hampshire* (1833). On the other hand, in Hursley church there is a monument signed 'G. Sampson architect' and dated 1731. Sampson built the central part of the Old Bank of England, and could have been employed by Heathcote.
C.L., 15 Nov. 1913.

444 *Hursley Park, Hampshire, 1718. Neale's* View *showing the house before enlargement.*

Hurstbourne Priors, Hampshire (demolished *c.* 1785)
Built for John Wallop, subsequently 1st Earl of Portsmouth, after 1712. Two early eighteenth-century paintings in possession of the present Lord Portsmouth show a large house with pavilions at right angles, and a long canal. This house, which may or may not be Thomas Archer's, was demolished *c.* 1785. It does not, however, accord with a plan preserved at Worcester College, Oxford, inscribed, 'A house designed for Mr Wallop at Husbourne, Hants, by Mr Archer 1712.' The Andover lodge is all that is left of the 1712 architecture. Of grey headers and red-brick dressings it has high arched recesses, circular windows and a parapet in a decidedly Archerian manner.

In the park is a strange mausoleum of flint with a Roman emperor standing on the dome.
C.L., 12 Sept. 1941.

Inkpen Old Rectory, Berkshire
A William and Mary rectory of brick, with coved eaves, steep roof and three pointed dormers. Symmetrical north and asymmetrical south front, on which some windows have mullions. The south front is tile-hung. Entrance hall with two Doric arches and staircase rising from the rear. On the walls twelve reliefs of Caesars' heads.

For over three hundred years the Brickenden and Butler families were rectors until 1933.

The special feature of this property is the miniature garden layout (*c.* 1695) made by Dr Brickenden, later Master of Pembroke College, Oxford, within a two-acre downland grove of elms, beech and yew. From an amphitheatre on the south side three vistas radiate. Four vistas converge at the south-west corner of the enclosure. There is a pleached lime walk along the side of the house.
C.L., 12 Feb. 1943.

The Ivy, Chippenham, Wiltshire
Described in J. Britton's *Wiltshire* (1814) as 'large and respectable'. It is, in fact, a very remarkable specimen of regional Baroque.

Main block added *c.* 1728 to the east of an older house (remodelled 1758) for a Chippenham attorney called Norris. The rich north front has a recessed centre and projecting wings of two bays each. Two-storeyed frontispiece with doorway of paired columns and a high arched window breaking into a pediment, which carries a panelled superstructure. The wings have large segmental pediments towering above the centre. Flanking urns stand above pilaster strips at the angles. The attic windows of the wings and the ground-floor windows of the centre are arched, the latter having carved keystones which rise into the stringcourse.

Beautiful oak and mahogany staircase and wainscoted drawing room with pilasters.
Kerry Downes—*English Baroque Architecture*, 1966.

Kemerton Court, Worcestershire
In a park-like setting an early Georgian front of imposing Baroque elegance built for the Parsons family. The house is of wafer thinness.

Front consists of four planes of two bays each, plus a central plane of one bay, all articulated by pilasters. The parapet is swept up in the middle and at the ends. The centrepiece is a nice play of segments. Queen Anne staircase and panelled rooms.

Architect—possibly Thomas White of Worcester, or whoever built Overbury Court nearby in 1739.

Kenfield Hall, Kent
A Queen Anne house of red brick, hipped roof and dormers. Although it is only of seven bays, with a three-bay centre under a pediment containing a single arched window, this house belongs to the Bourne Park, Goodnestone Park and Barham Court group. The identity of the architect, perhaps a Canterbury mason, is unknown.

Home of the Thomson family since the reign of Elizabeth I.

Kingston Bagpuize House, Berkshire
Built *c.* 1710–20 for Fettiplace Blandy, a boy who died before coming of age. William Townesend has been suggested as architect: certainly the golden stone for dressings was floated down the Windrush and Thames from a Burford quarry which he probably owned. John James's name has also been put forward. A bright brick is the material chiefly used.

East and west fronts identical. Seven-bay elevation with raised, pedimented, three-bay centre. The chimneys are concentrated into a pair of arched stacks flanking the centre block. Window-heads of first floor segmental, those of ground floor arched. On the roof-line are urns (Blandy arms or three urns sable with flames emitting). There are lower wings of two storeys each.

In 1865 the walled forecourt disappeared when the fine iron gates were moved to their present site.

Hall has two stone chimney-pieces. The staircase of Coleshill type rises in a long, gradual ascent. Sold 1938 by Colonel John Blandy-Jenkins.
C.L., 6 Nov. 1942.

Kingston Bagpuize Rectory, Berkshire

Designed and built 1723 by Dr George Clark of Oxford (according to Howard Colvin). A two-storey building of five bays, the central bay flanked by rusticated giant pilasters. Porch of rocky rustication, which may date from *c.* 1750.

N. Pevsner—*Buildings of England, Berkshire*, 1966.

Kings Weston, Gloucestershire

Sir Edward Southwell, Baronet, whose father had bought Kings Weston in 1679, pulled down the Tudor house and engaged Vanbrugh to build anew in 1710. Southwell was M.P. for Rye, Secretary for Ireland and a friend of Swift.

Vanbrugh's U-plan and south elevation, as shown in *Vitruvius Britannicus*, vol. I, were faithfully carried out. The front has an engaged portico of Corinthian pilasters with a characteristic lunette in the pediment. The west side is simple except for a three-sided bow rising its full height. The east side has on the ground floor a three-windowed tabernacle feature with broken pediment. But the outstanding device was a crowning coronal of arcaded chimney-stacks, a mighty and impressive composition. It has lately disappeared, and this splendid house now looks sadly distressed. The spectacular view over Avonmouth and the Bristol Channel, which like that from Seaton Delaval particularly appealed to Vanbrugh's sense of drama, is now obliterated by recent development of an ignoble sort.

George Townesend was master-mason. Structure finished in 1714. By 1719 the stairwell was floored. The stairs and galleries fill the entire space behind the hall. Vanbrugh made three flights rise seemingly unsupported. Ground floor and first floor contain arcades, some filled with grisaille paintings of statues and urns.

Vanbrugh's banqueting loggia, 'Venetian' loggia and machicolated brew-house survive after a fashion.

Robert Mylne made alterations, 1763–73. From 1832 to 1937 the house belonged to the Miles family.

C.L., 30 April 1927.

Kirkleatham Old Hall (or Free School), North Riding, Yorkshire

Part of a remarkable group built for Sir William Turner, Kt, philanthropist squire and once Lord Mayor of London. Turner's house was unfortunately demolished *c.* 1955. His hospital or almshouses, with the most complete and Baroque chapel in the north of England, may owe its original design to Wren. Its Baroque quality was enhanced by alterations for Cholmley Turner in 1742.

What was, however, the Free School, and is now called the Old Hall, was built 1708–9. Of two storeys with attic above the cornice. The recessed centre of five bays is embellished with a portal in the giant Doric order and elliptical pediment. It frames a boldly rusticated doorway carrying a tablet. On either side large roundel windows on the second floor. The composition is not at all provincial.

N. Pevsner—*Buildings of England, Yorkshire, The North Riding*, 1966.

Kirkoswald, The College, Cumberland

Thomas, Lord Dacre, founded a college for priests *c.* 1523. It was dissolved under Edward VI. Purchased in 1590 by the Fetherstonhaughs who are still owners.

In 1696 they added to a peel dwelling the stalwart, broad-fronted house of two storeys with projecting two-bay wings. Hipped roof and coved eaves. Front door of broken scroll pediment containing escutcheon. Steps of 1696 lead to a terrace at the rear.

C.L., 17 Nov. 1928.

Kislingbury Old Rectory, Northamptonshire

Of orange ironstone. Possibly by John Hunt of Northampton. According to John Bridges 'new built', i.e. 1710–20. Sir Gyles Isham attributes it to Francis Smith on the grounds of its resemblance to Lamport Rectory, 1724–30, in the same county.

Square with hipped roof and dormers (both unfortunately renewed). Finely moulded stone eaves cornice and

445 *(opposite) Kingston Bagpuize House, Berkshire, 1710–20.*

446 *(left) Kings Weston, Gloucestershire. By Vanbrugh, 1710. The main front.*

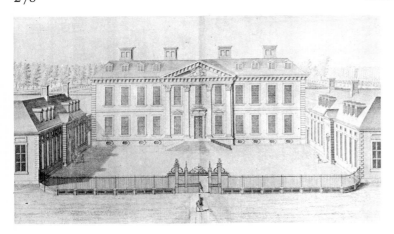

447 *Kiveton Park, Yorkshire, 1694–1704.*

central door with swan-neck pediment. The interior, somewhat altered, retains original stairs with twisted balusters and carved tread ends.
N. Pevsner—*Buildings of England, Northamptonshire,* 1961.

Kiveton Park, West Riding, Yorkshire

(demolished 1811)
For Thomas Osborne, 1st Duke of Leeds, who as Earl of Danby helped bring William of Orange to England. By William Talman 1694–1704 and modelled on Hugh May's Eltham Lodge, but more ambitious. It had eleven bays, the three central within a tetrastyle engaged portico with pediment. Eaves cornice, hipped roof and dormers. A forecourt was formed by a pair of single-storey pavilions at right angles. These had tall windows with panels above, hipped roofs and dormers.

Painted decoration by Laguerre and Thornhill. Mr Beard recounts that Thomas Young master-joiner, John Chaplin London joiner, Jonathan Maine carver, Jean Tijou French ironsmith, and John Baslow smith, all worked here.
Kerry Downes—*English Baroque Architecture,* 1966.

Langleys, Essex

Bought in 1711 by Samuel Tuffnell, a City man of much taste, and still owned by his descendant.

In brick, of straightforward H-plan, the hipped roof hidden behind a parapet with sunk panels, 1719. North wing incorporates a house of *c.* 1620. Centre of entrance front brought forward *c.* 1820, whereas the early Georgian work was preserved and reset. Doorway with broad segmental pediment, central window above with side volutes. The garden front a repetition of entrance front.

Saloon, *c.* 1720, of two storeys, decorated with fluted Corinthian pilasters and rich entablature. Plasterwork by Isaac Mansfield. Chimney-piece in two stages has affinities with the Jacobean style which Mr Tuffnell evidently admired, since he carefully preserved the 1620 library and dining room.
C.L., 9 Jan. 1942.

Langstone Court, Herefordshire

Built *c.* 1700 by the Gwillym family on to an older timber-framed house.

A small squire's or prosperous yeoman's home with forecourt, stone piers, iron gates and *clairvoie,* red-brick walls and stable block. Five-bay front all in brick, and hipped roof. A bow room added *c.* 1825. Panelled hall and parlour with deep 'Caroline' plaster ceilings, and staircase of sturdy balusters.

Since 1794 the property of the Jones family, and remarkably unspoilt in shape and setting.
C.L., 9 Nov. 1967.

Leeswood, Flintshire

A house, perhaps by Francis Smith, reduced in size *c.* 1800. Garden layout by Stephen Switzer *c.* 1715.

The so-called White Gates, or rather gates and long screen 'take their place among the finest pieces of ironwork in Europe' (G. Beard—*Georgian Craftsmen,* 1966). A 100-foot length of cornices, broken pediments, crests and vase finials of flowers by Robert Davies. In the central overthrow the Wynne arms; each pediment bears the family dolphin.

The White Gates and the Black Gates, only a little less magnificent, were made for Sir George Wynne, 1726–7.
C.L., 30 July 1943.

Little Glemham Hall, Suffolk

Dudley North transformed the old home of the Glemhams, leaving the Elizabethan gabled back more or less untouched, apart from some windows. He made the front into a long seven-bay, three-storey block with projecting two-bay wings. The whole is of red brick, relieved only by a pair of stone pilasters on ground level, which may be relics of the Elizabethan house. The roof-line is absolutely flat. The large windows are sashed. Date of the transformation is 1715–25 (rainwater heads 1717 and 1722).

Early Georgian hall with bolection-mould panelling and screen of Corinthian columns. Through an open arch is the staircase with twisted balusters, fluted Corinthian newels, inlaid strings and carved tread ends.

With a break between 1764 and 1829 Little Glemham belonged to the North family until 1920.
H. Avray Tipping—*English Homes,* Period IV, vol. I, *Late Stuart,* 1920.

Lockleys, Hertfordshire

Presumably finished 1717, the date on a hopper-head. Architect unknown. At the time the owner was Edward Searle, a London merchant. The property passed by purchase to a number of families, of which Dering was the last. Since 1924 it has been a school.

Entrance front has projecting wings of two bays. Two storeys of burnt brown and orange rubbed brick, finely pointed. Doric pilasters support an entablature over which is an attic storey under blank panels. Flat roof-line. Stone doorway with segmental head containing the arms of Dering (nineteenth century).

From the panelled hall rises the staircase of red mahogany balusters and tulip-wood inlay on treads and landings. Alterations at the rear were made by Sir Reginald Blomfield after 1911.
C.L., 10 July 1920.

Longparish House, Hampshire

Built about 1700 on the banks of the Test by the Hawker family. Home of Colonel Peter Hawker, diarist (1802–53) and sportsman. A simple house of truncated H-plan, altered throughout the eighteenth century. Of brick, now painted white. Windows have thick sashbars and dripmoulds.

Several Palladian doorways with pediments. Two rooms of unusual wainscot with polygonal-shaped panels and a central boss. Two early eighteenth-century staircases.

J. B. Burke—*Visitation of Seats*, vol. I, 1852.

Lowesby Hall, Leicestershire

A large house of the late seventeenth or early eighteenth century, once the property of Colonel John Hutchinson, regicide, who laid out the grounds. Now red brick with purple burnt headers. U-plan, two storeys and hipped roof. Garden side has curved steps with elegant wrought-iron railings. Ungainly windows in pediments of both fronts.

Hall with coved ceiling painted by (?) Verrio. Staircase curiously readjusted to fit a later corridor on entrance side. Well turned and twisted balusters and carved tread ends.

C.L., 8 May 1915.

Lumley Castle, Durham

In 1389 Sir Ralph de Lumley was given licence to crenellate the four-square castle with massive angle towers. In 1721 Vanbrugh stayed a week at Lumley with the purpose of making improvements in 'state, beauty and convenience' for Lord Lumley, afterwards 2nd Earl of Scarbrough.

The improvements merely amounted to refenestrating the south and west fronts, inserting the broad terrace and double-flight staircase on the west front, enlarging the Great Hall and forming the Library. The last is the only room solely to Vanbrugh's design. It is an undercroft divided into three aisles by piers of deeply V-cut rustication. It closely resembles the old entrance hall at Grimsthorpe Castle.

The ballroom with coved ceiling by the Francini brothers (cf. plaster volutes at the corners with stairwell ceiling at Biddick Hall) and panelled walls containing emperor's heads in roundels dates from *c.* 1740.

C.L., 18 June 1910.

Laurence Whistler—*Sir John Vanbrugh*, 1938.

Lyneham, South Devon

Built *c.* 1699. A rectangular granite block, seven bays long and five bays wide. A single projecting bay on south front; a wooden block cornice and hardly perceptible quoins. Two high granite chimney-stacks. Panelled rooms and pine staircase with fluted balusters. Rainwater heads dated 1768.

A drawing by Edmund Prideaux (1716) shows a roof balustrade enclosing the chimneys.

448 *Lyneham, Devon, c. 1699. Drawing by Edmund Prideaux.*

Market Bosworth Hall, Leicestershire

Built before 1700 for Sir Wolstan Dixie, 3rd Baronet, who inherited in 1692.

A long brick house of two storeys and flared roof. South front of eleven bays has a three-bay centre under a pediment with stone shield and garlands. The doorway is linked vertically with the window above it. Entrance front of nine bays with central pediment over elegant fluted pilasters.

Interior greatly altered, 1888.

N. Pevsner—*Buildings of England, Leicestershire*, 1960.

Marlborough House, St James's, London

The plate given in *Vitruvius Britannicus*, vol. I, shows a very different Marlborough House to that which we know today. Yet the two-storey block of 1709–11 still exists, submerged by the attic storey superimposed in the late eighteenth century, and again raised 1865–70.

The town house which Sarah, Duchess of Marlborough commissioned from Sir Christopher Wren was a deliberate contrast of economy with the extravagance of Vanbrugh's Blenheim which she detested.

Behind a French *cour d'honneur* is a long, low front in units of two bays separated by strips of horizontal rustication in the French style. In the projecting wings statues in niches. A crowning balustrade with gallant carved trophy of arms, banners, weapons and helm.

In the hall and on the staircase walls are scenes of Marlborough's military victories over Louis XIV painted by the Sun King's godson, Laguerre, in 1713.

C.L., 5 April 1962.

Medford House, Mickleton, Gloucestershire

A substantial smallholder's house of 1699 in vernacular classical. The entrance front is in russet Cotswold stone, the garden side in brick.

The front is set behind a shallow forecourt with piers carrying urns. Two wings and a slightly recessed centre, yet no break in the steep stone-tiled roof. Windows traditionally mullioned and transomed. Sophisticated front door with triangular pediment. Individual touches in the jewelled *œil-de-bœuf* windows and the semi-circular eave pediment bearing an urn.

Reginald Turnor—*The Smaller English House*, 1952.

Melbourne Hall, Derbyshire

A long leasehold from the Church was taken in 1630 by Sir John Coke, Secretary of State to Charles I. His grandson Sir Thomas Coke, Vice-Chamberlain to Queen Anne, fashioned after 1696 the incomparable garden, for which Messrs London & Wise supplied trees, shrubs and plants. Coke also consulted them about the formal layout. In 1704 he acquired the freehold. This small-scale garden was undertaken audaciously 'to suit with Versailles'. The wrought-iron arbour like a birdcage was made by Robert Bakewell of Derby 1706–11.

The Jacobean house was enlarged towards the end of the seventeenth century (south side), and again c. 1725 by Francis Smith. The seven-bay east façade, with central three-bay pediment, and lower windows with heavy key-

449 *Melbourne Hall, Derbyshire. The arbour, 1706–11.*

stones and Gibbs surrounds, was by William Smith, c. 1744, for George Lewis Coke; William Jackson was the builder.

Thomas Coke's youngest daughter was married to Sir Matthew Lamb, 1st Baronet, of Brocket. Through her Melbourne descended to the Viscounts Melbourne, the Earls Cowper and the present owner, the Marquess of Lothian.

C.L., 7 April 1928.

David Green—*Gardener to Queen Anne*, 1956.

Melbury House, Dorset

Acquired by the Strangways family 1500. House begun by Sir Giles Strangways at the end of Henry VIII's reign. Three wings round a court and the hexagonal tower are of this time.

Thomas Strangways rebuilt the east front and the centres of the north and south fronts. A portrait at Melbury is inscribed: 'Mr Watson, architect to Thomas Strangways Sen[r] Esq., who enlarged and adorned the house 1692.' He must have been a local mason-builder for the fronts are provincial, although charming. Of two storeys with dormers behind a balustrade. The east front has a tetrastyle centrepiece of Doric and Corinthian columns superimposed. The material used throughout is Ham stone.

In the Entrance Hall are two carved overmantels attri-

450 *Melbury House, Dorset. The east front, 1692.*

buted to Grinling Gibbons. The Grand Staircase has a ceiling painted by Lanscroon, and a vast canvas of Thomas Strangways's family in the garden by Thomas Hill.

In the eighteenth century Melbury was inherited by the Fox family who added the Strangways name to their own. Stephen Fox was created Lord Ilchester in 1741 and Earl of Ilchester in 1756.

Arthur Oswald—*Country Houses of Dorset*, 1935.

Milgate Park, Kent

A house of the Maidstone school (cf. Bradbourne).

Quadrangular, the rear range of Tudor brickwork. Side elevations *c.* 1695 for William Cage, whose grandfather William Cage bought the property (1624). These elevations have carved wood modillion cornices with neat breaks over the windows.

Front of claret brick and scarlet rubbed dressings. Fine coved wooden portal with carved cipher over the door. This was added on a slightly larger scale, presumably in Queen Anne's reign. Lead downpipes. Late Georgian bow added to west end.

Two-storey hall leading to spacious staircase, of which the upper walls and ceiling are decorated in style of Lanscroon (paintings blackened and practically invisible). Several rooms with pilastered chimney-breasts, and most rooms panelled.

Moat House, Sutton Coldfield, Warwickshire

Said to have been designed by Sir William Wilson, mason-architect, for himself and his bride, *c.* 1680, but a more likely date is 1700.

Very urbane and Baroque. Brick with stone dressings. Giant Corinthian pilasters support a cornice with balustraded parapet, from which a niche under a hood rises in the centre. Lucarne windows in the roof. Massive chimney-stacks at either end, and under one stack a sundial.

N. Pevsner—*Buildings of England, Warwickshire*, 1966.

Montagu House, Bloomsbury, London

(demolished *c.* 1822).

First built 1674–9 for Ralph Montagu (1st Duke of Montagu 1705) by Robert Hooke in 'the French pavilion way' according to Evelyn. Burnt down and rebuilt 1686–8, 'in doing which . . . little or no alteration could be made to advantage', according to Boyer (1710). Colen Campbell and George Vertue declared that the architect was a Monsieur Pouget, who has not yet been identified. Montagu's French proclivities are well known, and he certainly got a team of French artists to decorate the house. But it is not unlikely that Hooke was again involved in the architecture. Nevertheless the second Montagu House was decidedly more French-looking than the first (see also Fig. 50). It had a *cour d'honneur* defined by pavilions at

451 *(above) Montagu House, London, 1686–8 (destroyed).
An early 19th-century watercolour.*

452 *(right) Mothecombe, Devon, c. 1710.*

453 *(opposite) Oulton Park, Cheshire, 1715 (demolished).*

right angles and a linking wall with entrance.

The house consisted of three-bay projecting wings and centrepiece. A mansard roof, central four-sided dome, and horizontal angle rustication were further evidences of the French look. The interior was very richly decorated. The house had a strong influence upon contemporary taste. Stuart decoration.

C.L., 14 Sept. 1951.
Vitruvius Britannicus, vol. I, 1715.
J. Kip—*Nouveau Théâtre de la Grande Bretagne*, vol. III, 1715.

The Moot, Downton, Wiltshire
The terraced slope in the grounds is where the moots were held in Saxon times.

The yeoman Coles family settled in Downton, 1611. A descendant built the square house *c.* 1700. West front walls of alternate red stretchers and blue-grey burnt headers. The single-bay centrepiece under a pediment projects slightly and is of red brick only. The front door has a broken pediment. Central window with carved stone volutes to surrounds, which are broken into the wooden cornice (cf. Mompesson House, Salisbury). Hipped roof and dormers.

In 1927 the interior was gutted by fire, but reconstituted.
H. Avray Tipping—*English Homes*, Period IV, vol. I, *Late Stuart*, 1920.

Mothecombe, South Devon
For Sir J. Pollexfen, *c.* 1710. A small forecourt with wooden palisade. Two-storey stone house of five bays with hipped roof. Coved eaves and pilastered angles. Front door enters straight into hall. Pine staircase painted, corkscrew balusters. Vertical fielded panelling.

Additions for Lord Mildmay of Flete by Lutyens, 1923.
C.L., 26 July 1956.

Netherhampton House, Wiltshire
A face only, but what a lovely one! Between 1710 and 1720 a late seventeenth-century cottage was given a front of five bays and segmental headed windows with thick sashbars. The material is smooth ashlar, lichen-grey. The flat roof parapet carries three wreathed urns and sweeps down over single-storey wings. Over the front door a niche with rusticated surround.

Wrought-iron gates with armorial overthrow and screen, and pollarded limes. The home of Sir Henry Newbolt for twenty-seven years until 1938.

Newby Hall, Yorkshire
Built *c.* 1705 for Sir Edward Blackett, M.P. for Ripon, but looks a decade earlier. Belongs to the rectangular block type of house with projecting wings.

Of red brick and stone quoins. The chief feature is the central doorway on west and south elevations. A segmental broken pediment, very Wren-like, is repeated in each case over the window above. Paired columns adorn the west door; carved stone drops adorn the south door.

Newby was entirely redecorated and given wings by Robert Adam after 1767.
C. Hussey—*English Country Houses, Mid Georgian, 1760–1800*, 1956.

Newton Ferrers, Cornwall
Of rude granite, built 1686–95 for Sir William Coryton, 3rd Bart. One of the earliest Cornish houses of classical design. Centre of seven bays and two projecting wings. High pitched slate roof.

Two-thirds of the house were gutted by fire in 1940. Balustraded terraces, curved steps and garden piers, all in sparkling granite.
C.L., 17 Dec. 1938.

Ockham Park, Surrey

(mostly demolished 1950)

In 1710 the Jacobean manor house was bought by Peter King, later Lord Chancellor and Lord King of Ockham.

In 1725–9 King commissioned Nicholas Hawksmoor to build a grandiose seat. It was altered by Thornhill in 1729, Italianized in 1830 and burnt down in 1946. Only Hawksmoor's kitchen block and red-brick buildings survive after a fashion; they are in process of restoration. Hawksmoor's drawings still exist. A feature of the garden front was a blown-up Venetian window unit for the entrance.

Kerry Downes—*Hawksmoor*, 1959.

L. Whistler—*Architectural Review*, Oct. 1955.

Orleans House, Twickenham, Middlesex

(demolished 1927)

A small Thames-side house built for the Hon. James Johnston, one-time Secretary of State for Scotland. John James was the architect, 1710. The house stood to the right of James Gibbs's Octagon which survives (see Christopher Hussey—*Early Georgian*). It was illustrated in *Vitruvius Britannicus*, vol. I. The plan (corner fireplaces, linked flues) and elevations (window spacing, wooden cornice, projecting end gables) are demonstrative of James's peculiarities throughout his career.

Orlingbury Hall, Northamptonshire

Bought by Richard Young in 1705 and built soon afterwards. Of deep brown, almost orange, stone, and cream stone dressings. The entrance front divided into three parts of three bays each by giant Ionic pilasters. Each pilaster carries a frieze with triglyph, and the two inner support chimney-shafts. Was there meant to be a parapet? Instead there is a hipped stone roof with four pedimented dormers. Interior much altered.

J. A. Gotch—*Squires' Homes of Northamptonshire*, 1939.

Oulton Park, Cheshire

(demolished after 1926)

A large rectangular house built for John Egerton, a bachelor of sixty, in 1715, and gutted by fire in 1926 during the ownership of Sir Philip Grey-Egerton, 12th Bart. Of red brick and stone dressings. Architect unknown and design perplexing. The house had a few Vanbrughian features, viz. the north front centrepiece—wholly in stone—of four engaged Corinthian columns and broken entablature, supporting a broken pediment filled with carved trophies; and the elliptical pediments of the end elevations. The Dutch gables of the wings harked back to the Kew Palace Caroline style, and may even have dated from Lewis Wyatt's alterations.

Hall with fluted pilasters and groined ceiling had affinities with the halls of Beningbrough and Gilling. Carving in wood and moulding of plaster were of high quality.

C. Latham—*In English Homes*, vol. III, 1909.

Parliament Piece, Ramsbury, Wiltshire

Late seventeenth century but a good deal altered. South front of five bays and two storeys (front door removed to west side under Victorian portico). All in red brick on stone and flint base. Modillion eaves cornice, flared roof and pedimented dormers. Central brick stack of blind arcades. Casement windows, the mullions and transoms of wood.

Staircase (rearranged) of stout turned balusters and broad handrail.

Stables and long garden wall contemporary.

Plympton House, South Devon

Begun by Sir George Treby, at one time M.P. for Plympton and Chief Justice of the Common Pleas. How far he progressed with the house before his death in 1700 is uncertain. It was completed by his son George Treby, Secretary at War, *c.* 1720. In that year William Veale, mason, was in charge of the stonework and the completion of the chimneys.

The two main fronts are of Portland stone, and in the Palladian style. The south front has a central pediment containing a cartouche and swags. The sides are of red brick, still in the William and Mary fashion. Windows sashed.

The staircase is comparable with that of Puslinch, but has four balusters to a tread, evenly raked. The newels are fluted.

The house is contained within a series of garden walls which protect it from the town. Tiled dairy in the stable range.

C.L., 12 Aug. 1933.

Puslinch, South Devon

In 1726 James Yonge, son of James Yonge, F.R.S., a distinguished writer on medicine, married Mary, daughter and heiress of John Upton of Poselynche. She was tenth in descent from John Upton and Elizabeth de Mohun of Poselynche.

The present Puslinch seems to be earlier than 1726, and may have been built by Mary Upton or her widowed mother after John Upton's death in 1702.

Of brick and stone dressings with three-bay projection. Hipped roof and dormers alternately pedimented. Window-lintels of gauged brick. The front door leads straight into a large hall, of which the panelling has affinities with that of Antony across the Plymouth border in Cornwall. Behind, a fine contemporary staircase.

There are a number of portraits of the family, including Dr James Yonge (d. 1721), the friend of Hans Sloane, and a self-portrait by Northcote. Charlotte M. Yonge, a cousin, was a frequent visitor. Puslinch is still in possession of the Yonge family.

C.L., 18 Nov. 1933.

Pynes, near Exeter, Devon

Name derived from the family of Pyn, or Pine, who settled here *temp.* King John. The property was bought by Hugh Stafford in Charles II's reign and the house was rebuilt by his son in the early eighteenth century. The son's daughter married Sir Henry Northcote, 5th Bart. It has belonged to their descendants ever since.

Rectangular, red brick, and steep pitched roof. Over each bay of the projecting centre is a balustrade in the parapet. Tuscan pilasters at the angles of the centrepiece and the four corners of the block. Stairs and stairwell ceiling contemporary.

Large, ungainly extensions at the rear *c.* 1852 for Sir Stafford Northcote, 1st Earl of Iddesleigh and Chancellor of the Exchequer (1874–80).

A. E. Richardson and C. L. Gill—*Regional Architecture of the West of England*, 1924.

Rampyndene, Burwash, Sussex

Built 1699 by a timber merchant John Butler, and acquired in 1718 by ironmaster Thomas Hussey. It is, in fact, timber framed, although from the High Street it appears brick built and tile hung, with steep pitched roof and two huge panelled chimney-stacks. The windows are still casemented. A hood carved with birds and a cherub's head over the front door and flanking narrow windows. A block cornice runs under the eaves.

Hall and staircase occupy a third of the plan. Stucco hall ceiling rather coarse, but lively, in compartments of flowers and leaves. Stairs with thick handrail, yet elegant turned balusters. Wide first-floor landing and stucco ceiling over the staircase, marked '[J.B.] built this'.

Rampyndene looks back to the Inigo Jones rather than the Wren type of small domestic dwelling.

C.L., 1 March 1946.

454 *Rampyndene, Burwash, Sussex, 1699.*

Reddish House, Broad Chalke, Wiltshire

A small tradesman's dwelling of red brick and stone dressings, built 1700–2 for Jeremiah Clay, clothier and John Combes, mercer. Pevsner calls it 'not at all correct or polite', because presumably the giant pilasters are made to carry nothing. Nevertheless it is enchanting with its high roof and panelled brick chimneys, somewhat topsy-turvy. Steps up to front door with bust over. In the pediment an oval window set horizontally. The miniature front is practically dwarfed by elephantine yews of great age. In the attic are cock-fighting pens.

C.L., 21 March 1957.

Reigate Priory, Surrey

In 1703 Sir John Parsons, M.P. and Lord Mayor of London, acquired this Augustinian Priory, converted to a house in 1541. To the west of the hall he installed what may be the best painted staircase in England. In 1779 the Caroline house was rather feebly Palladianized.

The stairs rise round three sides of a spacious well, with a landing on the fourth side. Elegant and close-set twisted balusters and columned newels. Corinthian screen at the top of the stairs. Walls and ceiling of stairwell painted in continuous scenes by Verrio—*The Choice of Hercules* and *The Rape of Proserpine*. On the landing walls statues of the liberal arts in niches (monochrome).

C.L., 6 April 1918.

Roehampton House (Queen Mary's Hospital), Surrey

Built for Thomas Carey in 1712 by Thomas Archer. According to *Vitruvius Britannicus*, vol. I (1715), it had an enormous cleft pediment, somewhat resembling the one the architect gave to Monmouth House, Soho. Of brick with rusticated angles and vertical strips. Windows have aprons. Over the front door the very high window within a stone tabernacle lit the saloon which Thornhill decorated (*Feast of the Gods*), but which was destroyed in the Second World War. Above the entablature of the tabernacle eccentric bulbous trusses like orange pigs, typically Archerian, and on either side roundel windows.

Lutyens trebled the size of the house for A. M. Grenfell. It was necessarily altered again when it became a hospital. Consequently Archer's low, convex, quadrant arcades were somewhat overborne. The pavilions of the forecourt are replacements of Archer's.

C.L., 14 Aug. 1915.

Rosemerryn, Cornwall

Circa 1700–10. Two storeys and seven bays. Sash windows. Central Ionic doorway with pediment, the pilasters collared. Block cornice, hipped roof. Forecourt entered through wrought-iron gates between stone piers; on either side low walls with rails.

Sandywell Park, Gloucestershire

Atkyns compiling notes for his *History of Gloucestershire* (*c.* 1710) wrote: 'Henry Bret, esq. has a neat pleasant seat at Sandywell, and a new built house, with pleasant gardens.' The house is shown in Kip's plate—a five-bay square box with dormered roof, balustrade and cupola, probably 1680–90. The cupola has gone, but the block remains. To it, *c.* 1720, were added for the 1st Lord Conway, two-bay projecting wings, as shown in a plate (1770) in Rudder's *Gloucestershire*. The house of Rudder's plate still stands, only with Early Victorian additions to the east. The return south front, formed *c.* 1720, is of five bays and three storeys. Giant Doric pilasters at the angles and stone balustrade carrying urns. Windows have bold lintels and aprons. The doorway—now a window—has Gibbs surrounds. Handsome staircase (1720) and interesting garden hall (1680–90).

There are three fine garden gates of stone piers and finials, and on the west an ironwork screen.

The 2nd Lord Conway sold Sandywell in 1748.

455 *Roehampton House, Surrey. By Thomas Archer, 1712. The house was altered and extended by Lutyens in 1912.*

Scraptoft Hall, Leicestershire

Built for the Wigley family *c.* 1720. A pleasing specimen of Midland Baroque. Stone fronted with flat, swept-up parapet. The centre bay of front door, with scroll pediment and window above, is embraced by a giant order of Corinthian pilasters carrying pilaster strips on the attic floor. Keystones and aprons to windows.

Splendid screen and gates with overthrow (*c.* 1720–30) stand before the house.

N. Pevsner—*Buildings of England, Leicestershire*, 1960.

Serle's House, Southgate Street, Winchester, Hampshire

Now a town house, but when built for the Sheldons a villa in its own grounds. Date *c.* 1710–20. Architect unknown, but the style is so close to that of Chettle that Archer is the obvious guess.

Of red brick and rubbed brick dressings. Tuscan giant pilasters at the angles and on the projecting centre of the east side. They have oddly swelling capitals. The entablature has a coved frieze. Segmental headed windows on ground and first floor.

The centrepiece resembles in its quadrant curves that of the Chettle entrance.

On the west side there is an oval stairwell with stairs ascending in two arms from one flight. Graceful balusters resembling the Chettle ones. A Doric doorway, rusticated, leads to an upstairs drawing room. It has a swan-neck pediment over the door and a pair of wide niches facing the windows in the quadrant curves.

In 1781 bought by James Serle, and since about 1800 used as the headquarters of the Hampshire Militia.

N. Pevsner and D. Lloyd—*Buildings of England, Hampshire*, 1967.

Shenfield Place, Essex

Robert Hooke's *Diary* for 1689–90 contains several references to the modest house he was building for Squire Vaughan. On 3 June 1689 'With Vaughan's coach and 4 horses to Burntwood [Brentwood] thence to his seat . . .', and on 5 June, 'Vaughan here delivered him a draught for a house 40 feet square'. The present house is of these measurements. Richard Vaughan (d. 1728) married Elizabeth, sister and heiress of Sir Henry Appleton, Bart, of South Benfleet.

The house has been considerably altered and added to. Nevertheless the original foursquare block with widely spaced cornice modillions, hipped roof and dormers, remains. The most distinctive features are on the east and west sides, a pair of vast chimney-breasts in red brick and blue headers breaking through the eaves.

Simple pine staircase, some panelling and cornices survive.

Royal Commission Historical Monuments—*Essex*, vol. II, 1921.

Sherborne House, Dorset

In its own grounds in St Swithin's Street, Sherborne. Probably by a member of the Bastard family for H. S. Portman. A tall, compact house, colour-washed, with ashlar dressings. Central pediment and balustraded parapet, swept down to the side elevations.

Chief feature is the staircase. The tread ends display the Portman crest, a talbot, in marquetry over carved scrolls. Walls and ceiling painted 1715–20 by Thornhill, who was a Dorset man, and steadily patronized by Mr Portman. Walls depict within compartments of Corinthian columns, *Meleager and the Boar*; ceiling depicts *The Triumph of Diana* in prevailing soft grey-blue.

In 1849 the house was rented by W. C. Macready and often visited by Dickens.

Royal Commission Historical Monuments—*West Dorset*, 1952.

Shobdon Court, Herefordshire

(demolished 1930s)

Sir James Bateman, Lord Mayor of London, acquired the estate in 1705. He built Shobdon Court in the style of Clarendon House, Piccadilly, a nine-bay front with two-bay projecting wings. Five-bay centre under a pediment containing two oval windows and a stone escutcheon. All of red brick with stone dressings.

There was a two-storey hall with coved ceiling, the lower stage of Ionic pilasters. A gallery on columns.

The house was much tricked up in mid Victorian times. The windows were given rusticated lintels and the roof-line a parapet. The cupola (not shown in *Vitruvius Britannicus*, vol. II) was removed.

The 3rd Lord Bateman of the second creation died in 1931, when the house was pulled down.

C.L., 10 Nov. 1906.

Smedmore, Dorset

Inherited by the present owner through continuous descent since Henry IV's reign.

Sir William Clavell's Jacobean house was given a south front *c.* 1700. Stone, two storeys, blind parapet and dormers. The windows have bolection-moulded surrounds, and panels in dressed stone between each storey. Early eighteenth-century oak staircase. Bowed west front imposed 1761.

C.L., 19 Jan. 1935.

Somersby Manor Farm, Lincolnshire

In the Wolds and next door to the Tennyson family's rectory. Built 1722 for Robert Burton and, according to a contemporary design, one 'Robert Alfray', of whom nothing is known, 'invt: delin.' There are reasons for supposing that Vanbrugh was the true author (cf. Vanbrugh Castle).

Considerably altered, and the little pavilions linked by wide arches have disappeared. Of brick with four angle towers machicolated and embattled, and given round and round-headed windows. North front embattled. An ingenious arrangement of 'screens' passage, vaulted hall and narrow staircase.

L. Whistler—*The Imagination of Vanbrugh*, 1954.

N. Pevsner and J. Harris—*Buildings of England, Lincolnshire*, 1964.

456 *(above) South Littleton Manor, Worcestershire.*

457 *(left) Sprotborough Hall, Yorkshire, 1685 (demolished).*

South Littleton Manor, Worcestershire

To a low, gabled, lias stone building was added a rectangular block of deep plum brick. It has over a wooden cornice a steep pitched roof with top-heavy pedimented dormers. A pair of enormous chimney-stacks, each coupled and arched, flank a square lantern of three windows and a door. It bears a weather-vane dated 1721. The windows are casements restored early this century.

A narrow entrance hall leads to a sturdy staircase with twisted balusters. Small rooms to left and right of the front door.

Sprotborough Hall, West Riding, Yorkshire

(demolished 1926)

From the Fitzwilliams, who owned it since the Conquest, Sprotborough passed by marriage *temp*. Henry VIII to the Copleys. In 1709 it came through the female line to Joseph Moyle who assumed his metronymic.

A large house, rather French, built 1685 for Sir Godfrey Copley, 2nd Bart, over a long terrace. Seven-bay centre block with five-bay wings. Whole surface harled. On the entrance side, corner towers with leaded cupolas. The stringcourses over first and second floors continued through the segmental window-heads, giving a curious wavy roll to the centre block.

Large room of 73 feet with screen of columns at either end and boudoir decorated by Laguerre.

C.L., 11 Feb. 1922.

Stanhoe Hall, Norfolk

Built 1703 for Thomas Archdale, M.P., probably by Henry Bell of King's Lynn, with Stephen Kemp, stone-mason. Of brick and stone dressings. The seven-bay front has a slight three-bay projection. Two storeys, hipped roof and dormers. Central front door with broken pediment. Staircase of three twisted balusters to each tread.

C.L., 29 Sept. 1966.

Stansted Park, Sussex

(burnt 1900 and replaced)
In 1687 William Talman built for Richard Lumley, 1st
Earl of Scarbrough, a house which for its post-Restoration
look and lack of Baroque flavour makes his association
with contemporary Uppark highly plausible. Kip's view
is all we have from which to judge Talman's Stansted.
It was several times altered. The present house by Sir
R. Blomfield takes the place of the old house burnt down in
1900. Present owner the Earl of Bessborough.

Stedcombe Manor, South Devon

Built in 1695 for John Hallett who bought the property
four years previously. Halletts owned it until 1889.

The house is five-bay square, of two storeys, attic and
deep basement. The walls are of red brick, the quoins of
stone. The most striking feature is the square belvedere
built over the hipped roof for views of the sea and distant
hills. It has an arched window with heavy stone surrounds
on three faces.

Simple contemporary panelling. The drawing-room
chimney-piece is of elaborate carved woodwork in chinoiserie fashion (branches and birds) taken from a plate in
Lock and Copland's *New Book of Ornaments*, 1752.
C.L., 26 Dec. 1963.

Stoke Edith Park, Herefordshire

(burnt 1927 and subsequently demolished)
This beautiful and important house was designed and
begun by Speaker Paul Foley, and finished by his son
Thomas Foley. Celia Fiennes saw the gardens 'staked out'
in 1696 and the 'new house . . . building' in 1698. Red
brick with mansard roof, and on the north front stone

centrepiece of four Corinthian pilasters supporting a
pediment.

The outstanding features were Thornhill's painted hall
and staircase (1705).

Of the two-storeyed hall, ceiling and upper half were
treated as an open pavilion with mythological figures.
The lower half was painted in panels with grotesque
rocky landscapes by Isaac Bayly 1705 (cf. overmantel
panel of bedroom at Great Hundridge Manor). The staircase walls and ceiling entirely by Thornhill (*The Slaughter
of Niobe's Family*) who introduced elliptical arches flanked
by groups of Atlantes.

Saloon decorated 1771 in Adam manner.
Vitruvius Britannicus, vol. I, 1715.
Charles Latham—*In English Homes*, vol. III, 1909.

Stoke Mandeville House, Buckinghamshire

'A perfect example of the English house of *c.* 1700',
according to Nikolaus Pevsner, 'as good as any in the
country.' This concerns the exterior. Square in plan, of
red brick in Flemish bond, five bays and a hipped roof. The
eaves carved with outsize egg and dart. Of the two carved
wood door-cases the south has a frieze of flowers deeply
undercut and a rich shell hood on acanthus brackets.
N. Pevsner—*Buildings of England, Buckinghamshire*, 1960.

Swallowfield Park, Berkshire

The house which belonged to Flower, Lady Backhouse,
was rebuilt by Talman (1689–91) when this lady had
become the wife of Henry Hyde, 2nd Earl of Clarendon. In
1820 it was largely remodelled by William Atkinson for Sir
Henry Russell and the brickwork stuccoed over. The
shape of Talman's house remains—an H with shallow

458 *(right) Swangrove,
Gloucestershire, 1703.*

459 *(opposite) Tadworth
Court, Surrey, 1694–1704.*

and deep projections on west and east fronts; so does the red-brick court on the north.

On the garden side an oval vestibule with stucco dome (Edward Goudge worked here, 1690–1); but some of the plaster decoration is undoubtedly later.

The garden portal, removed from the house in 1820, must also be Talman's. This monumental affair, with broken segmental pediment, corbels in place of capitals, swags and draperies, derives from an Italian Mannerist source (John Harris suggests central doorway of Milan Duomo of 1567). The gardens were highly praised by John Evelyn (22 October 1682) before George London set about improving them in 1688.

Constance, Lady Russell—*Swallowfield and Its Owners*, 1901.

Swangrove, Badminton, Gloucestershire

A Cotswold 'maison de plaisance' on the Badminton estate. Built for Henry Somerset, 2nd Duke of Beaufort, 1703.

On one side are fields, on the other is a wood cut by intersecting rides shown in Kip's view of *c.* 1712. Four attendant pavilions and a tiny forecourt. A steep outside stair leads to a central 'great' room on the first floor. It is panelled. At one corner a small closet contains a marble cistern on a plinth. Water flows through a Chinaman's head.

A plain oak staircase descends to the ground floor and ascends to an upper room. Here the wainscot stiles are painted with vignettes of Chinese scenes in gold on brown imitating lacquer. The fields are missing. Doors and dado in contemporary grey marbling.

C.L., 16 Dec. 1939.

Swynnerton Hall, Staffordshire

William Fitzherbert married in Elizabeth I's reign Elizabeth daughter and co-heiress of Humphrey Swynnerton. Ever since this union Swynnerton has belonged to the Fitzherbert family of which the present representative is the 14th Lord Stafford.

Neale's *Seats*, vol. III (1820) claims that 'This handsome edifice was erected in the reign of Queen Anne.' Family tradition asserts that Francis Smith was architect. This is probable. Richard Trubshaw did work here in 1731.

Thomas Fitzherbert (d. 1765) will have been the builder, probably soon after his marriage in 1713.

The three-bay projecting centre has recognizable affinities with other Midland houses by Smith. Giant Doric pilasters carry an entablature, over which is a full attic storey. First-floor windows of centrepiece and wings are on brackets practically sitting on the pediments of the ground-floor windows. The pillared doorway leads straight into a two-storeyed hall.

Tadworth Court, Surrey

Built between 1694 and 1704 for Leonard Wessels. In the style of Uppark, i.e. hipped roof, dormers, and dentilled cornice, but in the opinion of Nairn and Pevsner, of higher quality. Yellow brick, and eleven bays long. A five-bay centre slightly projecting under a pediment, with well-carved doorway and swan-neck pediment, and with upper window and involuted side scrolls.

Two-storey hall with Rococo plasterwork over high panelling. But the ceiling, divided into stucco panels and central oval, is contemporary. Hall gallery with twisted balusters, *c.* 1700.

I. Nairn & N. Pevsner—*Buildings of England, Surrey*, 1962.

Thorpe Mandeville Manor, Northamptonshire

Probably for Richard Gostelowe by an unknown architect between 1702 and 1720. Of orange Hornton ironstone and grey stone dressings.

South front has a deeply projecting centre of three bays under a massive elliptical pediment which is broken and contains an urn issuing flames. It can only be described as Archer-like. Front door with scrolly pediment and escutcheon.

Behind the centrepiece a drawing room with bolection-moulded wainscot. Entrance hall with black and white marble floor, and oak staircase of twisted balusters and carved brackets.

Additions to the house by Oliver Hill in the 1930s. *C.L.*, 20 Aug. 1938.

Tintinhull House, Somerset

The west front was imposed upon a Charles I block for the Napper family *c.* 1700. It is a miniature classical composition of five bays in glowing, gold Ham stone. Centrepiece of three bays between Tuscan pilasters bearing pediment and eye-opening in a scroll frame. Ionic porch with semi-circular head. All the windows of mullion and transom casements. In the forecourt a pair of stone piers bear a displayed eagle apiece.

Reginald Turnor—*The Smaller English House*, 1952.

Trewithen, Cornwall

Begun soon after 1715 for Philip Hawkins. Certainly the pavilions were finished, if the centre block was not designed, by Thomas Edwards in 1738–40. Centre block of five bays and projecting wings of two bays, all whitened. High hipped roof with dormers over parapet. Facing pavilions of brick linked to centre block. Later work by Sir Robert Taylor, 1764.

C.L., 2 April 1953.

Trumpeters House, Richmond, Surrey

Called after two mediaeval figures of trumpeters formerly standing at the front door.

Built *c.* 1708 for Richard Hill, brother of Queen Anne's substitute for Sarah, Duchess of Marlborough, namely Abigail Hill, Mrs Masham. The ex-favourite herself rented the house in 1729. Was Wren the architect? Or another associated with the Board of Works?

The main river façade recalls Chelsea Hospital. Brick, eleven bays and a giant portico of two pairs of Doric columns with pediment. Tall, narrow sash windows. Two small pedimented end pavilions.

In one room fine Rococo ceiling with relief busts of Pope and Milton, *c.* 1740.

C.L., 21 April 1944.

Tutnall Hall, Tardebigge, Worcestershire

A rough-and-ready version of the Cound Hall type, having lost any pediment and parapet it may once have had. Queen Anne and red brick, the three-bay centre and two-bay ends separated by giant Tuscan pilasters and entablatures, embracing two floors and an attic.

Umberslade Park, Warwickshire

Acquired by the Archer family in the reign of Henry I. Andrew Archer rebuilt the house 1695–1700.

Francis Smith is now said to be the architect. He may well have been the actual builder employed, but there seems to be no reason why Andrew's brother, Thomas Archer was not the designer, if indeed he was responsible for Bramham. The plate in *Vitruvius Britannicus*, vol. III, shows two detached pavilions (were they ever built?) with distinct Baroque features, viz. rusticated strips, arcaded chimney-stack and pedimented centre gable (cf. Moat House, Sutton Coldfield).

460 *Tintinhull House,*
Somerset, c. 1700.

The main block of stone throughout is austere and plain. Rectangular, of 'double pile', blunt H-plan, no orders and vermiculated quoins. A balustraded parapet crowns the three storeys. Central window with swags of fruit turning into side scrolls. The hall has three-quarter Corinthian columns upholding a cornice with bold brackets. A crouching Venus by Van Nost (1702) within a niche. Dull staircase. Nineteenth-century alterations.
Victoria County Histories—*Warwickshire*, vol. V, 1949.

Uppark, Sussex

For a full account of this house see Christopher Hussey's *Mid Georgian* (1956) to which period the interior decoration properly belongs.

Nevertheless, the three main fronts and the two out of four detached pavilions intended remain unaltered since the house was built *c.* 1685–90 for the 1st Earl of Tankerville. Uppark is, as regards the exterior, a textbook William and Mary country house of small red bricks, stone dressings, hipped roof and dormers, deriving from the Dutch style introduced by Hugh May. If Talman was the architect, as is now reasserted, he was remarkably sparing of his usual Baroque touch. The carving of the pediment (the Fetherstonhaugh arms are an eighteenth-century replacement) in wood and of the door-case in stone is exuberant.

Of original interior work the staircase and dining-room panelling survive.

Uppark was bought 1747 by Sir Matthew Fetherstonhaugh, 1st Baronet.
C.L., 14 June 1941.

Vanbrugh Castle, Greenwich, Kent

One of the earliest of sham castles associated with the Picturesque movement. Sometimes referred to by Vanbrugh as 'The Bastille'. Built 1717–18 for his own use in the south-east corner (called Vanbrugh Fields) of Greenwich Park, where he also raised three other little follies, The Nunnery, Mince Pie House and the Gatehouse—all destroyed between 1902 and 1911.

On the edge of a bluff overlooking the Seamen's Hospital and the Thames. Of brick with square towers, a round tower, bows, battlements and machicolations, and outlying bastions. The castle, only faintly mediaeval in spirit, is in no sense Gothic. Rather it looks forward to the 'Gothick' Revival later in the century; and is more literary and dramatic than architectural.
H. Avray Tipping and C. Hussey—*English Homes*, Period IV, vol. II. *Vanbrugh and His School*, 1928.
L. Whistler—*The Imagination of Vanbrugh*, 1954.

Ven House, Somerset

James Medlycott, a Master in Chancery, bought the manor of Milborne Port in 1696. Between 1698 and 1700 he built himself a modest house with five-bay front facing west. Between 1720 and his death in 1731, aged seventy-three, he engaged Nathaniel Ireson to rebuild on a grander scale. Ireson's work incorporates the earlier house, of which the front has become one end of the new. Payments to Ireson occur in building accounts. Two prospects of the present house, dated 19 September 1739 and signed by one Richard Grange, are headed, 'the seat of James Medlycott, esq.', who by this time had been succeeded by his son, Thomas.

The rectangular block has two identical fronts of seven bays facing north and south. Two storeys are embraced by giant pilasters with attic floor above a sharp cornice, in the Buckingham House formula (closest parallel is Ireson's Crowcombe Court, Somerset, of 1734). Material red brick with stone dressings.

A two-storeyed hall with pair of stone fireplaces and painted ceiling. The curved screen and gallery may date from Decimus Burton's alterations *c.* 1836.

Wide, balustraded terrace garden and stone piers date from James Medlycott's time. Sold by Sir Hubert Medlycott, 7th Baronet, after the last war.
C.L., 24 June 1911.

Waddon Manor, Dorset

A wing of 1700 is all that is left of Henry Chafin's manor house burnt down in 1704. Of fine grey ashlar, wooden cornice and tall sashed windows. High-pitched slate roof. Walled forecourt, gazebo and classical gate-piers with ball finials.

Inside are two panelled rooms and an oak staircase with dog gate. Handrail ends in a fist-like scroll grasping a plain column. Painted King Charles spaniels on kitchen door.
C.L., 11 Nov. 1931.

Waldershare Park, Kent

The ghost of a fine Queen Anne house totally burnt out in 1913. The red-brick shell was reconstituted and the interior rebuilt by Sir Reginald Blomfield.

The centrepiece of south front retains its interesting outline of 1702–10 when built for Sir Henry Furnese, 1st Baronet, i.e. five bays of two storeys between stone Corinthian pilasters: attic storey carrying lead figures of Venus Jupiter, Saturn and Mars. The centrepiece, which is shown in T. Badeslade's *Noblemen's Seats of Kent* (1720), suggests Talman or Winde for architect.

Sir Henry Furnese's heiress granddaughter brought Waldershare to the Earls of Guilford.

461 *Waldershare Park, Kent, 1702–10. As restored in 1913.*

462 *(top) Warbrook House, Hampshire. By John James, 1724.*

463 & 464 *Wentworth Woodhouse, Yorkshire. The west front, 1725–8, and a detail of the central feature.*

Wallington, Northumberland

This traditionally Whig house was built in 1688 for Sir William Blackett, Bart, round a courtyard. Of honey-coloured sandstone, nine bays long and two storeys high. Hipped roof. The entrance front has a three-bay projecting centrepiece; the garden front two-bay projecting wings. The exterior of the house was embellished by Daniel Garrett c. 1740, and the interior 1740–3 in the Rococo style (plasterwork by Francini brothers).

Inherited from the Blacketts in 1777 by the Trevelyans. Given to the National Trust 1942.

C.L., 22 June 1918.

N. Pevsner—Buildings of England, Northumberland, 1957.

Warbrook House, Eversley, Hampshire

Strikingly individual house built for himself by John James, 1724. Of hair-thin pointed red brick with rendered dressings. A centre block of only three bays between pilaster strips under a pediment (the temple front motif) containing a Venetian window. On each end wall are six chimney-stacks in a row (if those at the angles are chimneys), the four central ones coupled by arches. Under each arcaded stack a small round-headed window. End walls of coarser purple brick.

Two pavilions, attached by a corridor of one bay each, are advanced on the entrance front. They have a blind lunette in the pediment. The rich oak staircase rises straight from the hall on the right of the entrance. Pedimented stucco panels and stucco ceiling.

On the garden side a formal canal in three arms meets in a pool opposite the centre block of the house and recedes in a wider stretch of water.

Additions to the pavilion wings by Lord Gerald Wellesley in the 1930s.

C.L., 11 March 1939.

Wellesbourne Hall, Warwickshire

Home of the D'Ewes family who changed their name to Granville after the marriage in 1740 of Anne Granville (Mrs Delany's sister) to John D'Ewes.

Circa 1700, red brick, stone dressings, hipped roof and dormers. South front with projecting wings. Possibly by the builder of nearby Alveston House.

In the hall a gallery with twisted balusters and string with acanthus scroll. Two shellwork chimney-pieces by Mrs Delany c. 1760.

Wentworth Woodhouse, West Riding, Yorkshire

For a full description see Christopher Hussey's Early Georgian (1955).

The 2nd Earl of Strafford left the property in 1695 to a sister's son, Thomas Watson. In 1716 Watson transferred it to his son, Thomas Watson-Wentworth, created Lord Malton, 1728, and Marquess of Rockingham, 1748. He was made Knight of the Bath, 1725. The carved insignia of the Bath without a coronet dates the west front after 1725 and presumably before 1728.

Among the recently acquired Newby Hall drawings in the R.I.B.A. is a plan of the west front which Mr John Harris believes to be in the hand of Vanbrugh (d. 1726).

It is not impossible that the west front, for which no original elevation drawing exists, was executed by William Wakefield. Of pink brick and light stone. It echoes two unusual features found in Wakefield's hall at Gilling Castle, namely the half blind Venetian window motif, and the niche door-head. Other features, the heraldic arms thrust into the entablature and the frilly window pediments, anticipate German palace Baroque of succeeding decades. Kerry Downes—English Baroque Architecture, 1966.

West Green House, Hampshire

Lieutenant-General Henry Hawley was an equivocal character, but a gallant soldier with a fine taste for architecture. He fought in Marlborough's wars and was present at Dettingen in 1743 and at Culloden in 1746. No one knows whom he commissioned to build West Green House, nor for certain when. Probably begun c. 1714.

Square in plan with hipped roof, and acutely pointed dormers. A deep plum brick with blue headers was used. West front remarkable for five roundels with busts. The north front has a pair. The middle of this front may have been altered c. 1720. It has a polygonal entrance bay with stout iron lampholder. Porch and flanking bays are embattled, and some windows have frilly and ogival heads in rubbed brick. The west front is extended by a screen wall of brick arches.

Interior plan made unusual by a huge coved room occupying two floors of the west front. Staircase round a top-lit well has iron S-scroll balusters—a mid eighteenth-century insertion. An elegant upper stair with fluted balusters. Nearly every room is panelled.

C.L., 21 Nov. 1936.

West Hanney House (Old Rectory), Berkshire

Dated 1727, but very bizarre and Baroque. Of blue glazed and red brick. The two-bay centrepiece of each front is swept up from the panelled parapet of the wings below to form a third storey. From the angles of each centrepiece rise tall chimneys, or dummy chimneys. The windows have segmental heads and prominent stone keys; several on the side fronts are blind.

Panelled rooms. Staircase with delicately turned balusters; and an ample first-floor landing.

C.L., 15 Jan. 1943.

Westwell, Tenterden, Kent

Date 1711 carved in stone in the little pediment over the first-floor central window, and 1718 embossed on two rainwater heads.

Built for John Blackmore (d. 1717) by an unknown artisan builder. A trim, tight, rectangular block of red brick. Cornice and quoins of orange-gold sandstone. The cornice rises into the small pediment already referred to. Panels with scalloped edges on the blank parapet, and aprons similarly treated under first-floor windows. These and the surrounds of two oval windows are in scarlet gauged brick. Two sentinel chimneys.

A wide arch in the Entrance Hall leads to the Staircase, which is of oak with ramped handrail, and twisted balusters.

C.L., 7 Nov. 1963.

Whiteway House, Chudleigh, Devon
Standing in a park, a large Queen Anne house, with alterations and additions of 1812 and 1815. All in red brick with stone dressings and stringcourses. A seat of the Parker family, Earls of Morley, for nearly two and a half centuries. A bust relief of Queen Anne within the pediment over the entrance.

Widcombe Manor, Bath, Somerset
Circa 1727 for Philip Bennet. This country villa-cum-town house has a front of great richness and fine quality. It is foreign to Bath architecture of the time, and its designer is unknown.

Ionic pilasters, fluted and coupled, articulate the angles and centrepiece, of which the heavy entablature carries a pediment with oval window and carved garlands. Behind a balustraded parapet rises a hipped roof with dormers.

The centrepiece is of channelled ashlar and its windows are small in scale. All the keystones are carved.

The elegant mahogany staircase has twisted balusters.

In the forecourt a bronze fountain is said to be late sixteenth-century Venetian.

'The Golden House' of Horace Vachell, novelist, who lived here until his death in 1955.
C.L., 28 Aug. 1937.

Woodperry House, Oxfordshire
Described by the 5th Viscount Torrington in 1781 as 'a neat snug box . . . resembling (in miniature) the Queen's Palace', meaning Buckingham House. Built between 1728 and 1731 for John Morse, a London banker, probably from designs of William Townesend of Oxford, the putative architect of Shotover, three miles away. Certainly payments were made by Morse to William King, mason, who had been Townesend's apprentice.

Five-bay centre block linked by quadrant arcades to pavilions at right angles so as to form a forecourt. The rusticated angle strips, segmental window-heads and the heavy strings of the arcades are still Baroque. Handsome iron screen and gates to forecourt.

In 1879–80 pedimented wings, in the same style as the centre, were added by one Sym of Oxford, for John Thomson, grandfather of the present owner.

Front door gives entry to staircase and, through an arched screen on the left, to the hall. The woodcarving of stair rail, landing and soffits, also of overmantels, window and door-casings is vigorous. Woodperry is in a sense a joiner's house.
C.L., 5 Jan. 1961.

Woolton Hall, Lancashire
North-west front in sandstone, built *c.* 1704 for Richard Molyneux whose father was at the time building Croxteth. Statues stood at the angles and over the pediment which is filled with carved military trophies. As at Croxteth this front has a somewhat thin quality. It contains rooms wainscoted in oak compartments with fluted Corinthian pilasters.

In 1774–80 Robert Adam rebuilt the north-east front for Nicholas Ashton.

Peter Fleetwood-Hesketh—*Murray's Lancashire Guide*, 1955.

Wotton House, near Aylesbury, Buckinghamshire
Begun 1704 and finished 1714 for Richard Grenville. Whoever the architect was—John Keene or James Thornhill(?)—he closely followed the Buckingham House formula. Wotton's single-storey pavilions with hipped roofs, dormers, lanterns and casement windows, survive intact. The centre block, however, was altered by Soane in 1820 after a fire had practically gutted the interior. Soane lowered the attic and the first-floor windows. Otherwise the red-brick exterior is little altered. Entrance front of eleven bays and two storeys with giant Corinthian pilasters of stone at the angles. The doorway has a segmental pediment (that on the garden side having splendid carved decoration).

Garden side is of nine bays, the windows being more widely spaced. The centrepiece rusticated and divided by four pilasters.

The forecourt is closed by railings and iron gates. Another fire in 1929 did much damage. Of the interior only the wrought-iron staircase balustrade is Queen Anne.
C.L., 1 July 1949.

Wrest Park Pavilion, Bedfordshire
Wrest Park house (entirely rebuilt 1834–6) was given a new front in 1676. Between 1709 and 1712 the 12th Earl (created Duke) of Kent got Thomas Archer to build a banqueting house at the far end of the long canal. It is the most Continental Baroque eye-catcher in England. Archer was clearly inspired by the plan and plate of Michelangelo's abortive design for S. Giovanni dei Fiorentini, Rome, given in Sandraert's *Insignium Romae Templorum Prospectus*. Borromini's S. Ivo, Rome, may also have been in his mind.

Archer's plan is a hexagon with segmental and rectangular attachments on alternate sides. The circular drum carries an ovoid dome. For the body of the pavilion yellow bricks, and for the rusticated angle pilasters red bricks are used.

The interior is deliciously painted in *trompe l'œil* by Louis Hauduroy (1712). Fluted Corinthian columns on either side of the six openings support an entablature; round medallions contain busts—all in grisaille and gold. In the drum are real and feigned eye-windows, also terminal figures, niches and urns. Three snail stairways ascend to rooms and descend to offices in the basement.
Vitruvius Britannicus, vol. I, 1715.
Marcus Whiffen—*Thomas Archer*, 1950.

465 *(left) Widcombe Manor, Bath, c. 1727.*

466 *(below) Woodperry House, Oxfordshire, 1728–31.*

467 *(bottom) Wotton House, Buckinghamshire, 1704–14.*

THE PRINCIPAL ARCHITECTS

For detailed particulars of architects of the Baroque period readers are advised to consult H. M. Colvin's *A Biographical Dictionary of English Architects, 1660–1840*, and those biographies and learned articles listed in the Bibliography (p. 299) of this book.

The abbreviated list given below is of those architects who were active between 1685 and 1715, and of their best-known country houses within this period. Some of their houses which were actually begun after 1715, but which can be described as Baroque, are included. Those already included in the *Early Georgian* volume are, however, omitted.

ARCHER, THOMAS (?1668–1743). Younger son of a Warwickshire squire. Travelled abroad *c.* 1689–93. Groom Porter at Court 1705. Purchased Hale estate, Hampshire 1715. His style derived from Roman Baroque architects, notably Borromini. He is not known to have built after 1720.

1695–1700	?Umberslade Park, Warwicks.
1699–1700	?Bramham Park, Yorks. (unspecified services)
1702–1705	Chatsworth, Derbyshire (Cascade and north front)
1706	Cliveden, Bucks. (alterations)
1706–16	Heythrop House, Oxon.
1707–11	Aynhoe Park, Northants. (additions)
1709–12	Wrest Park pavilion, Beds.
1710	?Chettle House, Dorset
c. 1710–20	?Serle's House, Winchester, Hants.
c. 1710–20	?Marlow Place, Bucks.
1712	Roehampton House, Surrey
1712	Hurstbourne Priors, Hants.
c. 1712	Wentworth Castle, Yorks. (east front alterations)
1715	Hale Park, Hants.
1716	?Beningbrough Hall, Yorks.

BASTARD, THOMAS (d. 1720). Joiner by profession. Progenitor of a family of Blandford builders in provincial Baroque during reigns of George I and II.

c. 1710	Sherborne House (Digby School), Dorset

BELL, HENRY (*c.* 1653–1717). Alderman and gentleman-architect active in King's Lynn, Norfolk, and the environs.

1691–96	?Kimbolton Castle, Hunts. (courtyard)
1712	?Cottesbrooke Hall, Northants.

BODT, or BOTT, JEAN (1670–1745). French Protestant who fled to Holland 1685. In England 1698 in service of William III. 1700 in service at court of Berlin.

c. 1701	Wentworth Castle, Yorks. (east front)

CLARKE, DR GEORGE (1661–1736). Fellow of All Souls. Secretary at War 1692–1704. Amateur architect in Oxford University.

1723	Kingston Bagpuize Rectory, Berks.

COLEMAN, WILLIAM. Joiner by trade.

1707	Kimbolton Castle, Hunts. (superseded by Vanbrugh)

DICKINSON, WILLIAM, JNR (*c.* 1671–1725). Worked at St Paul's and on City churches under Wren. Restored Westminster Abbey. A surveyor to Commission for Building London Churches 1711.

1704	?Herriard Park, Hants.

EDWARDS, THOMAS of Greenwich. Shipowner and (Cornish) mineowner. His architecture associated with Gibbs. Hence his several Cornish houses mostly belong in style and date to the Early Georgian period.

1710–21	?Antony House, Cornwall
c. 1715	Trewithen, Cornwall

ETTY, WILLIAM. Carpenter and master-mason of York. Worked for Vanbrugh, Hawksmoor, Campbell and Burlington.

1721	Newby Park, Yorks. (wing)
1721	Seaton Delaval, Northumb.
1726	?Aldby Park, Yorks.
1739	Castle Howard (Temple of Winds), Yorks.

GIBBS, JAMES (1682–1754). Tory and Catholic from Aberdeen. Much travelled in Italy and a pupil of Carlo Fontana. Although essentially a Baroque architect all his authenticated country-house work is Georgian.

1710–21	?Antony House, Cornwall (according to D. and S. Lysons, 1814)
1716	Cannons Park, Middlesex (redesigned south and east fronts)
1724	Wentworth Castle, Yorks. (redesigned gallery)

HAWKSMOOR, NICHOLAS (1661–1736). Entered Wren's office *c.* 1680 and associated with all the Surveyor-General's work thereafter. Clerk of Works at the several royal palaces. Secretary to Board of Works 1715–18 and 1726–36. Worked closely with Vanbrugh after 1702, but in his own right an architect of immense stature.

1696–1702	Easton Neston, Northants.
1699–1726	Castle Howard, Yorks. (with Vanbrugh)
1705–25	Blenheim Palace, Oxon. (with Vanbrugh and alone)
1725–29	Ockham Park, Surrey
1726	?Grimsthorpe Castle, Lincs. (chapel)
1729–36	Castle Howard Mausoleum, Yorks.

HOOKE, ROBERT (1635–1703). Founder Fellow of Royal Society and Secretary 1677–82. Brilliant scientist and inventor. Career as architect began 1666 and rightly belongs to Caroline period. Included here for possible authorship of:

c. 1683	?Boughton House, Northants.
1690	?Old Shenfield Place, Essex
1696	?Burley-on-the-Hill, Rutland

HUNT, JOHN. Statuary and mason of Northampton. Carved statue of Charles II on portico of All Saints church, Northampton.

1709–13	?Hinwick House, Beds. (certainly carved Diana relief)
1710–20	?Kislingbury Old Rectory, Northants.

IRESON, NATHANIEL (1686–1769). Master-builder from Warwickshire. Moved to Wilts. c. 1720; settled at Wincanton, Somerset, c. 1726. His architecture, which displays distinct Borrominesque touches, properly belongs to the Early Georgian period.

c. 1720–31	Ven House, Somerset (practically rebuilt house of 1698–1700)

JAMES, JOHN (c. 1672–1746). Son of a Hampshire vicar. Employed at Greenwich Hospital 1699–1736 as Assistant Clerk, and thereafter until his death, as Clerk of the Works.

1701	Appuldurcombe, Isle of Wight
1704	?Herriard Park, Hants.
1710	Orlean's (Secretary Johnston's) House, Twickenham, Middlesex.
1714–16	Cannons Park, Middlesex (replacing Talman)
1718	?Hursley Park, Hants.
1722–24	?Iver Grove, Bucks.
1724	Warbrook House, Hants.
1733–35	Baylis House, Slough, Bucks. (alterations)
1736	Eversley Manor, Hants.

JONES, HENRY (1649–1721). Northamptonshire carpenter. Accredited with a few local buildings, including

1712	Cottesbrooke Hall, Northants.

JOYNES, HENRY (c. 1684–1754). Resident overseer at Blenheim Palace under Hawksmoor 1705–15, and Clerk of the Works at Kensington Palace 1715–54.

1719–20	Carshalton (water pavilion), Surrey
1730–40	?Normanton Hall, Rutland
1742–48	Linley Hall, Salop.

LUMLEY, JOHN of Northampton. Employed by the Earls of Nottingham and Ashburnham, as 'supervisor'. Status otherwise unknown.

1697–1702	Burley-on-the-Hill, Rutland
1704–07	Ampthill Park, Beds. (designed)

POUGET, 'MONSIEUR'. Thought, probably wrongly, to be Pierre Puget (1622–94) who was born in Marseilles and was a pupil of Pietro da Cortona. Pouget, or Boujet (see footnote 1, p. 41) may possibly have been brought to England by the Francophil 1st Duke of Montagu to rebuild Montagu House, London.

1683–1709	?Boughton House, Northants.

PRICE, JOHN (d. 1735). With his son, also John, designed and built one of the most Baroque churches in England, St George's Chapel, Great Yarmouth, 1714–16. Surveyor to Duke of Chandos.

1720–21	Cannons Park, Middlesex (south and east fronts)

PRINCE, JOHN. Bricklayer and speculator. Also agent and surveyor to Edward Harley, 2nd Earl of Oxford.

1703–04	?Cound Hall, Salop.

SMITH, FRANCIS 'of Warwick' (1672–1738). Younger brother of William (q.v.). Successful and prolific master-builder in the Midlands. Much indebted to Gibbs under whom he worked. Majority of his houses fall within the Early Georgian period.

1695–1700	?Umberslade Park, Warwicks. (as builder)
1703	Calke Abbey, Derbs.
1706	Heythrop House, Oxon. (as master builder)
1713	?Swynnerton Hall, Staffs.
1719	Chicheley Hall, Bucks.
1721	Buntingsdale, Salop.
1730, 1737	Stanford Hall, Leics.

SMITH, WILLIAM (1661–1724). Elder brother of Francis (q.v.). Mason from Tettenhall, Staffs.

1697	Stanford Hall, Leics.
1703–11	Cottesbrooke Hall, Northants.

STRONG, EDWARD (1652–1724). Member of a large Oxfordshire family of master-masons in seventeenth and eighteenth centuries. Moved to London. Worked under Wren at City churches and St Paul's; and under Hawksmoor at Greenwich.

| 1702–03 | ?Addiscombe House, Surrey |
| 1705 | Blenheim Palace, Oxon. (as chief mason) |

TALMAN, WILLIAM (1650–1719). Younger son of a Wiltshire gentleman. 1689 Comptroller of King's Works. 1702 superseded by Vanbrugh. As a designer markedly original and diverse; as a person difficult and quarrelsome. His Thoresby Park plan and design (1683) became a prototype of country-house style throughout the ensuing Stuart reigns (see *Caroline* Notes).

c. 1681	Burghley House, Northants. (south front alterations)
1685–90	?Uppark, Sussex
1687	Stansted Park, Sussex
1687–96	Chatsworth, Derbs. (south and east fronts)
1689–91	Swallowfield Park, Berks.
1694–1704	Kiveton Park, Yorks.
1700–03	Dyrham Park, Gloucs. (east front)
1702–04	Drayton House, Northants. (alterations and frontispiece)
1705–10	Fetcham Park, Surrey
1713–14	Cannons Park, Middlesex (superseded)

THORNTON, WILLIAM (1670–1721). Joiner of York and restorer of Beverley Minster.

c. 1703–10	Bramham Park, Yorks. (joinery)
1708–11	Castle Howard, Yorks. (wainscoting)
1714–20	Wentworth Castle, Yorks. (joinery)
1716	Beningbrough Hall, Yorks. (joinery and ?architecture)

TOWNESEND, WILLIAM (c. 1668–1739). Most successful of Oxfordshire family of mason-builders; brother of George, who settled in Bristol. Employed extensively at numerous Oxford colleges and at Blenheim. Designed as well as built, but left few records of authorship. His style much influenced by Hawksmoor.

1709–c. 1720	?Haseley Court, Oxon.
c. 1710–20	?Kingston Bagpuize House, Berks.
1713–18	?Shotover Park, Oxon.
c. 1728	?Britwell Court, Oxon.
1728–31	?Woodperry House, Oxon.

VANBRUGH, SIR JOHN (1664–1726). England's most colourful and monumental Baroque architect. Began life in the Army. Incarcerated in the Bastille 1692. Became a playwright and, in 1704, Clarenceux King of Arms. Made Comptroller of Works 1702. Dismissed by Tories 1713. Knighted 1714 and restored to Comptrollership.

1699–1726	Castle Howard, Yorks.
1705–16	Blenheim Palace, Oxon.
1707–10	Kimbolton Castle, Hunts.
1710–14	Kings Weston, Gloucs.
1717–18	Vanbrugh Castle, Greenwich
1718	Audley End, Essex (staircase and stone screen)
1720–26	Seaton Delaval, Northumb.
1721	Lumley Castle, Durham (alterations)
1722	?Somersby Manor, Lincs.
1722–26	Grimsthorpe Castle, Lincs. (north front and forecourt)
1724–26	Eastbury Park, Dorset

WAKEFIELD, WILLIAM (d. 1730). Gentleman-architect, whose precise share in a number of Yorkshire houses has not yet been determined. Influenced by Vanbrugh and later by Campbell (viz. his Palladian Atherton Hall, Lancs., 1723).

1713	Duncombe Park, Yorks.
1715–25	Gilling Castle, Yorks. (west front and wings)
1725–28	?Wentworth Woodhouse, Yorks. (west front)

WILSON, SIR WILLIAM (1641–1710). Statuary mason from Leicester turned gentleman-architect of Warwickshire. Married a rich widow and was knighted 1682. Influenced by Wren.

1685–90	?Farnborough Hall, Warwicks. (west front)
1696	Four Oaks Hall, Warwicks.
c. 1700	Moat House, Sutton Coldfield, Warwicks.

WREN, SIR CHRISTOPHER (1632–1723). After Inigo Jones England's greatest Renaissance architect. For particulars of his important role in domestic architecture see O. Hill and J. Cornforth's *Caroline*. Nevertheless his two surviving houses come within our period.

| 1699–1702 | Winslow Hall, Bucks. |
| 1709–11 | Marlborough House, London. |

BIBLIOGRAPHY

A list of books and articles, excluding those references already given under *Notes on the Principal Baroque Houses*.

Ashton, John — *Social Life in the Reign of Queen Anne* (1897).

Baillie, Hugh Murray — 'Etiquette and Planning of State Apartments in Baroque Palaces', *Archaeologia*, CI, 1967.

Baker, M. I. and Collins, C. H. — *Life of James Brydges, Duke of Chandos* (1949).

Batten, M. I. — 'The Architecture of Dr. Robert Hooke', *Walpole Soc.*, XXV, 1937.

Beard, Geoffrey — *Georgian Craftsmen* (1966).

Bickley, Francis — *The Cavendish Family* (1911).

Booth, A. — 'The Architects of Wentworth Castle and Wentworth Wood-house', *R.I.B.A. Jnl.*, ser. 3, XLI, 1933.

Campbell, Colen — *Vitruvius Britannicus*, vols. I, II and III (1715, 1717, 1725).

Carritt, E. F. — *A Calendar of British Taste, 1600–1800* (1949).

Chapman, Hester — *Queen Mary II* (1953).

Collier, T. R. — 'The Patronage of Robert Benson', *Archit. Rev.*, Dec. 1965.

Colvin, H. M. — 'The Bastards of Blandford', *Archaeol. Jnl.*, CIV, 1948.
'Architectural History of Marlow', *Records of Bucks*, XV, 1947.
Biographical Dictionary of English Architects, 1660–1840 (1954).

Colvin, H. M. and Wodehouse, L. M. — 'Henry Bell of King's Lynn', *Archit. Hist.*, no. 4, 1961.

Croft-Murray, Edward — *Decorative Painting in England, 1537–1837*, vol. I (1962).

Downes, Kerry — *English Baroque Architecture* (1966).
Hawksmoor (1959).

Edwards, Tudor — 'Sir William Wilson', *Country Life*, 7 July 1950.

Fiennes, Celia — *The Journeys of, circa 1685–1703* (1947).

Finch, Pearl — *Burley-on-the-Hill* (1901).

Fraser, P. and Harris, J. — *The Burlington-Devonshire Catalogue of Drawings, Part 1* (1960).

Gray, H. St George — 'Nathaniel Ireson', *Country Life*, 22 April 1939.

Green, David — *Blenheim Palace* (1951).
Gardener to Queen Anne; Henry Wise (1956).
Grinling Gibbons (1964).

Gunnis, Rupert — *A Dictionary of British Sculptors, 1660–1851* (1953).

Habakkuk, H. J. — 'English Landownership, 1660–1740', *Economic Hist., Rev.* X, 1939–40.

Harris, John — 'Thoresby House, Nottinghamshire', *Archit. Hist.*, 4–5, 1961–2.
'Hampton Court Trianon Designs of W. & J. Talman', *Warburg & Courtauld Jnl.*, XXIII, 1960.
'Bodt and Stainborough', *Archit. Rev.*, CXXX, 1961.

Hiscock, W. G. — *A Christ Church Miscellany* (ch. 4 on 'William Townesend'), 1946.
'William Townesend', *Archit. Rev.*, Oct. 1945.

Honour, Hugh — 'Leonard Knyff', *Burlington Mag.* XCVI, 1954.

Hooke, Robert — *Diary of, 1672–80*. Ed. H. W. Robinson and W. Adams (1935).

Jenkins, Frank — *Architect and Patron* (1961).

Jourdain, Margaret — *English Interior Decoration, 1500–1830* (1950).

Kenworthy-Browne, J. — 'Easton Neston', *Connoisseur*, Oct. and Nov. 1964.

Lane, A. — 'Daniel Marot: Delft Vases and Gardens at Hampton Court', *Connoisseur*, CXXIII, 1949.

Lang, S. — 'Gibbs . . . and his architectural sources', *Archit. Rev.*, CXVI, 1954.
'By Hawksmoor out of Gibbs', *Archit. Rev.*, CV, 1949.

Lenygon, Francis — *Decoration in England from 1660–1770* (1914).

Little, Bryan — *James Gibbs* (1955).

Luttrell, Narcissus — *A Brief Historical Relation of State Affairs 1678 to 1814* (1857).

Lynton, Norbert — 'Kiveton and Laguerre', *Burlington Mag.*

Marot, Jean — *Le Petit Marot; Receuil des Plans Profils et Elevations Des Plusieurs Palais, etc. (1660–1670)*.

Mayhew, Edgar de N.   *Sketches by Thornhill* (1967).

Mingay, G. E.   *English Landed Society in the Eighteenth Century* (1963).

Niven, W.   'Marlow Place', *Archit. Rev.*, XXVII and XXVIII, 1910.

Oswald, Arthur   *Country Houses of Dorset* (1959). *Country Houses of Kent* (1933). 'The Work of Henry Bell and his Successors', *Country Life*, CX, 20 July 1951.

Ozinga, M. D.   *Daniel Marot* (1938).

Pevsner, Nikolaus   *Buildings of England*, various vols.

Plumb, J. H.   *England in the Eighteenth Century, Part 1* (1950). *Studies in Social History* (H. J. Habakkuk's chapter on 'Daniel Finch, 2nd Earl of Nottingham') (1955).

Robinson, H. W.   'Robert Hooke as Surveyor and Architect', *Roy. Soc. Notes and Records*, June 1949.

Saxl, F., and Wittkower, R.   *English Art and The Mediterranean* (1948).

Smith, H. Clifford   'John James', *Country Life*, 2 Dec. 1939.

Summerson, Sir John   'The Classical Country House in 18th century England', *Roy. Soc. Arts. Jnl.*, CVII, 1959. *Architecture in Britain, 1530–1830* (1963).

Tanner, Joan D.   'The Rebuilding of Chicheley Hall', *Records of Bucks*, XVII, Part 1, 1961.

Tawney, R. H.   'The Rise of the Gentry', *Econ. Hist. Rev.*, XI, no. 1, 1941.

Thompson, Francis   *A History of Chatsworth* (1949).

Tipping, H. Avray   *English Homes*, Period IV, vol. I, *Late Stuart* (1920, 2nd ed. 1929).

Tipping, H. Avray, and Hussey, Christopher   *English Homes*, Period IV, vol. II, *Work of Sir John Vanbrugh and His School* (1928).

Trevelyan, G. M.   *English Social History* (1944). *The England of Queen Anne* (1934).

Waterhouse, Ellis   *Painting in Britain, 1530–1830* (1953).

Webb, G. F.   'Baroque Art', *Proc. Brit. Acad.*, XXXIII, 1947. *Vanbrugh Letters* (1928). 'Henry Bell of King's Lynn', *Burlington Mag.*, XLVII, 1925. 'Thomas Archer', *Burlington Mag.*, XLVII, 1925. 'John and William Bastard', *Burlington Mag.*, XLVII, 1925. 'Letters and Drawings of Nicholas Hawksmoor relating to Mausoleum at Castle Howard', *Walpole Soc.*, XIX, 1930–1.

Whiffen, Marcus   *Thomas Archer* (1950). 'Thomas White of Worcester', *Country Life*, 7 Dec. 1945. 'Thomas Archer', *Archit. Rev.*, XCIV, Nov. 1943.

Whinney, M.   'William Talman', *Warburg & Courtauld Jnl.*, XVIII, 1955.

Whinney, M. and Millar, O.   *English Art 1625–1714* (1957).

Whistler, Laurence   *Sir John Vanbrugh* (1938). *The Imagination of Vanbrugh* (1954). 'Three Newly Discovered Designs for Kimbolton Castle', *New English Rev.*, II, May 1949. 'Talman and Vanbrugh . . . rivalry', *Country Life*, 21 Nov. 1952.

Wren Society   *Hampton Court*, vol. IV (1927).

INDEX

The figures in italics are plate numbers